The Short Oxford History of Italy

Early Modern Italy 1550–1796

The Short Oxford History of Italy

General Editor: John A. Davis

Also available

Italy in the Nineteenth Century
edited by John A. Davis

Italy since 1945
edited by Patrick McCarthy

Liberal and Fascist Italy 1900–1945
edited by Adrian Lyttelton

IN PREPARATION, VOLUMES COVERING

Italy in the Early Middle Ages: From Late Antiquity to the Coming of
  the Normans
Italy in the Later Middle Ages 1000–1300
Italy in the Age of the Renaissance 1300–1550

The Short Oxford History of Italy

General Editor: John A. Davis

Early Modern Italy

1550–1796

Edited by John A. Marino

OXFORD
UNIVERSITY PRESS

OXFORD
UNIVERSITY PRESS

Great Clarendon Street, Oxford OX2 6DP

Oxford University Press is a department of the University of Oxford.
It furthers the University's objective of excellence in research, scholarship,
and education by publishing worldwide in

Oxford New York

Auckland Bangkok Buenos Aires Cape Town Chennai
Dar es Salaam Delhi Hong Kong Istanbul Karachi Kolkata
Kuala Lumpur Madrid Melbourne Mexico City Mumbai Nairobi
São Paulo Shanghai Singapore Taipei Tokyo Toronto

with an associated company in Berlin

Oxford is a registered trade mark of Oxford University Press
in the UK and in certain other countries

Published in the United States
by Oxford University Press Inc., New York

British Library Cataloguing in Publication Data

Data available

Library of Congress Cataloging in Publication Data

Data available

ISBN 0-19-870041-5 (hbk)
ISBN 0-19-870042-3 (pbk)

10 9 8 7 6 5 4 3 2 1

Typeset in Adobe Minion
by RefineCatch Limited, Bungay, Suffolk
Printed in Great Britain by
T.J. International Ltd., Padstow, Cornwall

General Editor's Preface

Over the last three decades historians have begun to interpret Europe's past in new ways. In part this reflects changes within Europe itself, the declining importance of the individual European states in an increasingly global world, the moves towards closer political and economic integration amongst the European states, and Europe's rapidly changing relations with the non-European world. It also reflects broader intellectual changes rooted in the experience of the twentieth century that have brought new fields of historical inquiry into prominence and have radically changed the ways in which historians approach the past.

The new *Oxford Short History of Europe* series, of which this *Short History of Italy* is part, offers an important and timely opportunity to explore how the histories of the contemporary European national communities are being rewritten. Covering a chronological span from late antiquity to the present, the *Oxford Short History of Italy* is organized in seven volumes, to which over seventy specialists in different fields and periods of Italian history will contribute. Each volume will provide clear and concise accounts of how each period of Italy's history is currently being redefined, and their collective purpose is to show how an older perspective that reduced Italy's past to the quest of a nation for statehood and independence has now been displaced by different and new perspectives.

The fact that Italy's history has long been dominated by the modern nation-state and its origins simply reflects one particular variant on a pattern evident throughout Europe. When from the eighteenth century onwards Italian writers turned to the past to retrace the origins of their nation and its quest for independent nationhood, they were doing the same as their counterparts elsewhere in Europe. But their search for the nation imposed a periodization on Italy's past that has survived to the present, even if the original intent has been lost or redefined. Focusing their attention on those periods—the middle ages, the *Renaissance*, the *Risorgimento* that seemed to anticipate the modern, they carefully averted their gaze from those that did not—the Dark Ages, and the centuries of foreign occupation and conquest after the sack of Rome in 1527.

Paradoxically, this search for unity segmented Italy's past both chronologically and geographically, since those regions (notably the South) deemed to have contributed less to the quest for nationhood were also ignored. It also accentuated the discontinuities of Italian history caused by foreign conquest and invasion, so that Italy's successive rebirths—the *Renaissance* and the *Risorgimento*—came to symbolize all that was distinctive and exceptional in Italian history. Fascism then carried the cycle of triumph and disaster forward into the twentieth century, thereby adding to the conviction that Italy's history was exceptional, the belief that it was in some essential sense also deeply flawed. Post-war historians redrew Italy's past in bleaker terms, but used the same retrospective logic as before to link fascism to failings deeply rooted in Italy's recent and more distant past.

Seen from the end of the twentieth century this heavily retrospective reasoning appears anachronistic and inadequate. But although these older perspectives continue to find an afterlife in countless textbooks, they have been displaced by a more contemporary awareness that in both the present and the past the different European national communities have no single history, but instead many different histories.

The volumes in the *Short History of Italy* will show how Italy's history too is being rethought in these terms. Its new histories are being constructed around the political, cultural, religious, and economic institutions from which Italy's history has drawn continuities that have outlasted changing fortunes of foreign conquest and invasion. In each period their focus is the peoples and societies that have inhabited the Italian peninsula, on the ways in which political organization, economic activity, social identities, and organization were shaped in the contexts and meanings of their own age.

These perspectives make possible a more comparative history, one that shows more clearly how Italy's history has been distinctive without being exceptional. They also enable us to write a history of Italians that is fuller and more continuous, recovering the previously 'forgotten' centuries and geographical regions while revising our understanding of those that are more familiar. In each period Italy's many different histories can also be positioned more closely in the constantly changing European and Mediterranean worlds of which Italians have always been part.

John A. Davis

Contents

PART I   THE INSTITUTIONAL FRAMEWORK: LATE RENAISSANCE RESOLUTIONS

PART II   MATERIAL LIFE: ECONOMIC, SOCIAL, AND POLITICAL TRAJECTORIES

PART III IDEOLOGIES AND PRACTICES: COMPETING LANGUAGES, CONVERGING VISIONS

PART IV THE CHALLENGE AND CRISIS OF THE OLD REGIME

List of contributors

THOMAS J. DANDELET, Assistant Professor of History, University of California, Berkeley, is author of *Spanish Rome, 1500–1700* (2001). He specializes in the Spanish empire, the Mediterranean world, Rome and the papacy, and Spanish Italy. He is currently working on a history of the Colonna family from 1500 to 1700.

BRENDAN DOOLEY, Chief of Research at the Medici Archive Project, is the author of *Science, Politics and Society in Eighteenth Century Italy: The* 'Giornale de' letterati d'Italia' *and its World* (1991), *The Social History of Skepticism: Experience and Doubt in Early Modern Culture* (1999), *Science and the Public Sphere in Early Modern Italy* (2001), and *Morandi's Last Prophecy and the End of Baroque Politics* (2002). He is editor/translator of *Italy in the Baroque: Selected Readings* (1995), co-editor of *The Politics of Information in Early Modern Europe* (2000), and editor of *Giovanni Baldinucci, Quaderno: Guerra, peste e carestia a Firenze nel Seicento* (2000). He is currently working on the communication of occult knowledge in Medici Florence.

PAULA FINDLEN, Professor of History, Stanford University, is author of *Possessing Nature: Museums, Collecting, and Scientific Culture in Early Modern Italy* (1994), and co-author of *Merchants and Marvels: Commerce, Science, and Art in Early Modern Europe* (2001). She recently completed *A Fragmentary Past: The Making of Museums in Renaissance Italy* (forthcoming) and is finishing *The Woman Who Understood Newton: Laura Bassi and Her World*.

DAVID GENTILCORE, Reader in History, Department of History, University of Leicester, is author of *From Bishop to Witch: The System of the Sacred in Early Modern Terra d'Otranto* (1992) and *Healers and Healing in Early Modern Italy* (1998). He is currently working on two books: *Medical Charlatanism in Early Modern Italy* (Oxford University Press) and *The Regulation of Medicine in the States of Italy: the Protomedicato Tribunals, 1400–1800* (Ashgate).

R. BURR LITCHFIELD, Professor of History, Brown University, is the author of *Emergence of a Bureaucracy: The Florentine Patricians, 1530–1790* (1986) and the translator of three volumes of

Franco Venturi's *Settecento riformatore: The First Crisis* (1989) and *The End of the Old Regime in Europe, 1776–1789* (2 vols., 1991), of Emilio Sereni, *History of the Italian Agricultural Landscape* (1997), and of Sergio Bertelli, *The King's Body* (2001). He is currently writing an urban history of Florence.

JOHN A. MARINO, Associate Professor of History, University of California, San Diego, is author of *Pastoral Economics in the Kingdom of Naples* (1988). He is editor of *Early Modern History and the Social Sciences: Testing the Limits of Braudel's* Mediterranean (2002) and co-editor/co-translator of *Good Government in Spanish Naples* (1990). He specializes in the early modern history of Naples, Spanish Italy, and the Mediterranean.

JOHN JEFFRIES MARTIN, Professor of History, Trinity University, San Antonio, Texas, is the author of *Venice's Hidden Enemies: Italian Heretics in a Renaissance City* (1993). He is co-editor of *Venice Reconsidered: The History and Civilization of an Italian City-State* (2000). He is currently researching a book on 'sincerity' in early modern Europe, and specializes in the socio-cultural and religious history of early modern Venice and Italy.

GIANNA POMATA, Associate Professor of History, University of Bologna, is author of *Promising a Cure: Patients and Healers in Early Modern Bologna* (1998; Italian edn. 1994), and co-editor of three volumes: *Costruire la parentela. Donne e uomini nella definizione dei legami familiari* (1994), *Ragnatele di rapporti. Patronage e reti di relazione nella storia delle donne* (1988), and *Parto e maternità. Momenti della biografia femminile* (1980). She is currently completing *Dissimilar Resemblance: Sexual Difference in Early Modern Medicine* (Ashgate).

ANNA MARIA RAO, Professor of Modern History, University Frederick II, Naples, is author of *Il Regno di Napoli nel Settecento* (1983), *L'amaro di feudalismo* (1986), *Esuli. L'emigrazione politica italiana in Francia (1792–1802)* (1992). She is editor of *Esercito e società nell'età rivoluzionaria e napoleonica* (1990), and *Editoria e cultura a Napoli nel xviii secolo* (1998). She is a specialist in eighteenth-century politics and culture, the Enlightenment, comparative revolutions in early modern Naples, Italy, and France.

ANNE JACOBSON SCHUTTE, Professor of History, University of Virginia, is the author of *Pier Paolo Vergerio: The Making of an Italian Reformer* (1977), *Printed Italian Vernacular Religious Books: A Finding List* (1983), *The Autobiography of an Aspiring Saint: Cecilia Ferrazzi* (1996), and *Aspiring Saints: Pretense of Holiness, Inquisition, and Gender in the Republic of Venice, 1618–1750* (2001). She is co-editor of the *Archiv für Reformationsgeschichte/Archive for Reformation History*.

JON R. SNYDER, Professor of Italian Literature, University of California, Santa Barbara, is the author of *Writing the Scene of Speaking: Theories of Dialogue in the Late Italian Renaissance* (1989), *Dissimulation and the Culture of Secrecy in Early Modern Europe* (2002), and *Dissimulazione. Saggio sul comportamento celato nell'Antico Regime* (2002). He has translated Gianni Vattimo, *The End of Modernity: Nihilism and Hermeneutics in Post-Modern Culture* (1988). He is a specialist in Italian literature from the late Renaissance to the present.

GEOFFREY SYMCOX, Professor of History, University of California, Los Angeles, is author of *The Crisis of French Sea Power, 1688–1697* (1974), *Victor Amadeus II: Absolutism in the Savoyard State* (1983), editor of *War, Diplomacy and Imperialism, 1618–1763* (1973), and a major contributor to Einaudi's *Storia di Torino*, vol. iv (2001). He is currently working on a short study of Louis XIV (Laterza) and a history of Turin, 1675–1730.

Introduction: on the Grand Tour

John A. Marino

> Seeing the Villa Ludovisi again [and] more charmed than ever
> by Guercino's frescoes, [one feels] a sudden passion . . . a near
> exaltation [which] is somewhat like love at first sight [*un coup
> de foudre*]. An instant reveals to you what your heart had
> needed for a long time without recognizing it.
>
> Stendhal (1828)[1]

Guercino's fresco of *Aurora* in the Casino Ludovisi in Rome depicts
the charioteer Dawn ushering in a virile Day to dispel the furtive
Night. Guercino's *Dawn*, commissioned by the cardinal nephew of
the newly elected Pope Gregory XV (1621–3), celebrates the beginning
of his Bolognese compatriot Alessandro Ludovisi's pontificate as a
new golden age, while it marked the high point of baroque painting
among the Bolognese school in Rome—Annibale Carracci, Guido
Reni, Francesco Albani, Lanfranco, Domenichino, as well as the
young Guercino himself. Dawn, boldly streaking across the sky above
the pope's *casa*, a house in the sense both of family and of property
where social relationships and power politics were one, chases away
the darkness.

We might interpret Guercino's architectural framework supporting the exuberant colours of the morning sky figuratively as an alle-
gory for the universal politico-religious structures that undergirded

<hr>

[1] Stendhal, *Promenades dans Rome*, ed. V. Del Litto (Grenoble, 1993), 191 (30 April
1828).

the vibrantly creative world of early modern Italy. No longer seen as decadent 'forgotten centuries' obscured between a faded Renaissance and the delayed modernization of Italian unification, early modern Italy inaugurated a stable political system as well as a resurgent Church. The new institutional order imposed upon Italy by the Spanish victory in the Italian Wars and the religious reforms by the Council of Trent, moreover, reinforced the most fundamental bonds of Italian identity and solidarity, namely, the *casa*—family property, power, and patronage.

The pope's short two-year reign was, however, a false dawn darkened by the opening hostilities of the Thirty Years War that engulfed Italy in economic crisis and reoriented its relationship among the great powers. The true dawn—contrary to an earlier nationalistic historiography—linked the long-term politico-cultural movements of Renaissance humanism and religious reform in the sixteenth century with the eighteenth century's Enlightenment and political reform. Early Enlightenment thinkers such as Scipione Maffei, Ludovico Antonio Muratori, Giambattista Vico, and Pietro Giannone, as well as such Enlightenment reformers as Cesare Beccaria, the Verri brothers, Ferdinando Galiani, and the precocious school of 'moral' (soon to become 'political') economy founded at Naples in 1754 around Antonio Genovesi, developed their analysis of historical lessons and their programmes of ethical action in the evolving marketplace of information and knowledge. Eighteenth-century reformers responded to specific problems and local contexts with heightened urgency, increased militancy, and widening divisions between reformers and rulers. Early modern Italy did not break with the past, but elaborated and embellished, challenged and confronted the tradition as it constructed a distinctive path to modernity.

For Stendhal, who had first come to Italy in 1800 as part of Napoleon's army, 'love at first sight' is expressed in French (as in Italian) by the phrase 'a stroke of lightning'.[2] This metaphor is more than a romantic incantation to capture the 'sudden passion' or 'near exaltation' experienced on seeing Guercino's fresco. Stendhal extends the metaphor of the extreme improbability and complete devastation of being struck by lightning/love to the affective experience

---

[2] Stendhal greatly disliked this commonplace metaphor for 'love at first sight': 'This ridiculous word should be changed; nevertheless, the thing exists', cited in *Petit Robert* (Paris, 1978), 814.

of the baroque aesthetic—grandeur and magnificence, awe and consternation.

By the time of Stendhal's *Walks in Rome* in 1828, guidebooks and travel memoirs were compiled by repeating the second-hand observations of countless predecessors in order to quench the appetites of armchair travellers, no longer the cosmopolitan visitors making their rite of passage on the Grand Tour of Italy. During the heyday of the Grand Tour in the seventeenth and eighteenth centuries, the tutor-guide presented countless illustrations from the young traveller's classical education to elicit personal responses to literature, art, and architectural monuments of the Italian past. This moral education did not remain static, and as the new discoveries of Herculaneum in 1738 and Pompei after 1748 were unearthed to reveal new ways of understanding the ancient world, or the crisis of the Old Regime exposed the problems of the present—especially after the 1763–4 famine in Naples—so too the emerging modern world born of the republican and industrial revolution caused not only the observers but the object of their gaze to change. Goethe, as he reinvented and discovered himself during his Italian travels of 1786–8, expressed the quintessential romantic perception of Italy in the conclusion to his long description of Roman Carnival:

The long, narrow, full, crowded street [the Corso], reminds us of the paths of earthly life, where every spectator or participant, without a mask or with one, surveys from a balcony or stand just a meager space in front of, or next to, himself, proceeds only step by step in a carriage or on foot, is shoved more than he walks, is obstructed more than he willingly stands still, tries only the more eagerly to arrive at a place where life will be better and happier, then gets into straits again, and at last is crowded out.

If we may continue to speak more seriously than the subject seems to warrant, then we shall make the observation that the most intense and extreme pleasures, like those horses flying past, appear to us only for a moment, stir us, and scarcely leave a mark on our mind; that freedom and equality can be enjoyed only in the frenzy of madness; and that, in order to spur us to the highest pitch of excitement, the greatest delights must come into very close proximity with danger and let us wantonly savor, in their vicinity, feelings of pleasure mixed with fear.[3]

---

[3] Johann Wolfgang von Goethe, *Italian Journal*, trans. R. R. Heitner, vol. vi. of *Goethe's Collected Works*, ed. T. P. Saine and J. L. Sammons (New York, 1989), 'Ash Wednesday', 414.

What Carnival meant to Romans, however, depended on what kind of Roman you were. Cardinals ('princes of the Church') and their large households might entertain visitors such as the French nobleman Michel de Montaigne in 1581 from the balconies or temporary grandstands along the Corso. Their view of the daily races—of humans, not just horses—would be very different from that of Roman Jews (boys and old men) who were forced to run stark naked to the derision of the clamouring throngs.[4] Ritual humiliation for Jews, not the carnivalesque conceit of the 'world turned upside down', went hand in hand with identification badges or yellow hats, curfews, and residential enclosure in ghettos with walls, doors, or gates—in Venice (1516), Rome (1556), Siena (1567), Florence (1570), Ferrara (1627) and other Italian cities such as Reggio Emilia, Modena, and Padua.[5]

A traveller to Italy such as Montaigne in the late sixteenth century may have had another Bolognese guidebook, Leandro Alberti's *Descrittione di tutte l'Italia*.[6] Alberti profiled some 300 cities in nineteen regions. The voyager descended the Tyrrhenian coast from Genoa to Tuscany, Umbria, Campania, Terra di Lavoro, Basilicata, Calabria Inferiore, and Calabria Superiore, and then ascended the Adriatic coast from Terra di Otranto to Terra di Bari, Capitanata, the Abruzzi, the Marches, Romagna, Lombardy below and above the Po, the Veneto, Friuli, and Istria. Sicily and the islands were added in post-1561 editions, but the eventual unifier of Italy, Piedmont/Savoy, with its capital still in Chambéry and not moved to Turin until 1563, was excluded as not yet part of Italy. Such an itinerary challenges modern divisions of Italy into either a North/South dualism of developed and undeveloped economies or a tripartite regionalism of North, Central, and South defined by geographical/climatic commonalities and political/historical traditions. Instead, Alberti's

---

[4] M. Boiteux, 'Les Juifs dans le carnaval de la Rome moderne (XVᵉ–XVIIIᵉ siècles)', *Mélanges de l'École Française de Rome. Moyen âge temps modernes* 88(2) (1976), 745–87. My thanks to Bobbi Wirsh for her bibliography on Roman Carnival and the Jews.

[5] The word *ghetto* means 'foundry' and refers to the previous use of the site of the first Jewish enclosure in Venice. Paradoxically, forced segregation of the Jewish minority gave them more freedom within their confined area and fostered a closer community to help preserve the Jewish way of life. See also K. Stow, *Theater of Acculturation: The Roman Ghetto in the Sixteenth Century* (Seattle, 2001).

[6] L. Alberti, *Descrittione di tutta l'Italia* (Bologna, 1550) follows Flavio Biondo's 1453 model of 264 cities in 18 regions, and was originally dedicated to Henry II of France and his Medici consort, Catherine. It went through 10 subsequent editions in Venice between 1551 and 1631.

Italy is a geographical tour organized around the dominance of urban-based societies and the reciprocal relationship between town and countryside.

The rules governing land, labour, and exchange extended across political boundaries. Who owned and who worked the land, how it was cultivated, and where its products sold varied by climatic zone (mountains, plateaus, or plain) and regional custom. Towns were magnets drawing rural products for food and manufactures as well as immigrant populations to work, trade, study, and pray. Towns were the central places of markets and exchange, the centres of sharp social hierarchies and intense elite rivalries, the capitals from which urban patricians extended their sway over hinterland resources and formed regional states.

The various Italian states also shared traditions of law, language, and religion. Their very names—Roman law, Latin and Romance languages, and Roman Catholicism—all emphasize the imperial legacy of a universal government. The debates about the best forms of government—imperial versus local rule and principalities versus republics—took on added significance from 1550 to 1700 as most Italian states were either incorporated into the Spanish imperial system or came largely under its sway. Jurisprudence, learning, and religiosity were not dead letters. Their spread across Italy's political divides allowed for an easy circulation of people and ideas to accelerate and deepen the ties that bound the peninsula together.

The family, above all, was the binding force in Italian society, the source of support and identity for individuals. Kinship relationships through agnation (the vertical male line)—or when advantageous, cognation and affinity (both male and female relatives)—established the dominance of patriarchal, patrilineal families intent on producing male heirs to conserve their wealth. In a society with partible inheritance rather than primogeniture, marginalized wives, daughters, and second sons made family relations simultaneously complementary and conflictual.

The purpose of this book about early modern Italy is not to recount the warmed-over historical facts and artistic judgements from a long line of guidebooks. Rather, the history of early modern Italy establishes the context to understand the ideas and institutions, experiences, and examples that helped shape the present. In political thought, posthumous publication of Machiavelli's *Discourses* and *The*

Prince in 1531–2 and Guicciardini's *History of Italy* in 1561–4 established the principles for a realistic analysis of the state which was continued by Giovanni Botero and Paolo Sarpi in Italy and debated in republican discourse through the eighteenth century. Castiglione's *The Courtier* (1528), Della Casa's *Il Galateo* (1558), and Guazzo's *On Civil Conversation* (1574) provided models of comportment imitated in both city and court societies throughout Old Regime Italy and Europe. The plurality (some 40 per cent) of books published in early modern Italy, nevertheless, concerned religion and devotional literature. The formidable post-Tridentine Church from the 1580s emphasized confessionalization and social discipline, that is, centralized authority's efforts to define and enforce religious belief and practice. Late Renaissance books influenced audiences near and far, and had a life beyond their time.

The arts and sciences flourished in such early modern and Old Regime settings. Artists produced great works—whether the painting of Caravaggio and Carracci, the sculpture of Bernini, or the architecture of Borromini. Standards by which to understand art proliferated with Vasari's attempts to rewrite the tradition in his *Lives of the Artists* (1550), Cellini's archetypal portrait of the artist-as-genius in his autobiography (1558–62), or the design academy of Florence (1566). Foreign artists such as Rubens, Velasquez, and Poussin came to Italy for extended visits. Music gained equally high renown. Madrigals, organized conservatories, or the new collaborative form of music, dance, and theatre in the first operas, Peri's *Dafne* (1598) and *Euridice* (1600), gave rise to a European-wide musical culture centred in Italy. In literature, the epic poetry of Tasso and Marino, the prose novellas of Bandello and Cinzio, and the drama of Goldoni reached international audiences. In science and natural philosophy—from Della Porta's *Natural Magic*, the Jesuit mathematician Clavius' proposals for Gregorian calendar reform, Galileo's observations and experiments, and learned academies such as the Linceo (1603) and the Cimento (1657) to Laura Bassi's public experiments after 1732 and Alessandro Volta's invention of the first electric battery—Italians collected, classified, and hypothesized in the spirit of the new science.

The Italian diaspora was global. The Jesuit Matteo Ricci in China 1583–1610 would dream of becoming an intimate adviser to (and converting) the Ming emperor, the kind of influence achieved by Giulio

Mazzarino (Cardinal Mazarin) as first minister in France 1642–61 and by Carlo Broschi (the *castrato* Farinelli) in Spain 1737–59. In the fledgling United States, Lorenzo da Ponte, Mozart's great Italian librettist of the 1780s, taught Italian, lectured on Dante, and unsuccessfully promoted opera in New York City, where he died at the age of 89 in 1838.

The life led by common men and women in villages and towns, neither high-profile nor high-culture, were equally the stuff of dreams—from an obscure Friulian miller expostulating on his bizarre cosmology, Venetian artisans fist-fighting on bridges, and an itinerant exorcist plying the back roads of Piedmont to Roman Jewish boys caught roaming the streets after hours, Calabrian midwives accused of malpractice, and starving peasants everywhere fantasizing about food. Rounding out the portrait of Italians high and low, rich and poor, male and female, urban and rural sharpens our understanding of the possibilities and impediments facing them, reinforces our reconstruction of the relationship between material life and cultural creativity, underlines the peninsular exchange of people, goods, news, and ideas, and develops our sense of continuity and change over the long term of two and a half centuries. The history of early modern Italy, therefore, is a story of the construction and multiple responses to modernity that reveals the strengths and weaknesses of Old Regime society and polity.

Those weaknesses became ever more apparent in the second half of the eighteenth century as famines and wars brought home the economic, social, political, and cultural failings of the Old Regime. Reform from above under state ministers such as Giambattista Bogino in Savoy, Pompeo Neri in Milan, Francesco Maria Gianni in Tuscany, Bernardo Tanucci in Naples, or the Neapolitan Viceroy Domenico Caracciolo in Sicily became the order of the day for public administration. Even some members of the privileged orders in the clergy and nobility, who initially resisted change, joined the reform movement to address a wide range of fiscal, military, agricultural, educational, and penal problems. Such piecemeal reforms, however, often proved ineffective and illusory, for they could not resolve the fundamental contradiction between absolutism and liberty or between privilege and equality. The gradualism of government reorganization frustrated expectations and more radical political and social models pushed the Italian states to the crisis of war and revolution.

Even though the period appears to end, as it began, with foreign conquest—this time French, not Spanish—the ironies and surprises of early modern Italy teach us the importance of historical contingencies. If we return with Stendhal to take walks back in time to view Roman treasures and charms with his post-revolutionary eyes, we cannot help but have our breath taken away by fortune's turns! An obscure Corsican born in 1769, the year after his violence-riven island homeland was sold by Genoa to France, came to conquer Italy in 1796. He defeated the Piedmontese and Austrian armies to enter Milan in little more than a month. He brought the revolution, experimental republics, satellite kingdoms, or direct annexation. After enjoining the pope to journey to Paris, he crowned himself emperor in December 1804 and declared himself king of northern Italy four months later. And at the height of his power, with the dream of a new imperium and a new dynasty, Napoleon named his newborn son king of Rome in 1811.

Just as no cataclysmic break in Renaissance culture or 'loss of liberty' followed the French invasions after 1494, no liberator led the French armies 300 years later. If French and Spanish invasions and occupations conquered Italy politically, cultural exports from Italy had already conquered France, Spain, and the early modern world.

Acknowledgements

In the coordination of the dozen scholars' essays in this collection, one inevitably accumulates innumerable debts. Thanks first to the contributors themselves, who each went far afield in their essays as well as their suggestions and advice. In addition, it is a testament to the breadth and depth of early modern Italian studies to acknowledge consultation and assistance in planning and organization of the volume to the general editor, John Davis, the Oxford University Press staff, and to Judith Brown, Antonio Calabria, Jack Greenstein, Jules Kirshner, Tom Kuehn, John Martin, John Najemy, Ann Schutte, Domenico Sella, Cynthia Truant, and Stuart Woolf. Finally, I would like to remember two great scholars and teachers, Eric Cochrane and Franco Venturi, who live on in their students and their work.

PART I

THE INSTITUTIONAL FRAMEWORK: LATE RENAISSANCE RESOLUTIONS

Politics and the state system after the Habsburg–Valois Wars

Thomas J. Dandelet

In 1556, Pope Paul IV Carafa (1555–9), eager to drive the Spanish out of his native Naples, initiated an ill-fated war against the new king of Spain and Naples, Philip II (1556–98). Entering into an alliance with the French monarch, Henry II, the pope set the stage for a familiar conflict that proved to be the last sixteenth-century chapter in a long series of battles between the Spanish and French for supremacy in the Italian peninsula.

Over six unhappy decades earlier, the French invasions of Naples in 1494 had also led France and Spain to war. But if 1494 was the beginning of misfortune and war, 1557 was the end, at least for the sixteenth century. For it was in that year that the so-called Carafa war was concluded in favour of the Spanish. The French troops sent to aid the pope had been forced to retreat early in the campaign, and the Papal State was left to the mercy of the duke of Alba, the viceroy of Naples, who led the Spanish army. In the peace that followed, the pope was forced to accept terms decidedly favourable to the Spanish, notably an agreement from the papacy not to rebuild its fortifications and to treat Spain as an ally.

Combined with this victory and that of the battle of St Quentin, also in 1557, the treaty of Cateau-Cambrésis in 1559 between the Spanish and French formally acknowledged the Spanish monarch's sovereignty over his Italian territories and signalled an end to French military intervention in Italy for over fifty years. The period of the *pax hispanica*, or Spanish Peace, had begun, and the political boundaries of Italy that lasted with only slight alteration through the eighteenth century were established.

This opening chapter charts the main contours of the political history of Italy in the approximate half-century between the end of the Carafa war and the renewal of hostilities with Savoy and the French in the Monferrato war of 1613–17. This was a critical period for the development of Italian political life on both local and international levels—as well as for the recovery and flourishing of the Italian economy—largely because the Italian states enjoyed the almost unprecedented advantage of fifty years of internal peace. Locally, these decades were used to consolidate still fluid political institutions, while at the centres of power, theories of absolutism and the state matured into the dominant political ideologies of the seventeenth century.

While twentieth-century scholarship on Italy and the Spanish empire, particularly from the Italian and British traditions, has emphasized the weaknesses of the Spanish empire and the negative or regressive impact of Spanish rule on Italy, seen from the vantage point of the half-century from 1560 to 1610 this view is flawed and anachronistic. Clearly, many writers on the ground in Italy in the period did not see the Spanish empire as destined to decline and fall, or view its influence on the political and economic development of Italy as predominantly negative. Spanish rule was not an illusory power with feet of clay in those decades.

On the contrary, Italy in the age of the Spanish Peace revealed a surprisingly flexible, resilient, and effective form of imperial statecraft that represented one of the great success stories of the Spanish empire. This was not a zero sum game, moreover, and the Italian states witnessed a variety of positive internal and external political developments during the height of the *pax hispanica*.

It was clear to foreigners and Italians alike that Spain was the dominant power in Italy. In the words of one Italian observer, the Venetian ambassador Tommaso Contarini, 'The Catholic King possesses the Kingdom of Sicily, the Kingdom of Naples and the Duchy of Milan that are the most beautiful, the best, and the best part of Italy'.[1] More concretely, Milan served as the centre of the monarch's military forces in the peninsula and as the critical state connecting Spanish Italy with Spanish Flanders. At the same time, Sicily was a vital provider of grain and, together with Naples, provided men, revenue, and the strategic ports needed to control the central Mediterranean. Policies for all three states were formulated in Philip II's newly established Council of Italy, while Sardinia remained under his rule as part of the kingdom of Aragon. Moreover, the king also dominated indirectly and informally much of the rest of Italy, including the Papal States, Genoa, Florence, and the other smaller Italian states of Ferrara, Modena, Mantua, Parma, Mirandola, Urbino, and Savoy. The success of the monarch's informal imperialism was arguably as important for controlling Italy as the overt domination of his possessions. The Spanish monarch, in short, was the great power in Italy that shaped the political landscape. Subsequently, the Spanish empire and its Italian dominions formed the dominant pole of both political theory and political practice in the peninsula.

On a macro-political level, the Spanish empire provided the necessary military security and implicit or explicit threat to prevent both internal revolt and external invasion of Italy. It gave its client states of Genoa, Florence, and the Papal State, in particular, an extended period of time free of prolonged and expensive wars. These were five decades in which the institutions of the Italian states were built up and solidified, fifty years during which Spanish imperial absolutism bolstered the development of central features of the Italian state system such as military structures, finance, administration, communications, and diplomacy, while also borrowing both political theories and practices from the Italians. The Italian states thus became an integral part of the Spanish empire, and both shaped and were shaped by the political necessities of that global system.

It was in this same period that perhaps the central political development of the later half of the sixteenth century in Europe took definitive shape: the consolidation in both theory and practice of absolutism in both its ecclesiastical and secular forms. After Pope

---

[1] Biblioteca Apostolica Vaticana (hereafter BAV), Barb. Lat. 5370, os. 99–114. 'Sommario delle cose dette dall'Ecc.mo Sig.r Tomaso Contarini ritornato dall'Amb.re di Spagna nella sua relatione' (20 Apr. 1593), fo. 105.

Paul IV's failed war, the succeeding popes for the next sixty years entered into a close and mutually beneficial relationship with the Spanish monarchs that served to bolster the claims of both powers and to give them the time, money, and political stability further to develop the mechanisms of political power. The universalist claims and practices of the post-Tridentine papacy went hand in hand with Spanish imperial absolutism: frequently both Roman pontiffs and Spanish kings were supported by the same theorists, most noticeably the two neo-Thomist Jesuit theologians Francisco Suárez (1548–1617), who taught in Salamanca, Rome, and Coimbra, and Robert Bellarmine (1542–1611), who also taught in Rome.

Outside of the direct influence or control of Spain, the Republic of Venice alone kept alive the Renaissance ideal of the Republic and jealously guarded her political autonomy and privileges. While Venetian power waned after its defeat at the battle of Agnadello (1509), she continued to exercise a critical role not just in Italy but in the Mediterranean world more generally. Although increasingly a second-rate military power, the Republic was deeply aware of her distinctive form of government and political traditions. Positioned between the Mediterranean world's two great imperial giants, the Ottomans and Spanish, Venice was the other pole of Italian political theory and practice.

Still, while the distinction between the absolutist and republican political poles has been one of the defining features of Italian history in this period, the distance between the two primary powers in Italy was not as great as both contemporary and modern historians have sometimes made it appear. The tendency to romanticize the period preceding the Spanish domination as one of great political free-dom and republican political revival, and to see in Venice the last defender and reminder of that period, is a potent part of the myth of Renaissance Italy and Venice. Yet it is largely a myth. Throughout the peninsula, in city-states and kingdoms alike, the percentage of men who were politically enfranchised was remarkably small even before the age of the *pax hispanica*. In Venice, no more than two or three per cent of men had a vote in the great council, and the mainland territories controlled by the city had little more power than the towns and countryside of the kingdoms of Naples or Sicily.

Indeed, some contemporary political thinkers such as Giovanni Botero saw Venice not so much as a modern republic but as an old and medium-sized empire whose relative impotence assured her stability. For Venice, the challenge was to hold her Mediterranean possessions and trading monopoly in the face of the new large empire of the Ottomans, and her mainland possessions and prominent place in Italian affairs in the face of the Spanish empire. To this end, an increasingly small group of men made the major political decisions in Venice by following, in practice, not a republican political agenda but rather a pragmatic programme of doing whatever was necessary to maintain the power of the state. In other words, they followed the political philosophy known as *la ragion di stato*, or the 'reason of state' espoused in various forms by authors such as Machiavelli in *The Prince* and Botero in his *Reason of State*. Italian politics and the state system in the second half of the sixteenth century in general were shaped more by competing imperial systems than by a competition between republican and absolutist systems; more by the realistic power politics described by Machiavelli earlier in the century than by a struggle between lofty political theories.

Diplomacy, war, and the Holy League of 1571

The threat of the Ottomans, above all else, shaped Italian politics in the 1560s and 1570s, as it brought together the major powers of the Italian peninsula in a new and formidable alliance. In the early 1560s, the need to join forces against an expansionist Ottoman agenda in the central Mediterranean and to keep Italy at peace led the Spanish monarch to advise his ambassadors in Italy to cultivate the friendship and alliance of the Venetians. Writing to his ambassador in Rome, Don Luis Requesens, Philip II emphasized that 'with the Republic of Venice we have a good friendship and confederation', and further urged his minister to stress that 'we are and will be true friends and confederates'.[2] The Venetians, for their part, were eager to maintain cordial and constant diplomatic relations with the Spanish king and, when their mutual self-interest coincided, to be allied with him. Such was the case by the early 1570s.

---

[2] Archivo General de Simancas (hereafter AGS), *Estado, Roma*, leg. 901, unfoliated.

From the perspective of Spain's southern Italian viceroyalties, the Ottoman attack on Malta in 1565 and sporadic raids by Ottoman ships on the Italian coast underlined the continuing threat of the old enemy to the island of Sicily and the Apulian and Calabrian coasts. For Venice, at the same time, Ottoman expansion had been eating away at her trading colonies in the eastern Mediterranean for most of the century. The Papal State, too, was subjected to Ottoman raids particularly on its Adriatic coast, and Genoese ships likewise feared the Ottoman pirates. It was in the face of this common threat that the main Italian powers joined forces in the major act of military cooperation of the period, the Holy League of 1571.

The attack on Malta in 1565 had revealed both the strength and proximity of Turkish power and the importance of Spanish naval power in the central Mediterranean. For it was the Spanish troops and fleet of Don García de Toledo, viceroy of Sicily, that ultimately forced the Turkish fleet to abandon the siege of Malta. Pope Pius V (1565–72) justifiably continued to be preoccupied with Turkish naval power, and in 1566 pledged 3,000 paid soldiers for Malta's defence under the command of Pompeo Colonna, a double vassal of both the pope and Philip II.[3] In the following year he asked the king to send Spanish troops to help defend the island, and in 1568, under Philip's prompting, authorized a tax on the clergy of Naples that raised 30,000 *scudi* to build fortifications on Malta.[4]

With this defensive alliance growing throughout the early years of Pius V's pontificate, the pope was reluctant to hear any complaints against Philip II from unhappy subjects. When the Milanese senate sent an envoy to Rome in 1567 to protest Spanish taxation policies and seek papal intervention, the pope turned him away, saying that he had no intention of interfering with this business of the king, whom he called 'an obedient son of the Apostolic See'. Upon the insistence of the Spanish ambassador and the Spanish cardinal Pacheco, the pope went so far as to excommunicate the president of the senate when he persisted in resisting the king's financial demands. The pope also acknowledged the king's right to use force to extract the revenues if necessary.[5]

---

[3] AGS, *Estado, Roma*, leg. 902, unfoliated.
[4] BAV, Urb. Lat. 1041, fo. 50v.
[5] BAV, Urb. Lat. 1040, fos. 436v, 490v.

In a variety of ways, then, the pope used the substantial tools of power at his disposal, including the right to impose ecclesiastical taxes, excommunicate, and arbitrate or intervene, particularly in Italian and ecclesiastical affairs, to help the king consolidate his own power. Whether in Milan or Naples, the decisions of Pius V revealed explicitly or implicitly how the papacy often supported and contributed to an increasingly centralized Spanish monarchical authority. The joining of spiritual and temporal authority that characterized the papal monarchy in this period, and that led to such actions as excommunication for tax resistance, could be extended to the other monarchies as well when the pope cooperated. At the same time, such actions often strengthened the position and image of the papacy. Thus papal absolutism and Spanish absolutism, secular and ecclesiastical power, grew ever more complementary and interdependent.

So too did ecclesiastical and secular financial affairs and taxation, yet another realm of the early modern Italian state system that became more sophisticated and effective in this period. The largest share of most Italian states' budgets regularly went to military spending, and it was the extremely expensive war against the Ottomans that led Pius V to support special taxes on ecclesiastical revenues in Venice and the Spanish territories, in particular. When Pius approved the renewal of the sale of the Spanish *cruzada*, or crusade indulgence, in 1570, for instance, he required that the king use part of the revenue, estimated to be 334,000 ducats per year for five years,[6] to make the following contributions to the proposed alliance: 400 ships of various sizes, 10,000 infantry, 5,000 cavalry, and grain for the fleet.[7] Although this did not turn out to be the configuration of the Spanish contribution to the Holy League of 1571, Philip II did provide nearly half of the ships and two-thirds of the men, and paid for the majority of provisions for the alliance. Venice provided the other major contingent of ships and men, and the papacy provided a dozen ships and a few thousand men. The Genoese sent three ships and many men, and their prince, Gian Andrea Doria, commanded a significant number of the ships paid for by the Spanish monarch. Savoy also contributed three ships.

[6] BAV, Urb. Lat. 1042, fo. 34v.
[7] BAV, Urb. Lat. 1041, fo. 323r.

Before the real fight had ever begun, the alliance itself represented a victory for Italian statecraft, since it revealed the power of an increasingly mature diplomatic corps in the Italian peninsula. By the middle of the sixteenth century, Venice, the papacy, and the Spanish monarch had regular ambassadors in one another's courts, as did Florence and Genoa. Although the first permanent ambassador in Europe, that of the Spanish monarch in Rome, had only been established at the end of the fifteenth century, by 1571 the machinery of diplomatic relations had grown considerably.

Besides the regular embassies and ambassadors themselves, this included a regular mail service to shuttle back and forth the large volume of correspondence between the major Italian cities and Spain. By 1571 a regular courier was going twice a month between Italy and Spain by way of Sicily, Naples, Rome, Milan, Genoa, Barcelona, and Madrid. With a letter taking three or four weeks to make the journey one way, it was not a fast system. But it was the most regular communications system in early modern Europe. Its growing importance was embodied in the rise of the Tassis family, of humble Italian origins but with good horses, who were first hired to carry mail for Charles V in the 1540s. By the seventeenth century they had been made nobles by the Spanish king, and gave their name to the modern taxi. The papacy, Venice, Genoa, Florence and most of the other smaller Italian states also had couriers shuttling back and forth to the major cities of the peninsula, albeit on a less regular level.

With couriers dubbed nobles and Italian diplomacy reaching maturity by 1571, Lepanto also revealed that another major institution of the early modern state, the military, had attained new levels of organizational capability, logistical sophistication, and strength. When the 208 ships and 30,000 men of the Holy League faced the Ottoman forces in the Gulf of Lepanto off of the shores of Greece in October of 1571, they proved to be the superior force. With the advantage of six Venetian galliasses and 1,800 cannon, a type of floating arsenal that was overwhelming to the opponents, the Italian–Spanish coalition won a decisive victory that was celebrated throughout Italy as one of the century's great military moments.

While the Ottomans were able to launch another fleet the following year and take the prize of Cyprus, Lepanto effectively ended the contest for the central Mediterranean, with a stalemate establishing an Ottoman sphere in the eastern and a Spanish sphere in the western

Mediterranean. Although the Holy League of 1571 did not continue after Venice and the Spanish reached separate truces with the Ottomans in the mid-1570s, the two naval forces of the Venetians in the Adriatic sea and the Spanish-Italian fleet in the western Mediterranean effectively controlled the central and western Mediterranean sea for the next century.

The major innovation of the period was the constant fleet of roughly 100 ships that the Spanish monarchy continually had stationed in Palermo, Messina, Naples, and Genoa. Manned by Italian and Spanish sailors and often led by Italian princes such as Gian Andrea Doria of Genoa and MarcAntonio Colonna of Rome, this was the closest thing to a permanent navy that Italy beyond Venice had ever had.

Philip II was very aware of the politics and tax burdens of Italy and emphasized to the new pope, Gregory XIII (1572–85) in 1574 that the fleet, including the war and defence of Malta, cost him more than 2,000,000 ducats annually. This huge expense, together with the related logistical challenges of maintaining, manning, and supplying the ships, played a particularly significant role in shaping the politics of Italy and particularly the kingdoms of Sicily and Naples throughout the period.

The Spanish viceroys appointed to rule over the southern Italian kingdoms of Naples and Sicily, as well as the governor of Milan, were essentially military governors who spent a majority of their time seeing to the maintenance of fortresses and parts of the army and/or fleet, the recruitment of soldiers and sailors, and the collecting of various taxes to pay for these activities. While Milan played the role of the major military power among the Spanish possessions in terms of soldiers and fortresses, the ports of Naples, Messina and Palermo were also of major strategic importance. Overseeing the grain trade, too, was a central element of military strategy for Sicily since it was crucial to keep the ships supplied with food and to alleviate food shortages in other parts of Italy and Spain such as Genoa, Seville, Rome, and Savoy.

The bureaucratic state and patronage politics

All of these functions required a host of secretaries, lawyers, and tax collectors who played increasingly important roles in the day-to-day affairs of state. These *auditori*, as many of the lawyers holding state appointments or offices were to be called, grew in power throughout Italy in the later half of the sixteenth century as they increasingly came to dominate the representative bodies of different states. Many were able to purchase offices, titles, and estates and became a new nobility of the robe. In Naples, for example, the number of titles sold is estimated to have almost doubled between 1528 and 1601.

These men eventually dominated the three councils of Naples, and the senate in Milan. In Sicily, too, they held places in the parliament, and in Venice were in control of the fiscal machinery. In the Papal State, they held many of the most powerful positions in the curia. In Naples, these lawyers were often called *togati* ('men of the robe'), and the viceroyal administrations fostered them in all the Spanish territories in order to undermine the traditional nobility. As a middling administrative order, they were more dependent on the patronage of the state than the old nobility. Throughout Italy, in the Spanish and independent states alike, they formed the backbone of the administrative state of the early modern period.

The growing needs of a bureaucratic military state necessitated by a standing navy in the majority of the Italian states, on the other hand, sometimes served to reinforce traditional local political privileges. While growing political power at the centre could erode the rights of traditional representative bodies, as it did in the case of the Senate of Milan, or the Great Council of Venice, at other times the constant need for revenue also gave the towns and traditional corporate bodies more leverage with the powers at the top. In the case of Sicily in 1579, for example, representatives of the city of Palermo, who had just made a special contribution of 40,000 ducats to the king for the purchase of a new galley, wrote to the monarch requesting more judicial autonomy for the main court. The king subsequently wrote to the viceroy urging special care in honouring the traditional judicial privileges of the court.[8]

Increasing bureaucratic needs and a growing military state also led to the rise of one of the predominant features of the early modern Italian state, patronage politics. Widespread networks of patrons and clients, bound together by both public and private interests, were perhaps the most distinctive feature of later sixteenth-century Italian political life. With expanding numbers of financial and judicial offices, ecclesiastical benefices, military commissions, and lesser positions such as secretaries and notaries, the princes used these patronage appointments to build political factions and support. Political clientelism brought public and private interests together and was a central feature in the consolidation of the modern state. As larger numbers of people were bound to the central authority through various offices and income-producing positions, a social cohesion and consensus grew about the necessity and utility of a larger and more pervasive presence of state authority.

At the highest level, the Spanish monarchs were perhaps the most skilled players of the patronage game. The Venetian ambassador to Madrid, Tommaso Contarini, remarked in his report to the doge in 1593 that the Spanish king's political strategy with the Italian nobility was to tie them to himself with large stipends and honours. In this way the king took many of the best soldiers, captains, and other 'principal people' from the Italian states to serve the needs of the Spanish empire.[9]

In fact, in all the states of Italy there was increased jockeying for government offices that brought income and increased social status to the educated class. Government spending increased substantially in the period, and with it the positions available. Contarini reported that the Spanish monarchy's income and expenditures in Italy in the period was roughly 900,000 ducats in Sicily, 1,200,000 ducats in Naples, and 900,000 ducats in Milan. With a soldier's annual pay at roughly 30 ducats, a captain's at 600, and a high-ranking judge or royal official's at 1,000, the three million ducats of government spending represented employment and revenue for thousands of people.[10]

[8] Biblioteca Santa Scholastica, Colonna Archive, Personaggi Illustri, Buste AE, Letter 771, 23 Mar. 1579.

[9] BAV, Barb. Lat. 5370, 'Sommario . . . Tomaso Contarini' (20 Apr. 1593), fo. 105v.

[10] Ibid. fo. 100.

State income, however, could not keep pace with increased expenses. A detailed fiscal account from Naples in 1595 reported that total Neapolitan expenditures of 2,930,000 ducats exceeded income by 430,000 ducats. In addition, merchant bankers were owed more than 1,600,000 ducats of an already mushrooming public debt of almost 1,950,000 ducats. The 1595 Neapolitan budget projected that about half of state expenditures (almost 1,500,000 ducats) were earmarked for military, civil, and pension payments, while 39 per cent (more than 1,150,000 ducats) would be needed to service the debt.[11]

While the other Italian states spent considerably less than the Spanish, they too witnessed an expansion of administrative machinery and government spending in the period. Venice especially needed a great deal of money and men to keep her navy afloat, so much so that after Lepanto the Republic was straining under a huge public debt that pushed her to reach a separate treaty with the Ottomans. The papacy, too, was expanding its own administration, the curia, at this time, as well as its diplomatic corps, and its own budget reached the 2,000,000 *scudi* mark by the early seventeenth century, although as much as half went to service the debt.

The need to finance such debt led to an increasingly sophisticated set of financial instruments such as state bonds, or the papal *monte*, as well as large lines of state credit and international banking relationships. For the Spanish monarch, also constantly in debt, the Genoese bankers played a central role in the empire from Philip II's first bankruptcy in 1556 by providing the credit needed to keep the state's finances afloat in between the arrivals of bullion shipments from the New World. Subsequently, an international financial network developed that revolved around the mutually dependent Spanish military machine and Genoese financial and commercial enterprises.

---

[11] A. Calabria, *The Cost of Empire: The Finances of the Kingdom of Naples in the Time of Spanish Rule* (Cambridge, 1991), 76–8, cites the Neapolitan fiscal officer, Ferrante Fornaro, 'Brief Budget of Income and Expense and of what is due to Merchants and the Militia' (8 Nov. 1595), AGS, *Estado, Nápoles*, leg. 1094, fo. 124.

Disturbing the peace: the French revival

While this broad-based Italian–Spanish alliance dominated Italian political affairs in the 1570s and 1580s, a number of international and internal challenges to the status quo appeared in the 1590s. First among them was the re-emergence of the French monarchy as a potential arbiter of power in Italian affairs. After decades of civil war, the Protestant pretender to the French throne, Henry of Navarre, had agreed to convert to Catholicism in 1592, thereby paving the way for a united and reinvigorated France. The formal absolution of Henry IV by Pope Clement VIII in December of 1595 brought the French monarchy not only back into the Catholic fold but also back into Italian political affairs.

Even before his conversion, Venice had given support to Navarre's claim to the throne, thus indicating that at least one Italian state was eager to have another powerful European monarch to counter the Spanish hegemony in Italy. In Rome, too, it was clear that France would be challenging the dominance of Spain as the French monarch began sending more money to the papal court to build up a faction of French supporters in the college of cardinals. The grand duke of Tuscany, Ferdinand I, in the meantime, showed a new level of independence from Spain by marrying a French princess, and announcing the marriage of his niece Maria to the French king.

The first major political incident that revealed how the re-entry of the French had changed the equation of power concerned the state of Ferrara, then ruled by Alfonso II d'Este. When the childless prince died in 1597, Ferrara, technically a fief of the papacy, was claimed by Clement VIII, who wished to reincorporate it into the Papal State. Although Alfonso II had named his nephew Cesare as his lawful heir, Clement VIII did not acknowledge this claim, and the stage was thus set for a battle reminiscent of the earlier part of the century when the Papal State was expanding.

Although the Spanish monarchy originally sided with Cesare d'Este, the French king made a very public statement of support for papal claims, going so far as to say that he would send as many troops as necessary to aid the pontiff. With the papacy a far more important political ally than Ferrara, Philip II, then in his last year of life, quickly changed his position, paving the way for Clement VIII to reclaim Ferrara in May of 1598.

This victory for the papacy, together with the death of Italy's most powerful monarch, Philip II, later that year, sent a clear signal that the political landscape was shifting. The independent Italian states were increasingly emboldened to act out of own self-interest without consulting the new and inexperienced Spanish monarch, Philip III. And the papal prince, above all others, was moving to consolidate and expand both his temporal and spiritual powers. These developments set the stage for the volatile decade that followed, and for the most serious conflict of the entire period since the Carafa war, the Venetian interdict controversy.

The growing confidence and power of the papacy during the reign of Clement VIII served as a prelude to a yet bolder assertion of papal ecclesiastical prerogatives and political influence in the peninsula in the reign of his successor, Paul V Borghese (1605–21). Tensions between the papacy and Venice had been rising slowly but surely throughout the 1580s and 1590s, in large part because of Venice's failure to support the papal–Spanish political agenda in France and vis-à-vis the Ottomans.

In 1606, however, a more direct conflict broke out when the authorities in Venice arrested and tried two priests in the civic courts, an event that precipitated the Interdict controversy of 1606–7. Paul V saw the arrests as a direct infringement on papal authority, and matters came to a head in April of 1606 when the pope demanded the release of the two clerics being held by the civil authorities and the repeal of recent laws that had forbidden both the building of new churches without secular permission and the alienation of property to clerics. Venice refused. The doge, senate, and government of Venice were then excommunicated and the entire Republic placed under interdict. Priests were ordered to withhold the sacraments. Preparation for the threatening battle ensued on two fronts: real military preparations and ideological war.

On the first front, talk of open war between the two powers began immediately, and it was then that the true loyalties of France and Spain, as well as the dependency of Rome on the Spanish, were brought into full relief. Although Henry IV had initially attempted to play the role of mediator, the Venetians held fast to their positions, and the discussions in Rome became increasingly bellicose. In the meantime, Philip III wrote to the pope pledging his assistance to the Holy See. Repeated interventions by both Spanish and French ambassadors failed, and open preparations for war began.

In Rome, reports estimated that a full-scale conflict would involve 50,000 infantry and 4,000 cavalry at a cost of 600,000 *scudi* per month. It was obvious that the Papal State could not hope to finance a war of this magnitude, and it fell to the Spaniards to provide the bulk of the forces for the expected conflict. More specifically, Philip III ordered his governor in Milan, the count of Fuentes, to raise an army of 26,000 infantry and 4,000 cavalry to defend the papal interests. Early in 1607, moreover, Alfonso d'Avalos, a Spanish colonel serving in Milan, was called to Rome by Paul V and charged with organizing the papal forces. Shortly thereafter Alessandro Monti, a captain fighting for the Catholic king in Flanders, was called to Rome and put in charge of the papal forces.[12] These facts underlined both the central military importance of the duchy of Milan to Spanish power in Italy and the Spanish king's continuing role as protector of the papacy. Moreover, the threat of large-scale Spanish military intervention in Venice forced Henry IV to show his true sympathies. He subsequently ordered troops and cavalry raised to aid the republic, which further accentuated the fact that the Spanish monarchy was the sole power that Rome could truly depend upon. Even though an actual war was averted and a formal reconciliation between the papacy and Venice reached in April of 1607, the year of tensions had undermined many of the advances that the French had made in Rome in the previous decade and reaffirmed the continuing Spanish pre-eminence in Italy. It was also the major international event that demonstrated how dependent the bold claims of papal absolutism were on the practical military support of the Spanish monarchy.

On the ideological level, too, the Interdict controversy proved to be a seminal moment for the consolidation of developments in political theory and rhetoric that had been taking shape during the past century. More specifically, the Interdict led to the most elaborate and sophisticated exchange of competing theories of the state that had occurred to date, and set the terms of the debate in the century that followed.

Political theory did not drive political practice in the latter half of

---

[12] BAV, Urb. Lat. 1074, fo. 484v; Urb. Lat. 1075, fos. 61v and 128r.

the sixteenth century in Italy. Rather, most of the theoretical fundamentals of the three major political philosophies—Machiavellian political realism and 'reason of state', republicanism, and neo-Thomism at the service of absolutism—were already in place in the first half of the century. But it was largely the expanding powers and pragmatic necessities of the state, and particularly those of Spain and the papacy, that drove the elaboration and dissemination of the theories of absolutism and the application of reason-of-state arguments in the last decades of the century. Similarly for Venice, it was the papal and Spanish challenge to their autonomy that led their primary theorist, the Servite priest Paolo Sarpi, to use both the theory of the free republic and basic principles drawn from reason of state to explain and justify the Venetian government's claims.

The ideological debate between Venice and the papacy formally revolved around the old question of the relationship between the Church and state. More specifically, it focused on the rights of the papacy as the head of the Church to intervene in another state's ecclesiastical affairs. At its most fundamental level, the debate was about state power and sovereignty.

For the defender of Venice, Paolo Sarpi, state sovereignty was 'a power absolute by nature from which nothing can be exempted or excepted'.[13] It followed that the government of Venice could not abide papal intrusion into its affairs, an act that constituted an assault on its sovereignty. Writing anonymously, Sarpi further argued in his 'Treatise on the Interdict' that God intended that two forms of government, one spiritual and the other temporal, exist side by side, but ultimately independent of one another. The pope had no right to intervene in the affairs of a sovereign state whose absolute power was given by God; further, state power extended absolutely to jurisdiction over clerics and church property in the state's territory.

The central arguments from the papal–Spanish perspective were found in the writings of the Italian Jesuit Robert Bellarmine in *The Supreme Pontiff (1610)* and the Spanish Jesuit Francisco Suárez in *The Laws and God the Law Giver* (1612). These two theologians, both of whom taught in the Jesuit's Roman College in the late sixteenth century, were the primary exponents of a natural-law theory of the state

---

[13] W. Bouwsma, 'Venice, Spain, and the Papacy', in *A Usable Past* (Berkeley, Calif., 1990), 253.

that reached its peak in their writings. At the same time they were the main theorists for papal absolutism.

For Bellarmine, the pope had the ultimate authority, since only he had been given his power directly from God. Earthly governments such as princes and republics were given their power by the people, and although this power was absolute once given, it was still a temporal power that could be taken back if that power was abused. Such was not the case with the pope, whose power came directly from God as attested to in scripture, most especially in the famous gospel passage where Christ gives Peter the power of the keys of heaven.

The basic principle of papal spiritual supremacy over all other princes was already expressed in the advice given by another Spanish theologian, Melchor Cano, to Philip II at the beginning of the Carafa war fifty years earlier. This position was elaborated upon by the Salamanca theologians led by Vittoria, Ribadeneira, and Suárez, and the Spanish monarchy's adherence to it was central to their claim of being the main protectors of the Church. Defending theoretical papal supremacy thus became a cornerstone of Spanish policy and political theology throughout the period, even if they clashed frequently over practical issues of ecclesiastical jurisdiction and a range of other issues.

Perhaps the biggest practical difference between Spain and Venice was that the Spanish monarchy was steadily gaining control over the Church in its territories throughout the period, often with the support and help of the papacy. In Sicily, for example, the monarchy claimed the rights of papal legate that gave it wide-ranging rights over the local Church. Venice, on the other hand, was feeling increasingly threatened by a resurgent Rome and financially drained by money going to church-building and convent dowries.

Indeed, although the great theoretical disputes of the Interdict controversy revolved around divine intention, the interpretation of scripture, and the philosophical fine points of political power and sovereignty, with Christ, Plato, Aristotle, and Aquinas occupying centre stage, always lurking in the background was Machiavelli and the issue of raw power, realistic politics, and political necessities. Regardless of theoretical developments and the practical political advances made in Italy in the second half of the sixteenth century in terms of administration, diplomacy, and bureaucracy, the core Machiavellian purpose of all of the major Italian powers—pope, doge, Spanish monarch—remained the preservation and expansion of government power. And regardless of the occasional resistance to the expansion of state power and especially Spanish imperial power in Italy, the overwhelming drive was towards its validation and justification.

This was especially evident in one last political theorist who serves as a bridge between the sixteenth and seventeenth centuries, Tommaso Campanella (1568–1639). Campanella, a Dominican priest, prolific writer, and imaginative thinker, fell foul of the Inquisition in the 1590s. He wrote the first draft of *On the Monarchy of Spain* some time between 1594 and 1595 while under arrest in Rome, and revised it in forced exile in his Calabrian home town in late 1598. His own shadowy involvement in a minor uprising there in 1599 led to his imprisonment by the Inquisition in Naples, where he wrote his utopia, *The City of the Sun*, in 1602.

Written during his more than thirty years in prison, these works constituted a late Renaissance swirl of ideas drawn from a wide variety of ancient and contemporary writers as diverse as Plato and Botero. At their heart, both the metaphorical *City of the Sun* and the formal political treatise *On the Monarchy of Spain* promoted a universal Christian monarchy as the highest form of government. Given the circumstances of their production, it is no surprise that the monarchy destined for this role by the author was the Spanish monarchy.

Campanella wrote all of his prison works with the hope of proving his theological and political orthodoxy, and *On the Monarchy of Spain* subsequently represents perhaps the peak of Italian political writing that sought to justify and bolster both Spanish and papal absolutism. Unlike Suárez or Bellarmine, Campanella was not a scholastic theologian. On the contrary, his writing drew on a potent mixture of other strains of Renaissance humanism such as astrology, history, and rhetoric. Yet the aim of Campanella was much the same as that of his scholastic contemporaries. Indeed, he exceeded them in pushing for a universal Spanish monarchy, guided by the pope, ruling over all of Europe to unite Christendom and defeat the Ottoman threat.

Italy, moreover, was to play a critical role in this plan. For Campanella, Spain had no greater friend than Italy. With the pope acting as supreme spiritual adviser and the king's possessions in Italy, as well as the rest of the peninsula, supporting his leading political role in Christendom, Italy became wholly subservient to Spanish designs.

This was a world-view that clearly went beyond the more realistic aspirations of the Spanish monarchs themselves. But it did reveal how deeply the political fate of Italy had been tied to the Spanish empire in the minds of some. No Italian author would have thought to publish such ideas a century earlier, but by the early seventeenth century the political experiences of the previous five decades had made it possible.

Italian politics was married to Spanish imperial politics in the latter half of the sixteenth century, and it was a marriage that would last until the death of the last Spanish Habsburg, Charles II, in 1700. Like most arranged marriages, it was not marked by excessive love, and the cost of the dowry that many of the Italian states paid, namely their independence, was high. But the practical fruits born of the union—institutional development, peace in the peninsula, and security from the Ottomans—left many of the early modern Italian states more politically stable and prosperous than they had been for many years.

Even the war of Monferrato which broke out in the first decade of the seventeenth century and brought the French back into the peninsula could not disturb this fact. Too many people had tied their fortunes to the new Spanish status quo for any serious rebellion to take place. The jobs, salaries, and increased social status that many people had found in the Spanish-ruled, bureaucratic absolutist states were a potent combination that even appeals to national pride were unable to shake.

Religion, renewal, and reform in the sixteenth century

John Jeffries Martin

Varieties of religious experience

In 1573 Domengo di Lorenzo, an elderly shoemaker, was summoned before the Roman Inquisition in Venice to testify about his belief, shared by a few of his fellow craftsmen, that a great religious renewal was about to take place. The members of this small group of artisans (so the Holy Office learned) were convinced that the European and the Mediterranean peoples were on the verge of a New Dispensation. In particular, they believed that the time was ripe for the fulfilment of an ancient prophecy: soon there would be 'one sheepfold and one shepherd'. Concord would be restored to a world torn apart by the religious and confessional conflicts of the day.

Similar prophecies had frequently surfaced in Italian millenarian movements during the late medieval and Renaissance periods. But the story of Domengo's group also provides a glimpse into an important aspect of Italian religious culture in the decade immediately following the Council of Trent (1545–63). In Domengo's view, the Council had accomplished no good whatsoever, and he and his friends chose to ignore its decrees. For example, in explicit disregard

I thank Susan Boettcher, Caroline Castiglione, John Marino, and Anne Jacobson Schutte for their comments on earlier versions of this essay.

of the Church's stipulation that the Bible be read exclusively in the traditional Latin version known as the Vulgate, Domengo's group continued to read the Bible in an Italian translation. Moreover, though this information never reached the inquisitor, these artisans believed that the new 'shepherd' who would bring unity to their world was not the pope, but a Venetian nobleman. Clearly, this was a group that had lost faith in both Rome and the institutional Church.

This gap between the actions and pronouncements made at Trent by cardinals and bishops (most from noble families) and the beliefs of a group of artisans ten years later was not unusual. The relation between the official doctrines of the Church (themselves much debated) and the religious beliefs and practices of both the clergy and the laity was, after all, notoriously complex. Given that the Italian peninsula consisted of a patchwork of city-states, duchies, and monarchies, each made up of a great variety of social and cultural groups, Italian religious life was characterized above all by its diversity and by the frequent negotiations and renegotiations among different social groups over the meaning of specific religious symbols, beliefs, and practices. Italian religious culture was never, at least not until the late 1550s, a realm over which the papacy had much sway. As a consequence, it is best to think of the reform efforts of Italians, especially in the first half of the sixteenth century, as polycentric, emanating from diverse groups, institutions, and regions rather than as a coordinated response on the part of the Roman curia or the popes.

Until relatively recently scholars framed the discussion of the religious and ecclesiastical history of sixteenth-century Italy within the twin paradigms of a Catholic Reformation on the one hand and a Counter-Reformation on the other. The first of these terms emphasized the view that reform movements in the Catholic world had begun well before the challenge of Martin Luther; and, indeed, through this lens it is possible to discern various continuities between late medieval efforts at reform and many of the initiatives to renew the religious life in the early modern period. The notion of a Counter-Reformation, by contrast, tended to interpret the efforts for reform in Italy largely as a response to the threat of Protestant and other heretical ideas; and studies that have developed within this framework have stressed the repressive or even reactionary aspects of the Tridentine papacy and curia.

Yet neither the idea of a Catholic Reformation nor of a Counter-Reformation offers an entirely satisfactory account of the depth of the impulses for religious reform and renewal in Italian society. Both terms, in fact, tend to view religious change from the vantage point of ecclesiastical or institutional history. As a result they often ignore not only larger social, cultural, and political developments but also dynamic traditions within Italian spirituality that impinged powerfully on the lives of early modern men, women, and children. Furthermore, the juxtaposition of these concepts presents a much oversimplified narrative of early sixteenth-century Italian life as continuous with the ostensibly open and creative forces of the Renaissance, only to see this spirit of innovation shut down in the repressive climate of a Counter-Reformation that, some have argued, contributed decisively to the cultural decline of Italy. Not only is this narrative of cultural decline no longer viable, but it fails as well to identify certain common traits that underlay both the so-called Catholic and Counter Reformations. For, in fact, almost all reformers in sixteenth-century Italy shared a deep concern in fostering a more intense spirituality and at the same time a more disciplined religious culture over which a better-trained clergy would exercise greater control.

The political and cultural contexts of reform

The most decisive factor that led to an intensification in the desire for religious change was the impact of the Wars of Italy, a cycle of violence and diplomatic manoeuvring unleashed by the French invasion of the peninsula in 1494 which made much of Italy a theatre of war until the Treaty of Cateau-Cambrésis (1559). Pitched battles and marauding armies destabilized the already precarious balance of power in Italy, devastated much of the countryside, and led to a widespread sense, among many Italians, that the major political and ecclesiastical institutions of their society had failed.

The extraordinary influence by the Dominican Girolamo Savonarola exercised over Florence from 1494 until his execution in 1498 played upon this discontent. This intensely puritanical but charismatic friar used the pulpit to call for the reform of the Church; he urged the restoration of republican institutions in the wake of

Medici rule; and he mesmerized the Florentines with his prophecy that Florence itself was about to become the New Jerusalem and usher in an age of universal peace. But Savonarola was only the most conspicuous of the new prophetic reformers who crowded into Italian cities in this period. Hermits came down from the mountains to preach in town *piazze* for a renewal of piety; preachers saw in the crisis of this period evidence that ancient prophecies were on the verge of fulfilment; mystics, many of them women, seemed to reach up and touch the hand of God; finally, this was the era of the *sante vive* ('living saints') such as Colomba da Rieti, who protected her fellow Perugians from the plague, and Stefana Quinzana, who interpreted her own life's mission as the establishment of peace in an age clouded by almost continuous warfare. Many of these holy women—often honoured by the mark of the stigmata—were viewed as prophets; some were even invited to serve as counsellors to princes in the most elite courts of the day. Above all, however, they developed a model of spirituality that placed much emphasis on action in the world.

At the same time, major shifts in the cultural sphere were reshaping the religious lives of Italians. Italy—with its port cities, its merchants, and its relative openness to Jewish and Muslim traders—had long been fertile ground for the circulation of heterodox ideas. But, in Italy as elsewhere in Europe in the early modern period, it was the introduction of printing, the proliferation of presses, the diffusion of books, especially those published in the vernacular, and the growth of literacy that did most to alter and to expand the ways in which men and women, especially in the cities, participated in the religious life. The widespread diffusion of texts exploded not only among nobles and merchants but also among artisans, shopkeepers, workers, and even, on occasion, peasants and millers. An unprecedented flowering of devotional texts—lives of saints, legends of the Holy Family, treatises aimed at cultivating devotion to the Virgin Mary, books encouraging the saying of the rosary, and vernacular editions of the Bible—both provided readers with new spiritual models and led to a deeper internalization of piety and greater religious individualism. At the same time other texts, which both the religious and secular authorities would soon come to define as heretical, found their way into circulation. These included writings by Juan de Valdés, Desiderius Erasmus, Martin Luther, Huldrych Zwingli, and eventually the towering figure of John Calvin, whose theology was diffused in part in Italy in the celebrated treatise *Il Beneficio di Cristo* (1543), which became a bestseller among a wide range of readers, many of whom interpreted it (with some legitimacy prior to the Council of Trent) as an entirely Catholic work. To be sure, there were efforts to limit the availability of Protestant and other 'heretical' writings, but there was hardly the manpower to stop them from being printed, sold, shared, or read aloud among groups of friends. Printers and book-buyers alike found ways to conceal them under false titles or false names, to hide them from inspectors, and to smuggle them to new markets. Surely part of the excitement of the religious life of this period was the attraction of forbidden books.

Finally, throughout the first half of the sixteenth century, the popes and their advisers, ensconced in a world of power politics, wealth, patronage, intrigue, and inevitably preoccupied with the Italian Wars, seemed largely cut off from the spiritual concerns of the day. To be sure, the papacy was somewhat responsive to religious issues. In 1512 Pope Julius II (1503–13) convoked the Fifth Lateran Council to counter the efforts by a group of schismatic French cardinals to increase their power and influence in Italy by holding a largely Gallican council at Pisa in 1511. There is almost no doubt that both Julius and his successor Leo X (1513–21) as well as the ruling group within the curia saw the Lateran Council as a political necessity, but such a meeting did raise hopes among some that a genuine renewal would be possible. In an opening address to the delegates, Giles of Viterbo, the prior-general of the Augustinians, called for sweeping changes; and Tommaso Giustiniani and Vincenzo Querini, two Venetian patricians who had recently entered the religious life as Camaldolese hermits in the forests of north-eastern Tuscany, set out an ambitious programme for reform in their *Libellus ad Leonem X*. Nonetheless, by the time the Council ended in 1517, the delegates had only been able to agree on a few lukewarm measures. Its primary accomplishment was to strengthen the papacy in relation to church councils. The only other major action of the papacy in these years was its first, somewhat clumsy efforts to condemn Luther. Contemporaries were appalled by the degree to which the popes had seemingly abandoned their spiritual obligations. Machiavelli certainly exaggerated when he observed in *The Prince* that, 'owing to the bad example set by the Court of Rome, Italy has lost all piety and religion'. But his fellow Florentine Francesco Guicciardini captured the spirit of the times when he noted that 'reverence for the papacy has been utterly lost in the hearts of men'. And Giovan Francesco Pico made much the same point, writing that 'among many leading men of our religion there is either no worship of God or, indeed, very little'.

Papal detachment from spiritual concerns and the accelerated circulation of new religious ideas throughout the peninsula led to the opening up of spaces for the articulation of reform thought in various cultural institutions. The courts, the academies, the monasteries, and even the shops of printers and other artisans became cosmopolitan centres in which men and women of diverse social rank and nationalities found the freedom to discuss new religious concepts and gradually to put forth reform ideas of their own.

Many of the leaders of the efforts to bring about a renewal in the religious life concentrated, to be sure, on the interior or spiritual life of the individual Christian. This was the emphasis, for example, of Gasparo Contarini, a Venetian patrician with close ties to Giustiniani and Querini, who, as a young man, had undergone a religious experience that led him to place increasing emphasis on the role of grace in salvation—in ways that strikingly anticipated the teachings of Luther. A similar openness to the spiritual reform of the individual animated the circle of humanists, priests, friars, and aristocrats who gathered around Juan de Valdés (the Spanish mystic) and Bernardino Ochino (vicar-general of the Capuchins) in Naples in the period from 1535 to 1541. In the early 1540s another group formed at Viterbo around Cardinal Reginald Pole, then residing in Italy, and the poet Vittoria Colonna, one of the most influential aristocratic women of the period. Even some decidedly Catholic principalities became centres of evangelical ideas: quite openly at the court of Renée of France, the duchess of Ferrara; in a clandestine manner in the court of Cosimo I, duke of Tuscany. Academies too, from Naples and Rome to Siena and Modena, were important, providing spaces where humanists, professionals, and aristocrats could discuss and debate the new religious ideas. In addition, many religious institutions served as centres of reform: the Camaldolese Hermitage of Querini and Giustiniani; San Frediano in Lucca; the Benedictine Congregation of Santa Giustina in Padua; and San Giorgio Maggiore in Venice, also a Benedictine house. Finally, some printers freely published evangelical texts and circulated Protestant ones; they provided work, moreover, to aspiring writers, many of whom now tried to earn their living from their imaginations after the example of Pietro Aretino, himself the author of several popular satires of the papacy and a boldly pornographic indictment of nuns.

In general this was an elitist, cosmopolitan climate, one informed by a humanist critique of the abuses in the Church. And while many of these figures entertained a certain openness to Protestant ideas, these men and women, by and large, remained faithful to Rome. Their spirituality was Christo-centric, deeply personal, and stressed the importance of grace. Indeed, for a brief season, the ideas of Contarini and other evangelicals who shared his views (a group that has come to be known as the *spirituali*) seemed to offer hope for reconciliation even with the new Protestant churches, but, after the failure of the Colloquy of Regensburg in 1541 (where Protestant and Catholic legates failed to reach a common understanding) this hope was lost, and gradually a more rigorous, authoritarian coterie of reformers came to the fore within the Roman hierarchy. It was in this context, moreover, that Bernardino Ochino fled Italy to take up residence in Calvin's Geneva in 1542. Yet the texts by Erasmus and Valdés could also have radicalizing effects. For in addition to the *spirituali*, whose views remained irenic, reconciliatory, and evangelical, Italy also witnessed the emergence of both Socinian (anti-Trinitarian) and Anabaptist ideas. Moreover, neither evangelical nor more radical views were confined to the elites. In Italian cities, printers and merchants, weavers and cobblers made theological discussions part of their daily conversation. We have evidence of such groups in Naples, Rome, Florence, Milan, and Venice, as well as in numerous smaller towns and cities such as Lucca, Siena, Mantua, Modena, Verona, and Vicenza. To some church leaders, such as the Neapolitan nobleman Gian Pietro Carafa, bishop of Chieti, these movements were a warning sign that the new religious ideas had gone too far. As early as 1532, in a famous memorial meant for Clement VII, he called for the repression of the friars, priests, preachers, confessors, and books he saw as responsible for the spread of heretical ideas among the Italian populace.

Tradition and change in Italian piety

Not all efforts for reform drew on the ideas of Erasmus and Valdés, much less those of Luther and Calvin. Indeed, the greater part of the efforts to renew the religious life in the first half of the sixteenth century involved a large group of reformers who built on traditional Catholic practices, reinvigorating them and adjusting them to changed social conditions. Far more than the *spirituali*, these reformers were able to articulate a clear connection between their religious ideals and those of almost all groups in Italian society.

Saints' cults, which were exceedingly popular in Italy, demonstrate one facet of the way in which Catholic teachings were interwoven and transformed within the broader context of social and cultural life. Italians not only venerated saints; they also viewed the relics of the holy martyrs as powerful loci of the sacred that were diffused throughout their communities, in churches, shrines, and even niches along the exterior walls of urban buildings; and they called upon the holy dead for assistance in times of crisis. Women appealed to Santa Margarita at the time of childbirth; the faithful invoked San Rocco and San Sebastiano at times of plague; while the blind and those with failing eyesight called upon Santa Lucia. As a result, their shrines were often surrounded by ex-votos in various forms: miniature replicas of the body part that had been healed (an arm, a hand, a leg, the heart, and so on); small panelled paintings that narrated the cure; or brief writings that gave thanks to the saint for a miracle. Saints were also the charismatic figures around which various groups were organized. Each city and town had its own patron saints, and townspeople were able to exploit their saints either to express their discontent with their rulers (as in the popular appropriation of the cult of Santa Maria del Carmine in Spanish Naples) or to express their sense of civic unity (as in Venice around the cult of St Mark). Even smaller groups—guilds, confraternities, neighbourhoods, families—had their patron saints. The saints were foci of sacral power that impinged on the very identities of the faithful, so much so that, in the long run, Italian Christians were largely impervious to attacks on saints' cults. Nonetheless, the Council of Trent did attempt to regulate the secults. Trent invested the curia with greater control over the process of canonization, and, while allowing for the continued use of relics and icons, it developed strictures against their misuse—an important step in a climate in which both Protestants and Catholics had come to recognize how easily subject to abuse the trafficking in relics and holiness had become.

Other religious practices and rituals also wove Catholicism intricately into the lives of early modern Italians. Baptisms became occasions for the assertion of family honour; the higher the status of the godparents and the more ritual kin that the parents of the baptized infant could claim, the greater their standing in the community. Marriages too served as means for allying families and for increasing or conserving property and power. Funerals also made statements of one's family's public standing and, in some cases, as in early sixteenth-century Florence, they became elaborate theatrical celebrations explicitly designed to enhance the power of the Medici, who precisely in this period were attempting to impose their control over Tuscany. More quotidian rituals punctuated the lives of ordinary men and women as well. They took communion; they recited the rosary (an increasingly popular devotion in this period); and they made their confessions, usually to a priest or a friar. At moments of crisis, they took more dramatic actions. They formed communal processions to ward off plague; and they participated in public rites of self-flagellation, often drawing blood from their naked backs, in emotional civic dramas designed to bring God's favour upon their communities. The Italian urban landscape was filled with shrines, relics, icons, and various forms of religious theatre that brought the holy directly into the lives of people.

Beyond the city, in the Italian countryside, where the overwhelming majority of the population worked in agricultural production, there was a difference not so much in ideals about religious reform as in the very understanding of religion. Outside the towns, religion remained pre-eminently a practical matter. This was, after all, a world in which literacy was rare, and the quality of preaching deplorable. Peasants turned to priests for rituals that would protect their livestock and their crops; they drew on folk customs to ensure the safety of their families and fellow villagers; they engaged cunning women to settle disputes or to visit harm upon a neighbour. Eventually, the hierarchy would launch a campaign against these practices that it increasingly defined as superstitious, but the process was arduous, and often required not so much the suppression of a folk custom as the creation of a synthesis between rural customs and Christian doctrine. As late as 1664, a Roman priest commented on the religious ignorance of the peasants he encountered in the south of Italy: 'the majority do not even know the Lord's Prayer or the Creed, let alone the other things necessary to salvation.'

The social and economic changes of the period also led to calls for reform and renewal. As the population of the towns expanded, new forms of manufacture developed, the numbers of the poor increased, and the aristocrats began to style themselves as a privileged, landed elite. The poor, frequently uprooted by war or famine, crowded into the city in increasing numbers; there was a growing sense of civic disarray, and the religious elites sought to respond by channelling the energies of the laity into charitable activities such as poor relief and the care of the sick that would help mend the fabric of a society in crisis.

In this context new religious initiatives developed; and, although there were considerable differences among them, they were joined together by a heightened concern for charitable works, with a special emphasis on the spiritual direction of the laity by priests in religious orders. The first of these initiatives, inspired by St Catherine of Genoa (1447–1510) was the establishment of the Oratory of Divine Love in 1497. This group, made up of both laymen and women as well as priests, sought to connect the personal spirituality of each individual Christian to larger social concerns. Confraternity members took care of the sick, especially the *incurabili* (generally those suffering from syphilis), the poor, orphans, prostitutes, prisoners, and others who lived on the margins of society. In 1514–17 a number of clerics and laymen came together to establish a branch of the Oratory of Divine Love in Rome. The Theatines, a reformed order of priests led by Gaetano da Thiene and Gian Pietro Carafa, grew out of the Roman Oratory of Divine Love and was formally recognized by the pope in 1524. It too played a major role in fostering an active spirituality devoted to the care of the poor and the sick, especially the *incurabili*. Similar groups—the Barnabites, established in 1530, and the Somaschi, established in 1534—also sought to channel the charitable impulses of their members to the cure of those who lacked economic security. Exclusively female groups also had a similar emphasis. The Angeliche were inspired by Paola Antonia Negri and closely aligned with the

Barnabites; the Ursulines, established in 1535 in Brescia and inspired by Angela Merici, specialized in Christian education, though both orders, along with other female religious, were later cloistered. Emphasis on charity and active engagement in society also spread to more traditional religious orders. The Capuchins had first begun in 1525 when Matteo da Bascio, a lone member of a Franciscan friary in the Marches of Ancona, sought a return to a stricter observance of the mendicant life and an urban ministry to the poor and the sick. Recognized by the papacy in 1528, the order grew rapidly to 700 members by 1536 and to 2,500 by 1550, and counted over 450 houses scattered in towns and cities throughout Italy by the end of the Council of Trent.

By far the most significant of the new groups, however, was the Society of Jesus. This organization, which developed among fellow students at the University of Paris under the inspiration of the Basque nobleman Ignatius of Loyola, counted only ten members when it was established in 1540. The group placed itself in the service of the pope and chose Ignatius as its 'general'. Its members made it their duty to model their lives on the apostles, and they poured their energies into both education and Christian mission. By the time of Ignatius' death in 1556 there were more than 1,000 members; when the Council of Trent ended, the order counted well over 3,000 members. They established schools, imposed a strict discipline and a demanding curriculum on their students (especially on nobles/elites as future leaders), brought the Christian story alive through their dramas, and undertook missions to Asia, the Americas, and even the Italian countryside, especially in the South, which they called 'the Indies of down there'. Despite their vows of obedience to the papacy, however, they never hesitated to disagree with papal policies they found prejudicial to the larger interests of the Church. The Jesuits, for example, were among the most outspoken critics of Pope Paul IV's *Index of Forbidden Books*, a list they found too indiscriminate in its sweeping condemnations of such authors as Erasmus, many of whose works the Jesuits used in the classroom.

Other reformers, by contrast, worked within the context of the dioceses and parishes. Ever since the early sixteenth century Italian humanists had looked back to such late antique figures as Ambrose and Augustine as models for the bishops of their own age—an ideal that became especially attractive to prelates after the 1527 Sack of

Rome forced them to return to their own dioceses. These new ideals were influential on Jacopo Sadoleto (1477–1547), who took up residence in Carpentras, where he sought to reform the Church from within, as well as on Gian Matteo Giberti (1495–1543), who, after a distinguished career as a highly influential member of the papal curia, became bishop of Verona. Giberti, like Sadoleto, chose to reside in his see, where he disciplined his clergy, reformed religious houses, and took the cure of souls seriously. The next major effort for reform came early in the pontificate of Paul III (1534–49), when he appointed a commission of distinguished cardinals—among them Contarini, Pole, Carafa, Sadoleto, and Giberti—to draft a proposal for the reform of the Church. The document they produced, the *Consilium de emendanda ecclesia* (1537), called in particular for administrative reforms and the end of the common practice of holding multiple benefices, an arrangement that made many of the bishops and cardinals in Italy seem more preoccupied with their economic status than with religious leadership. But the papacy again failed to adopt the proposed reforms. It had economic and political interests of its own–even the reform-minded humanist Paul III was as eager to secure the duchy of Parma and Piacenza for his son Pier Luigi Farnese as Alexander VI had been to secure the Romagna for his son Cesare Borgia some forty years earlier.

Doctrinal and institutional reform

There were thus in Italy, by the middle decades of the sixteenth century, two distinct (though overlapping) tendencies among those intent on reform of the Church. One of these tendencies—best represented by those individual reformers such as Contarini—emphasized the possibility, by working to bring about significant institutional and doctrinal reforms within the Catholic Church, of reaching a settlement with the Protestants. On the other hand, among those who have often been called the *zelanti* or the *intransigenti*, there was a tendency to reject any possibility of compromise. Yet it is crucial to understand that the distinction between these two tendencies was more an argument about means than about ends. Both, after all, expressed a deep desire to reform the Church from within—from the papacy itself to the most insignificant parish. They both envisioned, moreover, a Church under the leadership of a reformed papacy, a renewed episcopacy, and better-trained clergy who would offer greater spiritual direction to the laity. To be sure, there were differences between the two groups. The *spirituali*, in particular, tended to emphasize faith over charity and innovation over tradition, while the *zelanti*, by contrast, stressed the central role of charity and tradition in the Christian life. Finally, there can be no doubt that it was from within this second group that we find those prelates such as Gian Pietro Carafa (the future Pope Paul IV (1555–9)) and Michele Ghislieri (the future Pius V (1566–72)) who gave their support, ultimately, to repressive measures. Both these pontiffs clamped down on dissent and attempted to enforce orthodoxy. They took a disciplinarian, even authoritarian approach to the imposition of Catholic beliefs and practices on the laity, and to a large degree their actions were shaped by their fear of the possible spread of Protestantism in Italy. It was these figures who published the various indexes of prohibited books, finally centralized in the Roman *Index librorum prohibitorum* of 1559, an authoritative but hardly enforceable list. In 1564 the original list became an updated and patrolled index, with professional theologians censoring texts and affixing imprimaturs, denying approval, or delaying approval until corrections were made. In addition, specially designated clerics inspected book-stores and confiscated banned texts; they arrested publishers; and they burned confiscated books in the piazze of Italian cities, in an attempt to warn the public of the pestiferous teachings such writings contained.

But their most decisive move was the formation in 1542 by Paul III of a commission of six cardinals whose task it was to stop the spread of heretical ideas in Italy through the establishment of inquisitorial courts whose authority (formerly under either the local bishop or a local mendicant house) was now seen to emanate from Rome. However, despite this effort to subject heresy to the control of the curia, the Roman Inquisition was never as centralized as its founders had intended. For one thing, it was the Spanish Inquisition which held sway in Sicily and Sardinia. Spain's two mainland territories—the kingdom of Naples and the duchy of Milan—successfully resisted the imposition of the Spanish and Roman Inquisitions and established their own inquisitorial courts, which remained largely under the authority of the bishop in Naples and the Dominicans in Milan, though in both these cases Rome and the local political leaders did have some say. Republican Lucca also managed to keep the Roman Inquisition at bay, and invested its local archbishop with the authority to pursue heretics. In Genoa and Venice, Holy Offices of the Roman Inquisition were established, but only on the condition that these tribunals seat lay representatives alongside the ecclesiastical judges. But many duchies in northern and central Italy, such as Tuscany under Cosimo I, were relatively quick to subject the control of heresy to Rome and to grant these tribunals considerable independence of action.

At first, the actions of the Inquisition against those suspected of heresy were relatively mild. Inquisitors sought to reconcile to the Holy Mother Church those whose writings or behaviours had cast their orthodoxy into doubt. Gradually, however, it became a more repressive institution, relying on anonymous denunciations and even torture in order to discern the 'truth'. To be sure, the Roman Inquisition, which was responsible for the executions of approximately 200 individuals, never approached the extremes of its Spanish counterpart. It did, however, represent a genuine effort to repress those expressions that it deemed as endangering the Roman Church. A fundamental turning point came when Gian Pietro Carafa became Pope Paul IV in 1555. This pontiff and his successors, in striking contrast to the popes earlier in the century, adopted rigorous policies towards even the suspicion of dissent. In 1557, for example, Paul IV ordered the arrest of Cardinal Giovanni Morone, whose early association with such figures as Contarini and Pole now made him appear suspect of heresy. And Pius IV (1559–65) also took a hard line, permitting the violent repression of Waldensian enclaves in the kingdom of Naples in 1560–61. Reasons of state also played a role. These pontiffs, after all, ruled over a vast territorial kingdom of the Papal States as monarchs, and the very structures of papal government were undergoing a rapid adjustment to the new pressures of sixteenth-century politics. The papacy established an increasingly elaborate bureaucracy, created permanent nunciatures (ambassadorships), and began the process of developing a system of 'congregations' or commissions, made up of cardinals, to advise the popes on various matters.

It was, however, undoubtedly the Council of Trent that constituted the major effort of the Roman Church in this period to clarify its teachings, to reform its institutions, and to subject both the clergy and the laity to a stricter discipline. This Council—which in three convocations (and a total of twenty-five sessions) was attended in its final stages by as many as 450 delegates, and closed with 255 signatories present (three-quarters of them Italian)—reached a number of doctrinal conclusions that together did much to uphold the authority of the Church. On the matter of the doctrine of salvation, for example, the delegates rejected Luther's teaching that the individual is saved by faith alone—a position that inevitably undermined the authority of the institutional Church—and emphasized an ideal, drawing to a large degree on the teachings of the great medieval theologian Thomas Aquinas (1214–74), whose far-ranging works bolstered the role of the traditional sacramental function of bishops and priests. The delegates also rejected the Protestant emphasis on scripture and upheld in its place the view that the Bible (which was to be read almost exclusively in the Vulgate) was to be interpreted within the framework of Catholic teachings, with Rome and its duly appointed theologians remaining the authorities in the explication of its meanings. Both these decrees clarified the salient differences between Protestant and Catholic theologies and made it clear that the Roman Church would continue to act largely as a mediator between the individual and God. Other decrees reinforced this view. The fathers at Trent upheld the seven sacraments (baptism, confirmation, the Eucharist, penance, marriage, ordination, and extreme unction); they reaffirmed the doctrine of transubstantiation (which held that the consecrated bread and wine of the Mass turned into the body and blood of Christ); and they insisted, again unlike the Protestants, on clerical celibacy, drawing a clear distinction between the priesthood and the laity.

While the doctrinal decrees taken at Trent clarified the theological differences between the Roman Church on the one hand and the new Protestant confessions on the other, the changes they adopted were also aimed at effecting significant change in the institutional structure of the Church. On these matters, even more than on the question of doctrine, the debates among the delegates grew heated. After all, the growing insistence by the reform party that cardinals, bishops, and other prelates should not hold more than one benefice and that bishops should reside in their dioceses threatened to undercut the power of the cardinals and bishops whose careers were made in Rome through patronage, nepotism, and their own efforts to achieve favour and influence within the papal court. In the end, the reform party won a few victories, while many cardinals and bishops and their families continued to find ways to accumulate multiple benefices, pensions, and privileges. Nonetheless, the delegates agreed that seminaries were to be established for the education and training of priests in order to improve the quality of preaching and pastoral care; bishops were to reside in their sees; parishes and other religious institutions were to be visited by the bishop of the dioceses in which they were located; and the religious lives of ordinary Italians were to be bound increasingly to their parishes, where they were expected to make their confessions and to take communion.

After Trent: renegotiating religious beliefs and practices

Although a few bishops, most notably Carlo Borromeo (archbishop of Milan, 1563–84) and Gabriele Paleotti (archbishop of Bologna, 1566–97) were quick to try to implement the reforms demanded by the Council of Trent, it would take at least two centuries of catechizing and proselytizing for the Church to bring about even a semblance of uniformity in religious beliefs and practices throughout the peninsula. Nonetheless, there can be little doubt that Trent, with its emphasis on the authority of the local bishop and the parish as the centre of religious life, had laid the foundations for a more individualistic and a more active notion of religious faith. Christians were to be baptized in their parishes, be married, make their confessions, take communion, and be buried there. Parish registers began to be kept on a more routine basis; and there was even an effort to institute confraternities such as the Brotherhoods of the Holy Sacrament that were explicitly organized to foster loyalty to the parish. Finally, the parish became a centre of religious education, at least ideally. Better sermons became a major source of religious instruction, the liturgy was regularized, and there was a new emphasis on catechesis, the effort to help the young in particular learn the rudiments of their faith. Such changes at times freed individuals from traditional corporate structures and, especially in conjunction with other cultural forces such as a gradual rise in the rate of literacy, may have resulted in new forms of religious individualism in early modern Italy.

At the same time, the Tridentine reforms also constituted the intensification of a process of *disciplinamento* (social disciplining) of the Italian populations through confraternities, the Inquisition, the confessional, preaching, and new catechisms—all of which, at least from the end of the fifteenth century, were aimed to bring the laity under closer spiritual direction by the clerical elites. The cumulative process of change and transformation was multi-faceted. It included, as we have seen, the failure of the *spirituali* to impose their moderating vision on the Church; the development of new religious orders that encouraged a revival of traditional piety within more strictly controlled limits; the emergence of a more rigorous party within the curia; the formation of a revitalized papacy with an increasingly centralized administrative structure; and, finally, the decrees and reforms of the Council of Trent. Moreover, the processes of social discipline set in motion by these changes were also frequently embraced by princes and urban magistrates, who had come to understand that the reform of the people served their more explicitly political interests as well.

We must be careful, however, not to take the model of *disciplinamento* too far. As we have seen, as late as 1573, ordinary Christians, like the cobbler Domengo di Lorenzo, believed that the Council of Trent had accomplished no good whatsoever, and he and his friends found ways to resist the changes Trent attempted to institute. A decade later, an obscure Italian miller in the Friuli developed a reputation for denying that the Holy Spirit governed the Church: 'priests want us under their thumbs, just to keep us quiet, while they have a good time.' And he too, like the Venetian cobbler, owned a vernacular Bible. Italian traditions and Italian social structures, that is, remained remarkably resistant to changes imposed from above, especially by priests. The Tridentine Church—which was as much a symptom as a cause of a new emphasis on social discipline and an increasingly absolutist political climate in early modern Europe—initiated more a period of institutional adjustments, shifts in piety, and gradual changes in the social significance of religious practices than it did the systematic cancellation of religious diversity or the systematic imposition of religious discipline. In the final analysis, the history of Catholicism after Trent, though shaped by doctrinal and institutional reforms, was above all a protracted process of negotiations and renegotiations over access to the sacred (and to power) among disparate social groups—a history, that is, not only of repression and consensus, but also of resistance and contestation.

PART II

MATERIAL LIFE: ECONOMIC, SOCIAL, AND POLITICAL TRAJECTORIES

3

Economic structures and transformations

John A. Marino

Asia and America remake Europe

Written in retirement 1537–40 and published posthumously twenty
years later, Francesco Guicciardini's *History of Italy* includes a short
digression on the explorations of the Portuguese and Spanish in the
chronicle for the year 1504, 'since this was one of the most memorable
things which happened in the world for many centuries and since the
harm it caused the city of Venice has some connection with Italian
affairs'.[1] The 'great detriment and damage' to the Venetian spice trade
monopoly through Alexandria by the Portuguese circumnavigation of
Africa and their military power in India and the Moluccas introduces a
learned disquisition explaining how the Portuguese voyages 'demonstrated the falsity of opinions and presuppositions' on traditional cos-
mography, and even more telling—in the final sentences suppressed
from the excursus for more than 200 years until the 1774 edition—how
the new discoveries prove that 'interpretations of the Bible [were]
contrary to truth'. 'Even more marvelous' were the Spanish voyages:
the initiative of the Genoese Christopher Columbus, the New World
peoples, the Spanish conquest and colonial enterprise, the mining,
panning, 'purchasing at ridiculous prices', and robbing of gold and
silver, how 'an endless quantity of gold and silver [was brought] to
Spain', even the later 1519–22 circumnavigation of the world.

[1] *The History of Italy*, trans. S. Alexander (New York, 1969), pp. 177–82.
Guicciardini's *History* is a participant's account of events from the 1494 French
invasions to the election of Alessandro Farnese as Paul III in 1534.

Guicciardini's concluding assessment begins with an encomium on the Portuguese, the Spaniards, and especially Columbus; but with his characteristically pithy juxtaposition, he immediately turns praise into blame. For Guicciardini, Portuguese and Spanish motivations in Asia and America were tainted because 'an immoderate lust for gold and riches' had 'lured [many] by the ease of taking possession of those islands and by the richness of the booty'. These bold achievements were a great opportunity lost to greed, and exhibited the same 'short-sighted' vice that he imputes to Italy's rulers who had provoked its calamitous wars after 1494. Guicciardini structures his analysis around his guiding assumptions on human nature: his belief in the perniciousness of unbridled passions unleashed in politics and economics and his pleasure in confuted Revelation and learning on terrestrial and celestial matters.

Guicciardini's authoritative history, published in 1561–4, confirms what and when late Renaissance Italy knew about the world-shattering contacts with Asia and America. Pirated accounts of Vespucci's voyages had first appeared in print in 1504 (in Latin translation in 1507), and Peter Martyr d'Angiera's Latin *Decades* of 1511 chronicled the early voyages and conquests. The Italian courtier Antonio Pigafetta's 1525 *Il primo viaggio intorno al mondo* presented an eyewitness account of his trip around the world with Magellan. Gonzalo Fernández de Oviedo's objective study for Charles V—the 1526 *Sumario de la natural historia de las Indias* or the first part of the *Historia general y natural de las Indias*, published in 1535 and reprinted in 1547, was translated into Italian in 1550–56. Also appearing in 1550–56 and republished five times before 1613, Giovan Battista Ramusio's three-volume *Delle navigationi et viaggi*, which was inspired by the Venetian humanists Bembo, Navagero, and Fracastoro, included translations of the ancient geographers, contemporary Iberian travellers, and Ramusio's own commentary.

For Guicciardini, the interrelationship of politics and economics dominates the story; and, at least four of his themes aid us in our understanding of the mental and material world of early modern Italy. First, the Italians swelled with local pride for some of their own; the Genoese Columbus, the Florentine Vespucci, and the circumnavigation of the world (no doubt derived from the Vincenza gentleman Pigafetta) were all mentioned by Guicciardini. He could have added that the Genoese-born/Venetian subject John (and his son Sebastian) Cabot and the Florentine Giovanni da Verazzano, working for the English and French respectively, were also part of this international enterprise. But more important than these adventurous pilots were the precedents pioneered by Italians: colonial models developed by both Genoese and Venetians in their Mediterranean empires, and financial mechanisms in the form of investment capital provided by the Genoese. Second, empirical discoveries called into question the received wisdom of religious preconceptions and philosophical speculations on the natural world. Politics, economics, science, and religion were not discrete realms but constantly over-lapped and affected one another. Third, the increased wealth of the Portuguese and Spanish changed the European balance of power and created an Atlantic-based economic system. The emergence of a global world economy and later sixteenth-century inflation from New World silver may have been beyond Guicciardini's ken, but he obviously knew about the threat to the Venetian Mediterranean monopoly, the rise of Antwerp, and the influx of gold and silver to Europe. And fourth, the emphasis on wealth, greed, and honour points to contemporary awareness—not just aristocratic disdain—of the ethical choices and moral implications of the actions of individuals and states toward native peoples and their domains.[2] Contact with the New World and Asia grew out of long-established Italo-Iberian initiatives in and out of the Mediterranean, challenged religious beliefs, and overturned the economic order; but above all, contact tested the moral character of men and society. It was not by chance that founders of the discipline of economics in the eighteenth century such as Antonio Genovesi and Adam Smith were professors of moral philosophy, whose inquiries into decision-making and ethics defined their subject first in Naples as 'moral', then in Scotland as 'political' economy.

---

[2] Montaigne's 1588 essay 'On Coaches', in Michel de Montaigne, *The Essays: A Selection*, trans. M. A. Screech (London, 1993), 344, captures the indignation over the lost opportunity and perverted purpose of European 'treachery, debauchery, cupidity, every kind of cruelty and inhumanity' toward the Indians. See also S. J. Stern, 'Paradigms of Conquest: History, Historiography and Politics', *Journal of Latin American Studies* 24: supplement (1992), 1–34.

The structural limits of the pre-industrial economy

The transformations in the early modern Italian economy—its relative decline in relation to that of north-west Europe—can only be understood in the context of the developing world economy and the larger political forces affecting the Mediterranean world and the various Italian states. Over the long term of the early modern period, Italy lost the early economic advantage it had enjoyed in the Middle Ages as north-west Europe incorporated the markets from new long-distance trade routes around the world and asserted itself as the centre of the first world economy. Guicciardini's astute geopolitical analysis at the end of the Italian Wars in the late 1530s had predicted the economic consequences of the new oceanic contacts with Asia and Africa, but Italian decline had not yet come to pass by mid-century because it was forestalled by the economic recovery of Italy after the Habsburg-Valois Wars. This late sixteenth-century 'Indian Summer' of the Italian economy, however, proved to be an ephemeral economic upturn; it has been described as the unsustainable recovery of a 'mature' or fully developed economy.[3] The Italian economy in the late sixteenth and early seventeenth centuries was no longer able to increase its production either in agriculture or manufacturing because, in the face of heightened competition from cheaper northern European goods entering the market, it could not lower its high labour costs and had reached the limits of its technological knowhow—or lost its ability to innovate.

The penetration of the medieval trans-Mediterranean trading circuit centred on Constantinople and the Italian Middle East by marginal outliers Genoa, Pisa, Amalfi, and Venice, or the dynamism of the pre-plague commercial, financial, and manufacturing quadrilateral around Venice, Milan, Genoa, and Florence, should not blind us to the fact that Italy was still predominantly an agrarian economy up to Unification. Although some twenty northern Italian cities

---

[3] C. M. Cipolla, 'The Economic Decline of Italy', in Brian Pullan (ed.), *Crisis and Change in the Venetian Economy in the Sixteenth and Seventeenth Centuries* (London, 1968), 127–45.

(Venice, Milan, Genoa, Florence, Brescia, Verona, Vicenza, Padua, Pavia, Piacenza, Cremona, Parma, Mantua, Ferrara, Bologna, Lucca, Pisa, Siena, Arezzo, and Perugia) counted more than 20,000 inhabitants in 1300 and 20 to 25 per cent of the population north of Rome lived in towns larger than 5,000 inhabitants, in southern Italy only five towns (Rome, L'Aquila, Naples, Messina, and Palermo) numbered more than 20,000 inhabitants and less than 10 per cent of the population—similar to that throughout Europe—lived in towns of 5,000 persons. Medieval Italian urbanization should remind us of two important facts that would be repeated in the early modern period. First, the economic portrait of pre-industrial Italy is described in relative terms, both vis-à-vis the rest of Europe and in comparison to itself, North and South. Second, the pre-industrial economy rose and fell in cycles, and the catastrophic decline and subsequent restructuring during the fourteenth-century crisis—which saw population fall 40 per cent from about 12.5 million in 1300 to about 7.5 million at the post-plague low point around 1450, and not return to pre-plague levels for more than two centuries until about the 1570s—was mirrored by the decline and restructuring during the seventeenth-century crisis. Even though the seventeenth-century shock-wave was much less precipitous and much shorter in duration (with less than a 15 per cent population decline from 13.3 million in 1600 to 11.5 million in 1650, and with population recovery by the end of the seventeenth century), Italy's restructuring and relative decline vis-à-vis northern Europe and between northern and southern Italy had far lasting results. Italy's economic peripheralization at the beginning of the new cycle of demographic and economic take-off in the seventeenth century ensured her subordinate place in the European state system, and exacerbated the problems of the dual economy that has plagued her to this day.

The precocious development of the Italian medieval economy from the rise of the commune in the eleventh century emerged through the efforts of Italian merchants and bankers who pioneered the tools and techniques of capitalism in the West as they exported their products and innovations. The Italian economy continued to expand in northern European markets during the Renaissance, in the power vacuum and political instability of the northern states. The consolidation of new monarchies in Iberia, France, and England, however, not only marked a political and military turning point but foreshadowed an economic maturation as well. At the same time, the pre-industrial economy was constrained by internal barriers or limits in demography, disease, soil, climate, energy, and technology. Understanding those constraints will help us understand the structural organization of land, capital, and labour in the rural and urban economy of pre-industrial Italy, and how the overwhelming realities and rhythms of daily life in the countryside and the city established the parameters for change and development.

The demographic facts of life (and death) set limits on population growth in Italy that endured up to the mid-nineteenth-century improvements in medication and health care. Because of slightly higher birth rates over mortality rates—of about 3 per 1000 in normal times—a demographic surplus would cause long-term population increase. Two self-regulating population mechanisms, disease and famine, however, held the early modern population in check. Plague was a recurrent threat from 1348 that struck early modern Italy exceptionally hard in the North and Centre in 1630–31 (with 61, 59, 50, and 49 per cent mortality in Verona, Padua, Parma, and Milan respectively) and in the South and Genoa in 1656–7 (with 150,000 and 45,000 deaths (50 and 60 per cent mortality) in Naples and Genoa respectively); but plague began to disappear by the second half of the seventeenth century. Typhus—a disease associated with malnutrition, homelessness, and poverty—along with malaria and measles, began to take greater toll in the seventeenth century. Bad harvests led to three serious famines, in 1590–91, 1648–9, and 1763–4 (with as many as 40,000 deaths in the city of Naples alone). Urban density and poverty made pre-industrial towns extremely vulnerable to disease and famine. The towns could not maintain their population by reproduction alone without the influx of rural migrants. The age pyramid of towns was skewed toward younger residents, since only one in two lived to adulthood: high infant mortality and childhood diseases caused one in four children to die in their first year and one in two to die before the age of twenty. Not only migration and mobility but also marriage patterns, inheritance, and property transmission were all affected by demography.

In the city, delayed marriage was a mechanism to ensure a sufficient but not excessive number of heirs. In the countryside, on the contrary, more hands were needed to work the fields in grain-growing regions, and males contracted marriages at younger ages to increase the rural labour supply. As these extra hands became excess labour without possibility of marriage and property of their own, rural migrants made their way to the city to replace declining urban populations.

The rural economy

The urban–rural continuum is a necessary component of the early modern city, not only for its population but also for its products. Grain for bread was the chief crop to be brought in from nearby hinterlands that the towns sought to control as they expanded to territorial states or imported from greater distances. Venice was fed by its mainland and overseas empire, Puglia became the granary for the city of Naples, and Sicily supplied far-flung urban markets. Likewise all raw materials, especially wood for fuel and construction as much as wool and silk for textiles, were essential in supplying the critical manufacturing sector of towns. Forests and fields, wheat and wool were subject to their own set of material and political constraints.

Forests reduced the arable, but were as important as the fields. Italy is without fossil fuels, coal, or peat, and its pre-industrial civilization was dependent on wood and stone. Wood provided needed energy for heat, fuel, and cooking as well as for construction of houses, tools, furniture, and ships. Forests were also the home to more animal life, in the form of wild game, than could be found as domesticated livestock. Even chestnuts and chestnut flour were important food supplements in the high hills and mountains up and down the peninsula around Bergamo and Brescia, Parma and Bologna, Tuscany and Liguria, Umbria and Lazio, to Naples and Calabria. About one-third of Italy's 30 million hectares were wooded, and it is estimated that the normal consumption of about 1 kg. of wood per day per capita would require between half to one hectare of forest.[4] With 13.3 million inhabitants in 1600, Italy's forest resources were exploited to their limit.

[4] P. Malanima, 'L'economia', in G. Greco and M. Rosa (eds.), *Storia degli antichi stati italiani* (Rome, 1996), 252, 264–5. See also, Karl Appuhn, 'Inventing Nature: Forests, Forestry, and State Power in Renaissance Venice', *Journal of Modern History* 72(4) (2000), 861–89.

Cereal yields were determined by the geography of the peninsula and the technology appropriate to it. Italy has little flat farmland and only two extensive plains (the Po Valley and Puglia in the southern heel); the majority of its area is made up of hills and mountains. A Mediterranean climate, characterized by violent autumnal and spring rains on light and rocky soil dried out by the sun and scarce rains through the rest of the year, supports fruit and olive trees, grapevines, and mulberry trees not viable in colder northern climes, but is less suitable for cereals. In Italy in 1500, 100 agriculturists could produce a grain surplus to feed themselves and thirty-three others, whereas in the Low Countries at that time the surplus reached some seventy-five other people. By 1800, with Italian yields at the same level they had been for centuries, the agricultural revolution in northern Europe allowed for the grain surplus to feed an additional 150 mouths above the number of agricultural workers.[5] In Italy, dry farming with little irrigation was the norm. Biennial rather than triennial rotation systems prevailed. Neither heavy ploughs nor the horses to pull them could be sustained by Italian soils or rainfall. Manpower and the hoe, rather than horsepower and the plough, limited the productive capacity of the land.

Traditional intensive agriculture concentrated on the Mediterranean complex of cereals, olive and fruit trees, and vines cultivated since ancient times. In the early modern period, three new crops became important. Mulberry trees and silk worms had been known in Calabria and Sicily from the tenth century, and made their way to the North by the fourteenth. Silk production increased dramatically in the second half of the sixteenth century, and the Veneto, Sardinia, and Lombardy became the chief producers of raw silk. Rice production in Northern Italy developed in the same period after 1550 on otherwise marginal, unproductive land, especially in Lombardy and Piedmont in the seventeenth and eighteenth centuries and in the Veneto in the second half of the eighteenth century. Maize had an important impact on diet in the Veneto and Lombardy, where by 1800 it accounted for about 50 per cent of available cereals. Maize had been introduced from the New World by the second half of the sixteenth century, but its spread began in the mid-seventeenth century from the Veneto and Lombardy to Piedmont, Emilia-Romagna, and

[5] Ibid. 256–7.

Tuscany, with its triumph in the eighteenth century. Maize was used in field rotation to restore fertility to fallow and, with its yields twice that of wheat, provided the closest thing to an eighteenth-century Italian agricultural revolution parallel to that in northern Europe. In all three cases, it is important to note, increased agricultural productivity resulted from an extension of arable. The limits of productivity increase would soon be reached with full utilization of all available marginal land.

Pastoral activity, similarly, supplemented agriculture by grazing livestock on marginal land. The expansion and contraction of the pastoral economy responded to a variety of external variables such as demography, climate, politics, and manufacturing demand for raw materials, as well as a number of internal variables such as tax policy, rural credit, and the availability of pasture. The bottom line was drawn by ecological limits: no more animals could be grazed than the land could support. Thus, in all three rural environments— forests, agricultural plots, and pasture land—the pre-industrial rural economy was ruled by material facts and political choices.

The urban economy

The division of labour among the city's dense population made the city what it was—a centre of production and exchange. Demand for food consumed about 80 per cent of private expenditure for the mass of people, and together with clothing and shelter accounted for almost all their consumption. Expenditures on consumer goods and services for a well-to-do middle-class notary in Verona in 1653–7, on the other hand, showed growing disposable income of up to 25 per cent, but with still almost half of expenditure on food.[6] Between 55 and 65 per cent of the urban labour force engaged in these three sectors fundamental for survival—food, clothing, and shelter. In 1552 Florence and 1660 Venice, 13 and 17 per cent respectively engaged in food distribution and agriculture, 41 and 43 per cent in textile and clothing trades, and 6 and 4 per cent in construction.[7] At the end of the sixteenth century, twenty-four of Venice's 107 guilds (36.8 per cent

---

[6] C. M. Cipolla, *Before the Industrial Revolution: European Society and Economy 1000–1700*, 3rd edn. (New York, 1994), 25, 28.

[7] Ibid. 64.

of guild members) worked in the textile industry of wool, silk, cotton, and linen cloth, the dynamic heart of the manufacturing economy in the pre-industrial city.[8] The majority of Venetian guildsmen (56 per cent in the good times of 1595) worked in the non-export trades. As the textile industry declined through the seventeenth century to number slightly more than one-quarter of the guild workforce, the non-export sector of Venetian guilds increased to two-thirds of the labour force. Hard times reduced the city to its primary identity as a place where its residents exchanged goods and services among themselves. Another 15–20 per cent of workers were employed in specialized crafts such as metallurgy, woodwork, and leatherwork. A final 20 per cent engaged in miscellaneous work, with professionals (bankers, lawyers, doctors, and notaries) constituting about one-quarter of this category in larger cities.

The urban manufacturing sector had three chief components that put limits on production. Raw materials (wool, silk, cotton, and linen for textiles, metal from mining, wood from forests, leather from livestock, etc.) linked the city to the countryside. Capital and credit financed commerce and industry and blurred the boundaries between merchants and bankers who tried to control all aspects of the manufacturing process, especially by turning independent craftsmen into dependent employees through credit and indebtedness. And finally, labour in the person of salaried employees was constantly maintained by rural migrants. Textiles are exemplary of the relationship between raw materials, all phases of the manufacturing process, and labour in the dyeing process—about one-third, one-half, and one-fifth of production costs respectively.

Limits or impediments to manufacturing were omnipresent, and high costs in manufacturing could mount up. The devastating winter of 1611–12 in the Tavoliere di Puglia that killed two-thirds of the transhumant sheep in winter pasture, and the constraints of animal demography that required at least a decade to recoup the losses, coincided with the decade of major decline in Venetian woollen production. Politics could likewise depress the manufacturing sector, as the first war of Monferrat in Piedmont and the Thirty Years War in Germany disrupted local production and long-distance markets

---

[8] R. Rapp, *Industry and Economic Decline in Seventeenth-Century Venice* (Cambridge, Mass., 1976), 76–7, 97, 103.

respectively. Although some entrenched guilds may have been able at times to control workers' wages, the quality or design of their products, and even resist technological innovations, the constraint of high labour costs seems to have been the chief factor in making Italian manufactures less competitive than northern European goods. The wide range of employment opportunities in the Italian cities, even as formerly leading industries declined and disappeared, allowed displaced workers to find jobs in construction, luxury or skilled crafts, retail trade, and domestic service, so that no widespread unemployment and its consequent effect on lowering wages appeared. In absolute terms, the Italian cities continued to be vibrant centres of internal and local or regional exchange, even as they lost their former international markets. A final cause of high costs, similar to the problem of high wages, was opportunity cost for innovation. Opportunity costs to retool or invest in new equipment and techniques were high for established industries, as they found themselves in competition with more efficient new rivals and new products from northern Europe, which had entered the market with the most up-to-date machines and methods.

The one viable way to escape the limits constraining industrial production was for entrepreneurs to try and control the labour market by transferring manufacturing production to the countryside. The rise of rural industries—proto-industrialization or the putting-out system—took advantage of cheap peasant labour. Because the agrarian calendar kept agricultural workers seasonally under-employed and women workers often in the home, low wages and piece rates could keep production costs down. At the same time, the absence of guild organization freed manufacturers from restrictions on labour, product quality, or technological innovation. Such rural enterprises included Brescian metallurgy and firearms manufacture as well as iron smelting along the Tuscan coast and even in Calabria, paper production around Lake Garda and also Voltri, west of Genoa, woollens in the Alpine valleys of Venetian Lombardy north of Bergamo and throughout rural towns from Piedmont and Tuscany to the Abruzzi, silks in the countryside between Verona and Trent, cotton and flax (fustians) in the countryside north-west of Milan, and the formerly secret technology of silk-throwing in the Venetian Terraferma (mainland Italy). By 1679, silk manufactures in the Milanese countryside counted 266 hydraulic mills and by 1700,

125 operated in Piedmont.[9] The geographical distribution and infrastructure of pre-industrial production had been dramatically transformed by the seventeenth-century crisis.

Conjunctures: the shift from the Mediterranean to the Atlantic

In the short term, the Italian economy began to recover from the Italian Wars of the early sixteenth century by about mid-century, and continued to prosper under the Spanish hegemony to the second decade of the seventeenth century. The geographical explorations with Venetian pepper trade losses after 1504, Venice's 1509 defeat at the battle of Agnadello with the complete loss of its Terraferma territories, and the aggressive expansion of the Turks in the eastern Mediterranean with the erosion of Venice's overseas empire proved to be only momentary setbacks, and not the beginning of the inevitable decline of Venice or even an end to the dynamic economic underpinning of Renaissance Italy itself. Modern research has shown that the Venetian pepper trade, which did suffer a temporary disruption as a result of the Portuguese voyages around Africa to Asia, was never cut off, and that the Portuguese defeat in Asia at Aden in 1513 prevented the closing of Venice's Red Sea route through Ottoman Egypt. In fact, by the mid-sixteenth century Venice had regained about half the market share of the spice trade in Europe. In the same way, Venice gradually regained the lost Terraferma possessions by the 1520s and returned to its position as the strongest independent state in the peninsula. Even the Turkish threat diminished after the successful defence of Malta against the Turkish siege of 1565 and the détente established with the Holy League's war of 1570–73, despite the loss of Cyprus, allowed Venice to play off the Ottomans in the east and the Spanish in the west.

The *pax hispanica* permitted the Italian states to return to their former local, regional, and international economic activities in trade and finance. Textiles led the manufacturing sector. Production of

[9] D. Sella, *Italy in the Seventeenth Century* (London, 1997), 41–6.

Florentine woollens doubled from 1553 to 1560 and registered more than 33,000 cloths in 1572; Venetian woollens increased 9.6 per cent per annum from 1521 to 1569, and grew from about 10,000 cloths at mid-century to a peak of almost 29,000 pieces in 1602; and after the 1559 treaty of Cateau-Cambrésis, Milan, Como, and Bergamo (which produced 26,500 less expensive cloths in 1596) developed significant production. Increased silk production was even more dramatic: four-fifths of workers in Naples were involved in the silk industry in 1580; 50,000 women worked in silk in the state of Milan in 1593; and silk production also boomed in Genoa and Venice. Similarly, Milanese armour, Brescian armaments, Venetian and Milanese printing industries all expanded. In commerce, Medici patronage to the small coastal town of Leghorn (Livorno) saw its annual numbers of incoming ships rise eightfold between the 1570s and 1600, thereby displacing Genoa as the chief Tyrrhenian port, while Venice regained its dominance in the Adriatic. Finally, Genoa emerged as a financial powerhouse as the Spanish crown's banker by replacing the Augsburg Fuggers after Philip II's first 'bank-ruptcy' (a debt crisis requiring refinancing and rescheduling of loans) in 1556. The Genoese held Spanish imperial finances in their hands until the 1620s, were the major underwriter of Spanish wars, and became the chief beneficiaries of Spanish New World wealth in repayment for their loans.

The demand for manufactures reflected continued demographic growth, which also required increased agricultural production to provide sufficient foodstuffs and raw materials for the growing urban population. Since seed–yield ratios did not increase agricultural productivity, increase in the arable from reclamation projects such as those in the Veneto, Piedmont, and the Tuscan Maremma were necessary. More land under cultivation, increased sheep-rearing in the Abruzzi, and diffusion of mulberry trees and silk worms in northern Italy provided the wheat, wool, and silk to fuel the economic recovery.

Sure signs of the coming economic downturn, however, began to appear with the famines after 1585 and into the 1590s. A series of bad harvests, poor weather, over-cropping and soil exhaustion, the land boom that installed new landlords and disrupted old village hierarch-ies, and the consequent rise in prices pointed to more serious prob-lems ahead. In manufacturing, cheaper foreign textiles challenged traditional high-quality clothes and new producers began to compete in the Italian market. In trade, Venetian and Genoese shipbuilding declined; and increased tonnage, especially Dutch and English vessels, made its way into Italian ports to take over the carrying trade. Even Venice's long-time monopoly in the Levant markets gave way to France, which had received commercial privileges from the Ottomans in 1569. After the 1570–73 Holy League war, France began to displace the Venetians with about 1,000 French ships in the eastern Mediterranean, which accounted for half of France's total trade by the early seventeenth century.

The effect of the five- or sixfold price rise in the sixteenth century, even before the dramatic increase of American silver shipments after 1570 increased the European money supply, cannot be over-emphasized. This inflation—the so-called 'Price Revolution'— extended across Europe even into the Ottoman empire, where the absence of customs duties on silver imports brought large quantities of cheap European silver into the Levant market after the 1580s. Higher prices were not matched by higher wages or increased rents, so that landlords and property-owners as well as salaried employees and peasants found their real income fall and the power of credit markets rise. The credit shock of the second decade of the seventeenth century and the outbreak of the Thirty Years War burst the bubble of the Italian boom.

The reconfiguration and consolidation of the economy during the seventeenth-century crisis from about 1620 to 1660, with marked recovery especially after 1680, changed Italy internally from an exporter to an importer, from a manufacturing to a service-oriented economy, and from urban production to countryside putting-out industries. The gap between its northern states and southern kingdoms widened; above all, Italy changed in relationship to the other European states.

Italian urbanization created a multipolar economy in the North as competing states and cities within them vied for agricultural resources and raw materials as much as for markets for finished goods. The movement to rural industrialization accompanied a decline in the percentage of the population living in towns with more than 10,000 inhabitants, from 15 to 13 per cent, and these smaller second-tier and provincial towns were those most likely to lose out. In the South, nodes of economic activity in Puglia, the Abruzzi, the

Salerno fair, and Naples itself connected with different northern states such as Venice, Florence, and Genoa to form trade networks outside and apart from strictly national or state orbits. Imports outweighed exports, and resultant trade deficits weakened states already in a downward economic spiral. Further, large producers squeezed out small ones and a more hierarchically divided society emerged. Such decentralization and inequalities made Italian markets all the more attractive and vulnerable to Dutch, English, and French commercial expansion.

Comparative eighteenth-century population growth illustrates the relative decline of Italy. Over the course of the eighteenth century, Italian population increased by more than one third, from 13.4 million in 1700 (approximately what it had been in 1600) to 18 million in 1800. Italian recovery, however, could not keep pace with the rest of Europe's two-thirds population increase. In absolute terms, Italian population and its economy continued to grow, albeit at a slower rate than the leading states of north-west Europe.

Capital cities, with resident patricians and judicial and administrative bureaucracies supported by service industries, continued the tradition of the Italian urban exceptionalism—numerous cities with large populations and high densities.

- Turin was transformed after it became the Savoyard capital in 1563. By 1700 its population had doubled to 42,000; it then almost doubled again, to 82,000, by 1770.
- Milan, devastated by the plague of 1630, lost half of its 130,000 inhabitants, its population falling to about 66,000. And even though much of its textile industry had disappeared from the city to find a place in the putting-out industries of the Lombard countryside, by 1688 population in the capital had returned to 126,000. With the Austrian succession in 1715, Milan became the capital of the imperial presence in Italy and a cosmopolitan, intellectual centre linked to Europe across the Alps.
- Venetian mainland possessions, from the Friuli through the Veneto to eastern Lombardy, sent half of their income from land to lay and religious proprietors in the island-city, where investors had diverted their capital from trade to the land. Crete, the jewel of Venice's overseas empire, was lost to the Ottoman Turks in 1669 after a protracted war of twenty-five years, and Venice was only able to regain

most of its Dalmatian coast and Ionian island possessions after 1684. By the 1720s, the Turkish wars and northern European military and trading incursions had even wrested Adriatic supremacy from Venice, now an administrative capital of rentiers dominated by service industries and monopoly protection in its internal market.

- After Genoa lost her privileged financial position in the Spanish empire with the 'bankruptcy' of 1627, unsuccessful attempts to re-establish trading links to the eastern Mediterranean, and the competition from the French port of Marseilles, Tuscany's Leghorn, and Savoy's Nice and Oneglia, squeezed the Ligurian capital into the second rank in Italy itself.

- In Tuscany, the decadence of the last Medici dukes paralleled the economic stagnation that had overtaken Florence, Siena, Pistoia, Arezzo, and Pisa. Only after the Lorraine regency (1737–65) and the reforms of Leopold II (1765–90) were sagging fortunes revived.

- Rome continued to grow in size, its population reaching 160,000 by 1750. Bloated by great families and clerical lords with their syco-phant retainers, large numbers of administrators, lawyers, and artisans in the service sector, an army of the poor and hangers-on, and seasonal waves of pilgrims (especially during the quarter-century Holy Years), Rome's parasitic economy consumed rather than produced wealth.

- In seventeenth-century Naples, Spanish policy shipped wealth out of the city and kingdom to protect Milan and the North. With its 1647 revolt and devastating 50 per cent mortality from the 1656 plague, Naples had to await the independent kingdom under Charles of Bourbon (1734–59) for needed reform.

- In Sicily, Palermo and Messina followed Naples in being slow to recover from the seventeenth-century crisis, and likewise looked to Charles of Bourbon for economic stimulus. Even Messina's former export staples of grain and silk were in sharp decline.

In sum, the numerous Italian capitals set the economic tone of their respective territorial states.

A new urban creation, the free port, challenged the old commercial and shipping powers. Trieste under Austrian patronage, Ancona in the Papal States, and Leghorn in Tuscany received special exemptions from customs duties and began to attract international shipping. Trieste's privileges date from 1719, but only after 1760 under Maria

Theresa's reforms did the Adriatic port enjoy a real expansion in trade. Ancona received its customs exemption in 1732 and contributed to the pressure put on Venice in the Adriatic. Leghorn, officially a free port in 1675, grew spectacularly from 16,000 inhabitants in 1700 to almost 50,000 in 1785. It became a foreign base for English, French, and Flemish merchants for storage and transport of products such as olive oil and fish. As an international and extra-territorial port, it stood apart from much contact with the rest of Tuscany's towns. In all three ports, Jews, Armenians, and peoples of all nationalities with contacts and connections around the Mediterranean—even pirates and criminals in Leghorn—were granted special exemptions in the name of trade and commerce.

At the end of the early modern period in the decades between 1780 and 1850, with the dramatic economic transformation of industrialization—the development of steam and other energy sources—the relative decline of the Italian economy, its decentralization, the shift from urban manufacturing to service industries, and the rise of rural industrialization increased Italy's marginalization among Europe's great powers. This restructuring of economic activity in Italy after the seventeenth-century crisis underlines the fact that industrialization was as much a socio-cultural as a technological fact.

What at first may seem to be the weakness and disunity of the Italian states may, in fact, be seen as their greatest asset for future success. The decentralized, multipolar Italian economy and its cacophony of voices calling for reform in the eighteenth century suggest that, though Italy was no longer at the centre of a Mediterranean or European economic world, it still participated as a secondary player in the new world economy. The sites of the new rural industrialization (north-eastern Piedmont, the region north-west of Milan, the Bergamasque and Brescian valleys, the coastal region near Genoa), not by chance, were eventually to become the heartland of later Italian industrialization. The infrastructure created in the ruins of the seventeenth-century crisis would prove a sturdy foundation for what was to come.

Similarly, second-class economic status did not inhibit Italians from playing an active role in the eighteenth century's cosmopolitan marketplace of ideas, where many reformers and intellectuals distinguished themselves by addressing problems of economics, law, and ethics. Whether in dialogue with their Scottish or French Enlightenment peers, Italian reformers from Naples to Milan made a significant contribution both to European social thought and to the reform of their local society. In Naples, Ferdinando Galiani's 1751 *Della moneta*, Antonio Genovesi's writings and pupils (a roll-call including Francesco Longano, Traiano Odazzi, Giuseppe Maria Galanti, Domenico and Francesco Antonio Grimaldi, and Francesco Maria Pagano), and Gaetano Filangieri's 1780s *Scienza della legislazione* as in Milan, together with the Tuscan economist Pompeo Neri's 1750–58 census of Lombardy, Pietro Verri's 1763 *Discorso sulla felicità*, Cesare Beccaria's 1764 *On Crimes and Punishments*, and the Verri brothers' periodical *Il Caffè* (published in Brescia for only two years, 1764–6), pointed the way to a unified understanding of politics, culture, economy, and society. The goal was a reform of the fundamental basis of social life and the restoration of power to the market to establish justice and equality.

Family and gender

Gianna Pomata

In 1739, at the age of 50, Lady Mary Wortley Montagu left England, husband, and children to settle in Italy. *'Je franche le pas hardiment pour un autre monde'* ('I am boldly taking the step to another world'), she wrote to the man she hoped would share her new Italian life, Francesco Algarotti, the ambitious author of a book on Newtonian physics for the female reading public, *Newtonianesimo per le dame* (1737). Lady Montagu loved ideas, and she loved to travel. She had written to her sister ten years before: 'I have a mind to cross the water, to try what effect a new heaven and a new earth will have upon my spirit.'[1] But why try for a 'new heaven and a new earth' in Italy, of all places? Why would a keen observer of women's condition across cultures, such as Lady Montagu, choose to spend in Italy, to paraphrase the title of Kazuo Ishiguro's novel, 'the remains of her day'?

Lady Montagu's choice suggests that Italy might have been perceived in the first half of the eighteenth century as a country where gender roles offered comparatively more freedom to a woman of intellect, weary of family ties. This may well seem surprising: much evidence suggests that in the early modern period the family structure of the Italian aristocracy became even more markedly patrilineal and patriarchal. In 1684 Cardinal De Luca, a prominent Roman jurist, published a book-length comment on a law passed by Pope Innocent XI in 1680. The law aimed at radically excluding women from intestate succession by upholding municipal law, which excluded women, over Roman law, which did not. After an extensive inquiry into the statutes of over 1,000 municipalities, De Luca established that the

[1] R. Halsband, *The Life of Lady Mary Wortley Montagu* (Oxford, 1956), 179.

exclusion of women was mandated in 187 communities of the Papal State, as well as in major Italian cities such as Florence, Genoa, Lucca, Mantua, Milan, Naples, Pisa, Siena, and Turin. On the grounds of this evidence, backed also by the customs of several European countries, he argued that women's exclusion from inheritance in favour of the male line was 'a universal custom, not only of Italy but of all other people who live by the law'.[2]

De Luca's comments highlight an issue that was crucial to both family and gender in early modern Italy: the tension between a patrilineal and a bilineal view of kinship. His text also deals with the central paradox of early modern Italian law on gender issues: the discrepancy between Roman law and municipal law in matters of property devolution. Roman law and municipal law coexisted in early modern Italy's legal pluralism, but they were at odds on women's inheritance rights. Although Roman law excluded women from all legal and political positions on the grounds of their inability to act on behalf of others, it did acknowledge their right to own and dispose of property, and gave daughters and sons equal inheritance rights to their father's estate. In Italian history, it was not Roman law but late medieval city statutes that seem to have detracted most from the legal condition of women. Starting in the age of the communes, municipal statutes increasingly limited women's inheritance rights (fundamentally by excluding daughters from inheritance on the grounds that they received a dowry at marriage—the so-called *exclusio propter dotem*) and sought to impose some form of male guardianship over all women, especially in property matters. The rationale that jurists gave for the exclusion of daughters from inheritance was the so-called *favor agnationis*: the preservation of the family, as defined by agnation or the male line. Roman law distinguished between agnation (a relation through a male person) and cognation (a relation through either a male or a female person). But the concept of agnation, as defined by Roman law, had never implied women's exclusion from inheritance: on the contrary, a daughter's inheritance rights were based precisely on her agnatic tie to her father. To make things more complicated, all distinction between agnates and cognates in matters of succession had been abolished at the very time when the great collection of

[2] G. B. De Luca, *Commentaria ad Constitutionem Sanctae Memoriae Innocentii XI, de statutariis successionibus* (orig. 1684; Venice, 1734), 25.

Roman law, the *Corpus juris civilis*, had been assembled and codified. A new law (Novella 118) passed by Justinian in 543 had eliminated all legal advantage formerly enjoyed by agnatic kin in succession.

It was especially this Byzantine law that De Luca decried as 'contrary to the laws and customs of the Romans and the Italic people'. Rewriting legal history, De Luca orientalized bilateral succession as a sad consequence of the transfer of the Roman empire to the east: a 'Greek custom' introduced by Justinian under his wife Theodora's baneful influence. The truly Roman, Italic custom, he argued, was the exclusion of women from inheritance in favour of the male line: when the *Corpus juris civilis* was rediscovered in the twelfth century, most Italian cities reacted by passing 'laws of their own that excluded women from succession'. In spite of the enormous prestige of Roman law, De Luca concluded that in matters of women and property, municipal law should take precedence over Roman law.

Two faces of the family: *casato* and *parentado*

De Luca's comments lead us to what is perhaps the most fundamental feature of the Italian family in this period: the tension between agnatic and cognatic views of kinship: one centred on the vertical chain of fathers and sons–the patriliny, or *lignaggio*; another, more horizontal, that included cognates and affines, the kin created also through women. Such different conceptions of the family implied a different social value for each of the sexes. Whereas the agnatic view of the family wiped women out of the family map, the cognatic view included them as agents in the construction of kinship ties.

The agnatic and the cognatic principle coexisted, with varying balance, throughout Italian history from antiquity to the end of the *ancien régime*. The two principles did not represent successive stages in the evolution of kinship but two coexisting ways to think about the family, which could be complementary but also in conflict with each other. In the first case what was stressed was the vertical transmission of name, patrimony, and rank through the male line; in the second, the extension of the family's network of influence and power through marriage alliances and the exchange of women and dowries. This double conception of the family was reflected in the vocabulary of kinship of late medieval and early modern Italy, where key terms were *casa*, or *casato*, referring to the agnatic line,[3] and *parentela*, or *parentado*, referring instead to the ties of cognation and affinity created through women.

This double image of the family as *casato* and *parentado* can be often found in family chronicles: in Donato Velluti's fourteenth-century *Cronica domestica* it is clear that the agnatic, vertical image of the family competed with a horizontal one which included cognates and affines.[4] Typically, however, family memory privileged the male line and included women only when they had been the instrument of important marriage alliances. In Giovanni Rucellai's fifteenth-century *Ricordi* the main topic is the family's male genealogy, but occasionally the author mentions the cognatic kin (and the women through which it was acquired) whenever this kin brought new political alliances, and thus an increase of the power and influence of the family.[5] Similarly in the seventeenth century Virgilio Spada, a member of a provincial family that had managed to join the ranks of the Roman nobility, in his official family chronicle emphasized the continuity of the patriliny, dating it back to the eleventh century; but in less official writings he also stressed the *parentadi* contracted through women.[6] In fact, in spite of the dominant patrilineal image of the family conveyed by family histories, the systematic use of cognatic kin to extend the political influence of the family has been documented in several contexts, such as sixteenth-century Brescia and Ravenna and, in the case of family fortunes linked to ecclesiastic careers, in seventeenth-century Rome.

But beyond the inherent tension between *casato* and *parentado*, is it possible to measure the relative strength or weakness of agnaticism in various Italian contexts? How truly 'universal', as claimed

---

[3] Andrea Capano, *De fideicommisso masculino sive de memoria nobilium in familiis conservanda* (Naples, 1649), 48: 'Agnatio, Casata sive Casa et domus in materia fideicommissi et primogenii sunt sinonima.'

[4] Ch. M. De la Roncière, 'Une famille florentine au XIV siècle. Les Velluti', in G. Duby and J. Le Goff (eds.), *Famille et parenté dans l'Occident médiéval* (Rome, 1977), 227–48.

[5] R. Barducci et al., 'Genealogia e parentado. Memorie del potere nella Firenze tardo medievale. Il caso di Giovanni Rucellai', *Quaderni storici* 86(2) (1994), 365–403.

[6] C. Casanova, *La famiglia italiana in età moderna. Ricerche e modelli* (Rome, 1997), 212–13.

by De Luca, was the patrilineal bias of the family in early modern Italy?

A first answer to this question comes from the comparative studies of family and gender in Renaissance cities, which suggest that agnaticism was not equally strong everywhere. A comparison between Renaissance Florence and Venice—the two contexts most intensively studied—is very instructive. Christiane Klapisch-Zuber's detailed study of Renaissance Florence has persuasively shown how the Florentine family structure presented a strong agnatic bias, which heavily limited women's rights to property and children, their experience of sexuality (including childbearing and nursing), their social identity and sense of self. Married at an early age, the Florentine woman from the propertied classes did not own either her dowry or the rich clothes and jewels which bedecked her during the wedding ceremony. She bore children who would be taken away from her soon after birth to be entrusted to a wet nurse in the countryside. If she became a widow, pressure from her paternal family would likely force her to remarry, and thus lose contact with her children, who legally belonged to their father's *casato*, or agnatic family. As in all strongly patrilineal contexts, so too in Renaissance Florence women were structurally located between male lineages: they moved in and out of *case* where they never permanently belonged.

Klapisch-Zuber's picture of Florentine wives' and widows' limited autonomy contrasts, however, with the better status of women in other Italian cities, especially the Renaissance Venice described by Stanley Chojnacki. The Venetian case strongly suggests that variations in the rules regarding the devolution of property may have been a key factor in women's status. In Renaissance Venice wives were free to bequeath their dowries to whom they willed, whereas in Florence they were required by law to leave them to their children or husband. In Venice, women's control of their dowries defined them as economic actors in relation to their families, society, and the state. Moreover, the *exclusio propter dotem* was less radically agnatic in Venice than in Florence: Venetian statutes gave women the right to inherit from their intestate fathers in the absence of sons, whereas Florentine daughters could inherit only in absence of all other male agnates—descendants, collaterals, or ascendants. In view of this better chance Venetian women had of receiving property from intestate succession, it is not surprising to find evidence in Venice of significant private wealth in female hands. Nor is it surprising to learn that Venetian women tended to write wills much more often than their Florentine counterparts. As concerns the low number of women among testators, in fact, the Florentine case contrasts not only with Venice but also with other cities like Pisa, Siena, and Assisi.

The range of local departure from Roman law seems to hold the key to the varying status of women in different cities, at least in terms of property rights. The already mentioned difference between Venice and Florence, for instance, can be seen as a more or less radical departure from Roman law: less radical in Venice, where dowered daughters kept inheritance rights from fathers (in absence of sons) and married women were left the right to freely dispose of their property in their wills; more radical in Florence, where women almost entirely lost their inheritance rights from their fathers, and were permanently under the guardianship of a male *mundualdus* (a legal figure deriving from Lombard, not Roman law).

There is strong comparative evidence, therefore, that women's property rights were inversely related to the legal and social strength of the patriliny and the tightness of the agnatic control over property devolution. In seventeenth-century Rome, Renata Ago has noted how women's assertive claim to individual property rights (backed by new trends in jurisprudence) acted as a counter-force to the ideology of the patriliny.

Further studies of women's property rights in local contexts will allow us to draw a more accurate map of agnaticism in early modern Italy, but the first rudiments we have of such a map suggest that agnaticism was less ubiquitous and unmitigated than assumed by De Luca. Nor should we replicate De Luca's mistake of basing such a map exclusively on written norms. Unwritten, customary norms could point in other directions. For instance, at Forni di Sopra in Friuli in 1538–9 litigation over inheritance appealed to two conflicting sets of rules: an unwritten custom that allowed daughters to inherit from intestate fathers when there were no sons, and the local statutes, which in such cases favoured male agnatic collaterals over daughters. It is interesting to note that in this village there was a high level of male emigration.[7] In other contexts with high male emigration,

---

[7] C. Povolo, 'Eredità anticipata o esclusione per causa di dote? Un caso di pluralismo giuridico nel Friuli del primo '500', in L. Accati, M. Cattaruzza, and M. Verzar Bass (eds.), *Padre e figlia* (Turin, 1994).

such as the mountain communities around Como, we find a strong cognatic bent: men sometimes took on a double surname adding the wife's family name to their own, sons and daughters had equal access to inheritance, 14 per cent of marriages were uxorilocal, and women were described as 'viragos' who 'buy and sell, rule the household, go to market, plough the fields, cut grass and wood, harvest the wheat and carry it home on carriages'.[8]

Most importantly, we should beware of projecting the agnatic pattern of the aristocracy onto the family of the lower classes, of which we know considerably less. It is true that between the sixteenth and the eighteenth century among small farmers and sharecroppers of central Italy, women as a rule were excluded from inheriting the bulk of the family property (house and land). But in other areas such as Puglia, in southern Italy, where the property of land among the peasantry was highly fragmented and men were very mobile because of seasonal work, house and land were often transmitted as a daughter's dowry—possibly a sign that the family assigned a higher value to its women, who were the family's stabilizing element during men's prolonged absence for work.

1560–1700: triumph of the patriliny

Much recent research suggests that a shift in the uneasy balance of *casato* and *parentado* occurred, in the Italian aristocracy, in the second half of the sixteenth century. Both in northern and in southern Italy, at about the same time (the 1560s–70s), aristocratic families started to adopt a much more marked patrilineal structure, characterized by male primogeniture and the concentration of wealth by *fedecommesso*[9] within the *casato*'s main line, with exclusion from inheritance not only of daughters but also of younger sons (cadets). The traditional practice of marrying all sons to multiply the *casato*'s branches, and most daughters to contract useful matrimonial alliances, was discontinued. Marriage was now reserved for the

---

[8] R. Merzario, *Il capitalismo nelle montagne. Strategie familiari nella prima fase di industrializzazione nel Comasco* (Bologna, 1989), 61.

[9] *Fedecommesso* was a testamentary provision that specified a line of heirs over several generations, entailing property to them.

first-born son, the heir to the *casato*. All other sons were destined to celibacy, and to a military or ecclesiastical career. A major consequence of this was the drastic reduction of the *casato*'s collateral lines (and, in the long run, the demographic decline of the aristocracy).

Historians have associated this process with the oligarchic *serrata* of the aristocracy, namely the closing off of access to noble rank, which accompanied state centralization and the transfer of patrician fortunes from financial and mercantile wealth into land. In the preceding centuries, when in most Italian cities the political structure was not yet stably dominated by a single family or small group of families, the competition for power among factions gave great political value to the creation of extended networks of kinship by means of marriage alliances. In this context, the spreading of *parentado* was crucial for the family's acquisition or preservation of political power. Hence the multiplication of the *casato*'s collateral branches by the marrying off of all sons. The establishment of the oligarchic power of a few families, in contrast, favoured a vertical vision of the family, limited to the *casato*'s main branch. Although cognatic and affinity ties remained significant (for instance, an aristocratic origin on the mother's side was a factor in nobility status), their political and strategic value diminished. The social identity of the aristocracy was increasingly based on the continuity of the patriliny rather than on extended networks of *parentado*, as shown by the more pronounced patrilineal bias of family memory in late sixteenth and seventeenth-century genealogies.

This process has been studied in political and legal traditions as far apart as Milan and Florence, and it appears remarkably similar. It also happened in the kingdom of Naples, where the traditional strategy of the feudal aristocracy had been the extension of the *casato*'s influence thanks to the multiplication of collateral branches: the more numerous these branches, the more powerful the family. This strategy had implied generalized marriage for cadets and most daughters. Feudal property was divided up among all sons. Daughters' dowries were kept within the family thanks to carefully orchestrated endogamy within the *casato*'s collateral branches: marriage would be arranged systematically between cousins (or even between couples of brother and sister). This pattern changed significantly in the second half of the sixteenth century, when the feudal aristocracy adopted male primogeniture and women were excluded from the transmission of feudal property. The exclusion of women from feudal succession (in favour of male collaterals) was sanctioned by a royal edict in 1595, but this rule had already been adopted, in practice, by the major aristocratic families: testamentary practice shows that the patrimony descended to first-born sons until the end of the male line, then passing to a collateral male line. At this point, matrimonial alliance became less important, the rate of celibacy of cadets and daughters sharply increased, and the level of dowries declined.

This shift in the structure of the family—a stronger patrilineal emphasis and a diminished significance of *parentadi*—had important consequences for women, which have been highlighted in another context (late sixteenth and seventeenth-century Romagna) by Cesarina Casanova. She describes how, in a situation of intense and often violent conflict for political power among families and factions in the early sixteenth century, the establishment of *parentadi* through marriage was crucial to the political fortunes of the family. Sons and daughters were usually married in order to multiply kinship ties, and they all received a portion of inheritance. In this context, precisely because they could inherit the family's patrimony, women were often the pawns of a ruthless and even brutal competition for *parentado*: entire patrimonies changed hands because of the abduction and forced marriage of heiresses. But if women could be victims in this situation, they could also be important political actors. Women were included in the ritualized peacemaking, or *paci*, between rival families: for instance, a mother's consent would be required for reconciliation with a faction responsible for the murder of her sons. Even more significantly, since men were often exiled when the opposing faction was in power, women could become head of both household and faction in their stead. Subsequently, at the turn of the sixteenth century, when the Romagna families, like the rest of the Italian aristocracy, adopted primogeniture and the limitation of the family to the patriliny, there was a marked diminution of marriages, especially of women, and consequently, according to Casanova, a devaluation of women's political role.

Daughters and cadets: the price of patriliny for women and men

It would be misleading, however, to stress only the consequences of the new pattern for women: these consequences, especially the drastic limitation of marriage, affected both daughters and younger sons. The destiny of daughters and cadets, in fact, had shown remarkable similarity even before the post-1560 shift to primogeniture. For instance, in Renaissance Venice Stanley Chojnacki has called attention to the plight of patrician bachelors as 'subaltern patriarchs'. In Venice, patriarchy was the principle that linked governmental and private spheres in securing elite hegemony. But while the culture celebrated the integrated public and private roles of the patriarch as father and husband, in practice nearly half of male nobles who reached adulthood appear to have remained bachelors. Because of dowry inflation (the high price of creating ties of affinity) patrician families limited the number of marriages of their sons as well as their daughters. These forced bachelors formed a sort of 'male periphery of patriarchy': although they took part in governmental activities, they were confined to lesser offices. In some respect, Chojnacki argues, their position was as marginal in the patriliny as that of their married sisters, though within an overall structure that favoured men of whatever marital status. Interestingly, like their married sisters, they sometimes showed bilineal social orientation (benefiting in their wills, for instance, their sisters' children). Also, like their unmarriageable sisters, they were often forced into the religious life.

In early modern Italy, in fact, religious profession was a container for excess female population: in Venice in the period 1581–1642 the percentage of nuns among patrician women averaged over 70 per cent. But the petitions sent to the Roman office of the papal penitentiary (*Sacra Penitenzieria Apostolica*) for dispensation from monastic vows show that being forced to make a religious profession was not an exclusively feminine fate. Men also were often coerced into an ecclesiastical career, as an alternative to the military, increasingly in the late sixteenth century by the demands of primogeniture. In the requests they made for the annulment of vows, men also claimed to have been driven into a religious profession by the violent pressure of their families.

For these men, as for their sisters, things got worse after the Council of Trent. Traditionally, the Roman curia had granted such unwilling members of the religious orders a permit to live out of the monastery for study, family, or health reasons. After a papal bull of 1558 all such former monks were ordered to return to their monasteries, under threat of losing church benefices. Those who did not obey were to be marked out and all Christians were forbidden to give them hospitality, on penalty of excommunication. In view of all this, we may well say that some males also paid a high price for the patriliny: the requirements of the *casato* implied the hierarchical privilege of males over males, not only of males over females.

In the seventeenth century, the enforced celibacy of daughters and cadets already caused by the dowry inflation was further exacerbated by primogeniture and the triumph of the patrilineal family. Among the Milanese aristocracy in the years 1600–49, for instance, the percentage of celibates, men and women, is stunning: 49 per cent of the men, 75 per cent of the women. (We may remember that at about the same time over 70 per cent of patrician women in Venice were nuns.) Just as daughters had to be compensated with a dowry for their exclusion from inheritance, so cadets were entitled to a life income. Like the dowry, the cadets' *vitalizio* (living allowance) could be burdened by conditions imposed by the father's testament, such as that the beneficiary could marry only within certain branches of the *casato*. Although the cadets' *vitalizio* could be a heavy encumbrance for the family (leading in some cases to serious financial crisis) a clear trend in the seventeenth century is the steady decline of cadets' *vitalizi*, paralleled by a similarly declining trend for daughters' dowries. The two seem to be consequences of the same phenomenon— the decreased significance, in the family's strategy, of matrimonial alliances once primogeniture was generalized. Visceglia has described these parallel trends in the kingdom of Naples throughout the seventeenth century: more and more aristocratic daughters became nuns, and those who married received dowries that were much inferior, by the end of the seventeenth century, to those of the beginning of the century. Similarly, she notes a declining trend for the cadets' *vitalizi*. Both trends, she argues, were a consequence of the same strategy, namely the family's choice to shift onto its weakest members—daughters and younger sons—the costs of the crisis of feudal rent.

But it was especially women's property rights that were most dramatically curtailed. Visceglia stresses that throughout the seventeenth century not only did the amount of the dowry decline, but the methods and times of payment of the dowry changed for the worse. The percentage of the dowry paid in cash went down, while the period in which the payment was to be completed became longer. More and more often dowries included credits which were uncertain and difficult to get. Moreover, the quit-claim (*rinuncia*) usually included in marriage contracts or monastic professions, whereby the woman gave up, in exchange for her dowry, any future claim to inheritance, became much more radical and generalized. Originally, the woman would renounce only the paternal or maternal inheritance if her brothers had male heirs. In the seventeenth century the renunciation becomes total and unconditional: 'she renounces all family inheritance also in the name of her successors . . . under penalty of suspension of the dowry payment.'[10] To this should be added the negative consequences for women of the new possibility of commercializing the dowry. Traditionally the dowry had been legally protected as inalienable property: but starting in the second half of the seventeenth century it became an accepted practice to sell or otherwise alienate dotal property, and often this was done in favour of men's, not women's, economic interest.

Visceglia's study of male testaments in the kingdom of Naples in this period shows that the role of women in the family's patrimonial strategy becomes more and more marginal. In the early sixteenth century a woman would get, beside her dowry, also the *dovario*[11] (consisting usually of one third of the husband's property) and various legacies plus, if her children were minor, their guardianship and the usufruct of the husband's patrimony. From the end of the sixteenth century, in contrast, the widow's power as administrator of her husband's property is restricted—even her use of house and household items is limited (husbands' testaments suggest the widow moves

---

[10] M. A. Visceglia, *Il bisogno d'eternità. I comportamenti aristocratici a Napoli in età moderna* (Naples, 1988), 90.

[11] Similar but not entirely equivalent to the English dower.

to a smaller house, her jewels are left to the eldest son, she gets fewer legacies).

A comparative study of male and female testaments in Turin 1650–1710 by Sandra Cavallo shows similar trends. As in the kingdom of Naples, also in Piedmont at the turn of the eighteenth century there seems to be a crisis of women's property rights, in connection with an increased agnatic bent of the family. Cavallo's study shows that women testate much less than men (they are one third of the whole sample), and increasingly their ownership of their dowry or extradotal property seems purely nominal. In men's wills, usufruct on the husband's property is left to widows under condition that they give up their right to dowry and extradotal goods in favour of off-spring. The very term 'usufruct' seems to signify in this context not that the widow will be entitled to administer the husband's property but that she will receive a living allowance from it. In parallel, women's testaments reveal that their real control over property is much more limited than their nominal ownership. Mostly, women bequeath only personal objects: these seems to be the only items which they feel free to dispose of. On the other hand, Cavallo notes, women's wills seem to be more 'individualized', less stereotypical than men's. While men's legacies conform much more closely to family expecta-tions, women's legacies have a more marked individual character. Precisely because they were more marginal to the family, women seem to have developed a more individualized sense of self, less shaped and conditioned by single-minded loyalty to the family as patriliny.

1700–96 and beyond: crisis of the patriliny

Since daughters and cadets paid the highest price for the *casato*'s aggrandizement, it is not surprising to find that resistance to the inequities of the patriliny came from them. We find evidence of this in testamentary practice. While fathers' wills privileged the first-born son, women and cadets often testated in a more egalitarian way. Visceglia's study of the Neapolitan nobility shows that some *fed-ecommessi* were created to provide for young cadets, and this was usually done by women or older cadets. She finds that mothers used testamentary legacies to balance the inequality among children required by primogeniture: they may even privilege the cadets over the first-born son. Furthermore, marriage contracts show that mothers contributed regularly to their daughters' dowries with amounts that were even superior to what they left to cadets by will. Although one cannot speak of a female devolution of the maternal property for the Neapolitan nobility, there was clearly among women the desire to balance the distribution of property among children.

At the turn of the seventeenth century, there are clear signs that the imperatives of the patriliny were increasingly resented by some family members. In her studies on seventeenth-century Roman patrician families, Renata Ago has shown how hierarchies of status, privilege, and autonomy among family members used to be counterbalanced by a strong corporate sense of the family as a 'team unit', which was expressed also in ceremony and ritual. For instance, women, because of their lack of formal power, were employed as brokers and envoys in risky transactions and negotiations, in which the direct involvement of the male head of the family would have imperilled the family prestige in case of failure. Thus differences of power and resources among family members were used strategically as a family asset. But at the turn of the seventeenth century this corporate sense of the family was shaken by new individualistic trends. A telling sign of heightened stress within the patrilineal family is the rise of litigation over property devolution. It was precisely the mounting number of lawsuits contesting women's exclusion from inheritance by pitting Roman law against municipal law that led several Italian princes, among them Pope Innocent XI, to pass new laws upholding the rights of the agnatic family against the more egalitarian Roman law. More research is needed on this issue, but it seems likely that this mounting tide of litigation was fuelled by women's and cadets' increased resistance to their exclusion from inheritance. In all the lawsuits of Bagnacavallo families in the eighteenth century, for instance, the bone of contention was women's inheritance rights. In this period women seem increasingly prone to protect their property rights (or even those of the family) against wasteful husbands, sons, or sons-in-law. In eighteenth-century family chronicles we meet women such as Countess Laura Bigini, married to Girolamo Vitelloni, who separated from her inept husband and resettled in Rome, 'where she devoted herself to filing and following up several lawsuits of great consequence in favor of the Vitelloni family, to the admiration of everybody'.[12]

Women's new attitude to property finds an echo even in Italian literature. We can hear a strikingly new note, for instance, in the poems of the Bolognese Teresa Zani (1664–1732), who deliberately represents herself in her poetry, no more as the pining lover of Petrarch's convention, but as a wealthy heiress, the owner of landed property (lovingly described in a sonnet), and as a young woman who claims, thanks to this economic independence, the right freely to choose a husband according to inclination and not family interest. Beside voicing this unconventional view of womanhood in her poetry, Teresa Zani did not hesitate, later in life, to file a lawsuit against her deceased husband's family over property matters. A keen sense of property rights seems to have been at the heart of her authorial and personal identity.[13]

Perhaps the most striking evidence of the crisis of the patrilineal family in the eighteenth century is the tremendous drop in the rates of celibacy. In the period 1650–1799 among the Milanese aristocracy, the rate of male celibacy went from 50.5 per cent to 36.5 per cent, and even more striking is the figure for women: from 48.5 to 13 per cent. In fact women were the leaders in this trend: their rate of celibacy had already begun to decrease significantly (to 34.5 per cent) at the beginning of the eighteenth century, when the corresponding rate for men was still 50 per cent. There are other eloquent signs of the crisis of the *casato*'s model of marriage. Although the Catholic form of divorce, that is, separation '*a mensa et thoro*' ('of table and bed') was granted very sparingly, there is evidence that it grew more common in the eighteenth century, possibly thanks to wives' greater economic independence. In one of the few contexts where this issue has been studied quantitatively, the city of Siena, the number of separations doubled: from 1.22 per cent in 1600–40 to 2.12 per cent in 1750–99.

Much more pronounced is the growth of another sign of patrilineal stress: the diffusion of clandestine marriages in the early eighteenth century. Among the Venetian patricians there seems to be a veritable epidemic of such marriages, leading the city government to claim control over this issue in order to repress it more severely

---

[12] Casanova, *La famiglia italiana*, 200–01.

[13] E. Graziosi, *Avventuriere a Bologna. Due storie esemplari* (Modena, 1998), 141–237.

than the ecclesiastical authorities were inclined to do. Besides the spread of clandestine marriages, the Venetian aristocratic family of the eighteenth century shows multiple signs of the crisis of patrilineal and patriarchal hierarchies: requests for marriage annulment or separation advanced especially by women, loss of authority of fathers over sons, of husbands over wives.

In the early eighteenth century foreign visitors noticed a peculiar addition to the Italian aristocratic family: the *cicisbeo*, or *cavalier servente*, a gentleman who regularly escorted a married lady in all social occasions and who was rigorously not her husband. The *cicisbeo* was often chosen by common agreement of husband and wife when drawing up the marriage contract, the lady's right to have one being sometimes included in the stipulations therein. English, French, and German visitors in this period all expressed their astonishment at this singular Italian arrangement of marital roles. They exclaimed at the extraordinary sexual liberty of Italian gentlewomen, and declared that all stereotypes relating to Italian husbands' proverbial jealousy were in need of serious revision. As for foreign women in Italy, they seem to have taken to the custom rather good-humouredly. When Mrs Thrale visited Italy at the end of the eighteenth century, she first insisted on being accompanied by her husband in all social occasions, but then bowed to Italian ways by selecting a *cicisbeo*, although with English propriety she chose an 80-year-old clergyman.[14]

It might have been some inkling of this custom, together perhaps with the news of another Italian oddity of the times, the granting of university degrees to women (Laura Bassi received her doctorate from the University of Bologna in 1732), that lured Lady Montagu to Italian shores in 1739. Strange as it may seem to us in hindsight, Italy might have appeared at that time as a land of greater freedom for women, a land where gender orthodoxy was being overhauled. But Lady Montagu's high hopes were bound to be disappointed, and not only because Algarotti chose basely to desert her. Although the French custom of *salons* where women were intellectual leaders was spreading to Italy in the early eighteenth century, many obstacles still

---

[14] *Thraliana: The Diary of Mrs. Hester Lynch Thrale, 1776–1809* (Oxford, 1951), ii, 622, quoted by M. Barbagli, *Sotto lo stesso tetto. Mutamenti della famiglia italiana dal XV al XX secolo* (Bologna, 1984), p. 334. On *cicisbei*, see ibid. 331–36.

hindered women's participation in the intellectual life, and cases such as Laura Bassi's were destined to remain few and far between.

Moreover, much of gender orthodoxy was going to remain in place throughout the eighteenth century and beyond, although the patrilineal family had certainly started an irreversible decline. A recent book by Roberto Bizzocchi follows up this decline through the life and personal records of four men belonging to a Pisan aristocratic family, the Bracci Cambini, from the middle of the seventeenth century to the middle of the nineteenth.[15] The tension between heirs and cadets is the recurring motif of these life stories. The founder of the family, Leonardo, had been himself a rebellious cadet, who rejected celibacy and a military career, choosing instead to claim his portion of inheritance and marry. He thus established a new branch of his *casato* but he did it in a new and individualistic way, cutting all links with the main line. Leonardo managed successfully to move from cadet to patriarch, becoming the head of a new patriliny and the father of sixteen children. His diary chronicles the family affairs and bears few traces of his personal tastes and individuality: a 'feeling for the *casato*' was his ruling passion. A century later, the diary of another cadet of the family, Lussorio, shows little interest in family affairs and very strong scepticism as to *casato* values. Lussorio rejected his role as cadet much more radically than Leonardo: he married for love, not to establish a new patriliny, and bequeathed his property to his wife, ignoring the *casato*'s males in his will. In the following generation the stories of two brothers, Nemesio and Atanasio, show that the conflict between heir and cadet had become irremediable. Nemesio, the elder brother, tried to restore the *casato*'s ideology by adhering to nineteenth-century Restoration values and by tyrannizing over the women of the family and his younger brother, Atanasio. Following time-honoured *casato* practice, Atanasio has been pressured to enter monastic life and to sign a quit-claim, *rinuncia*, over his portion of inheritance. The letters he writes to his brother from the convent, reporting the crisis of his religious identity and asking his brother for support, make sad reading. Nemesio pettishly sticks to his hierarchical role as head of the family, and rejects Atanasio's entreaties for brotherly sympathy. The rebellion of this cadet is much more radical

---

[15] R. Bizzochi, *In famiglia. Storie di interessi e affetti nell'Italia moderna* (Rome, 2001).

than the previous ones: in 1861 Atanasio leaves the convent and joins Garibaldi's troops. In the same year, he files a suit against his brother, asking for the annulment of his religious vows and his *rinuncia* to inheritance. He won the suit, and in a further act of defiance against the patrilineal logic he chose as heir the son of his sister, a cognatic kin.

Atanasio's story exemplifies the successful revolt of cadets against the inequities of the patrilineal family. In the case of women, however, the force of agnaticism proved stronger and more persistent. Even after the norms of the Napoleonic code that gave daughters equal inheritance rights in intestate cases (*ab intestato*) had been extended to the newly unified kingdom of Italy in 1865, the persistence of patrilineal attitudes regarding daughters' access to inheritance has been documented in several contexts. In the second half of the nineteenth century upper-class Neapolitan fathers made wills much more often, in order to limit daughters' inheritance as far as possible. An attempt to circumvent the new norms is also found in the same period among peasant families of the Bolognese countryside, where daughters are pressured into signing quit-claims renouncing their legal portion of inheritance (*legittima*) in exchange for their dowries: very much business as usual. Research on dowries in the Bolognese nobility at about the same period shows that, although fathers' obligation to give a dowry to daughters had been abolished in 1865, the practice persisted. For Italian women, the decline of patrilineal ideology and practice proved extremely slow.

The social world: cohesion, conflict, and the city

R. Burr Litchfield

Italian society of the early modern period was a society of orders transforming itself gradually, but unevenly, into a society of classes. The traditional orders of medieval society (nobles who fought, clergy who prayed, people who worked) had, to be sure, been undermined to a large extent, especially in the North, by the commercial and proto-industrial experience of the medieval and Renaissance communes with their merchants, artisan workers, vibrant urban culture, and control over the surrounding countryside. Italy remained the most urbanized region of early modern Europe, with seven cities in the sixteenth century (Genoa, Milan, Venice, Florence, Rome, Naples, Palermo) that had 50,000–150,000 inhabitants, and sixteen others with more than 20,000. But the persistence of corporative bodies—feudal nobles, the urban magistracies that were restricted to patrician or noble 'citizens', the guilds, the clergy and religious orders, even the numerous confraternal religious associations—still associated individuals with separate institutional groups. The transformation toward a society of classes proceeded with a varying rhythm. The consolidation of the regional states was a significant factor, but underlying economic trends were also important. Change proceeded more quickly in the fading economic prosperity of the late sixteenth century, more slowly in the seventeenth century, and again more rapidly in the eighteenth century. There were striking regional differences, especially between the cities of the North and Centre and the still feudal society of the South and the islands. However, corporative cohesion remained significant, in civil institutions, religious life, the ceremonial that affirmed the social hierarchy, and in action during periods of crisis that sparked underlying conflicts.

The social hierarchy: feudal nobles

Aspects of change appear when one considers the situation of nobles in the different states. Despite the urban development of the Renaissance, feudal (or semi-feudal) nobles still occupied a significant place. In the possessions of the duke of Savoy (Piedmont, Savoy, Nice) a feudal-military class and serfdom persisted. In the Papal States, the kingdom of Naples, and Sicily, feudal barons with great landed estates worked by servile peasants absolutely predominated. Throughout Italy, even in places where the communes had acted against feudal nobles, titles and feudal jurisdictions continued to be created through the eighteenth century. However, feudal nobles were being gradually transformed through their relationship to the court society of regional capitals: the courts of the dukes of Savoy in Turin, of the Este in Ferrara and Modena, the Gonzaga in Mantua, the Medici in Florence, patrician nobles in Genoa and Venice, the papal curia and the courts of cardinals in Rome, and the entourage of the Spanish governor of Milan and viceroy in Naples. An intense debate continued about the nature of 'nobility' throughout the period. Was nobility immutable, something conferred by descent from a blood lineage (*nobiltà del sangue*), or, as some Renaissance humanists had held, was it conferred by particular virtue and talent?

Nobility is the 'antiquity, splendour, and illustriousness' of families, 'coats of arms, titles, dignities,' Scipione Ammirato wrote in defence of the autonomies of Neapolitan feudal barons in 1580. But in the sixteenth century feudal nobles were absorbing the court culture of the regional states, and treatises in the tradition of Baldassare Castiglione's *The Courtier* of 1528 taught them court manners. Sons of feudal families were pressed into honourable service in the courts of local rulers, as gentlemen of the chamber, masters of the household, stewards, carvers, cup-bearers, and masters of the horse.

At the same time the princely courts also gave scope to the military tradition of nobles, for instance in the new knightly orders designed in part to fight the Turks, such as the order of the Knights of Saint Stephen founded by Cosimo I de' Medici, grand duke of Tuscany, in 1562, or the order of the Knights of Saints Maurice and Lazarus founded by Emanuele Filberto, duke of Savoy, in 1571. Some nobles aspired to admission to the socially exclusive order of the Knights of St John of Jerusalem, especially after the defeat of the Turkish siege of Malta, their headquarters, in 1565. Titles sometimes revealed a military career, not so much in the service of the pope in Rome (who nonetheless granted the title of prince to several old Roman feudal dynasties) but certainly in the service of the Habsburgs, where the military career of a younger son could garner at least the title of count.

The number of new titles and fiefs granted to aspiring families also increased, especially in the Spanish Habsburg possessions in Italy, the kingdoms of Naples and Sicily, and the duchy of Milan, where fiscal need made the infeudation and sale of previously free villages a tempting source of revenue. In the duchy of Milan, among 275 fiefs conferring titles that existed in the first years of the eighteenth century, 175 (64 per cent) had been created after the death of King Philip II of Spain in 1598. In the kingdom of Naples, the number of barons with titles grew from 118 in 1590 to 341 in 1640 and 434 in 1675. In some other states, such as Tuscany, the number of infeudated communities was smaller, but still noticeable. The high point in the creation of new fiefs was the 1640s, the moment of greatest fiscal need during the Thirty Years War. These new feudal holdings were without question much smaller than those once possessed by independent feudal lords in the fourteenth and fifteenth centuries; they were often hardly more than an appendage to a rural estate, and involved little more than the right to administer justice in the subjected community. Sometimes the new feudal lord was welcomed as a patron and protector. A tenant of Prince Trivulzio in the duchy of Milan said of his lord's management of Melzo in the 1670s: 'to attract people to come and settle here . . . he promised exemption from half the taxes for three years.'[1] But the new fief holders were also resented. The

---

[1] Quoted in D. Sella, *Crisis and Continuity: The Economy of Spanish Lombardy in the Seventeenth Century* (Cambridge, Mass., 1979), 170.

countryside of the kingdom of Naples was alive with peasant unrest before the outbreak of the revolt of 1647 in the Neapolitan capital, not to mention the brigands, who preyed on merchants between Naples and Rome, along the border between Tuscany and the Papal States, and in the mountain passes between Genoa and Lombardy, and who sometimes used noble fiefs as a base of operation. The people of Chianni and Rivalto, in Tuscany, south-east of Pisa, whose villages had been infeudated as a marquisate to the Riccardi family of Florence in the seventeenth century, represented in the 1770s that they no longer wished to remain under the Marchesi Riccardi. The ducal police had to be dispatched to return them to order.

The new titles and feudal possessions were sold, which opened the way to upstarts, often wealthy urban patricians like the Riccardi, a fact that contested their claim to 'nobility of blood'. In the 1760s, Giuseppe Parini, a figure of the Enlightenment who helped to revive the assumption that nobility should be founded on virtue and talent, complained about the *compri onori* ('bought honours') of Milanese nobles. But despite the erosion by capitalism a noble ethos and life-style persisted: the rural castle or villa, the sumptuous urban palace with the family coat of arms displayed on its façade, the horde of servants, duels fought to defend family honour (although duels were condemned by the Council of Trent), and the enormous dowries required for an honourable marriage that sent many unmarried younger sons in search of a career in the army or the Church, condemned many unmarried daughters to the obscurity of life in a convent, and led to the extinction of many families through lack of heirs.

Urban patricians

Another development in the court society of the sixteenth and seventeenth centuries was the transformation of urban patricians into nobles. Typically, the government of the Renaissance city had been reserved for an enclosed group of wealthy merchants, or in some cases city-dwelling nobles. In Venice, Florence, Genoa, Milan, even Naples, and in smaller cities—Siena, Lucca, the cities of the Venetian hinterland, and in Venice's subject cities along the Dalmatian coast, such as Ragusa—patrician families preserved significant wealth during the early modern period, and in the context of princely courts they aspired to 'noble' status. A long debate continued as to whether participation in commerce disqualified patricians from 'nobility'; a nervous relationship continued between merchant patricians and feudal court nobles. One Florentine merchant, Roberto Pepi, wrote around 1600 of the 'cavalaresque and lordly' city of Naples 'with many barons and other titled persons' but warned that 'one must be cautious there, because the many pleasures can easily distract youths from trade'.[2] A jurist of the early eighteenth century (Agostino Paradisi) surveyed the statutes of fifty-three towns in the north and found that two-thirds of them considered participation in trade to be an impediment to noble status.[3] Nonetheless, by the mid-seventeenth century the patricians of most capitals succeeded in having themselves declared 'nobles' as a group, at least to the extent, as one Genoese writer living in Naples (Paolo Mattia Doria) stated at the turn of the eighteenth century, that families 'who possess old wealth are nobles, as are those who have long remained distant from any mechanical or servile trade; thus the honoured citizen [whose family qualified to hold office] and the noble are the same thing'.[4] Often patrician families earlier enriched through trade and industry made large investments in landed estates between the late sixteenth and late seventeenth centuries, a decision that was both consistent with anticipation of a noble life-style and economically prudent in troubled times, since land provided a smaller but more certain income, especially when protected by a family entail. Of the 202 patrician families remaining to be registered as nobles in Florence in the 1750s from the priorate of the fifteenth-century republic, about half possessed a fief or noble title, or had been admitted as knights to the order of Saint Stephen under the Medici dukes, which implied ownership of a significant landed estate. The Venetian republic forbade its citizen nobles (those who sat in the *Consiglio Maggiore*) from assuming titles such as prince, duke, marquis, or count. But this did not prevent them from acquiring large landed estates in the Venetian hinterland, or from expanding from their urban palaces to

[2] R. Burr Litchfield, 'Un mercante Fiorentino alla corte dei Medici. Le 'Memorie' di Roberto di Roberto Pepi (1572–1634)', *Archivio storico italiano* 47 (1999), 750.

[3] See C. Donati, *L'idea di nobiltà in Italia. Secoli XIV–XVIII* (Bari, 1988), 302.

[4] Ibid. 308.

monumental country villas, such as Strà of the Pisani or Masèr of the Manin.

Cittadinanza and grosso popolo: professions, traders, and guildsmen

Below the patricians in the urban social hierarchy, and more intermingled with them at the beginning of the period than at the end (although the commercial involvement of some patricians continued), was the world of retail traders, service providers, masters in artisan industries, and men engaged in professions. The organization of trades into guilds continued from the Renaissance city but began to disappear in the last half of the eighteenth century. Typically, small producers in the cloth industry were organized in guilds (wool, silk, and linen cloth), as were small retail shops of different sorts (apothecaries, mercers), those engaged in alimentary trades (butchers, grocers, bakers), large varieties of other small artisans and tradesmen, and professionals such as notaries and doctors. But guild organization varied considerably from place to place. In seventeenth-century Florence there were only eleven 'official' guilds, due to an amalgamation of trades under the republic and Medici duchy, but a hundred or more trades were organized in Venice, 82 in Genoa in 1628, 71 in Rome in the 1620s, 45 in Milan in 1659. Turin, a new city in the sixteenth century, had no guilds until they were imposed by Duke Carlo Emanuele I in 1582; it had nine major guilds in 1650, 24 in 1740, and 91 in 1791.

The urban middle class inherited its corporative identity from guild membership (which often passed from father to son). Guilds provided a degree of mutual assistance among members, who were also subject to the guild tribunals. Street fights, and other contests sometimes developed between workers in guilds that maintained traditional rivalries. But the guilds were gradually declining in significance. With the crisis and then the fall of textile production of Florence, Venice, and Milan, the numbers matriculating into cloth guilds diminished, and the more bureaucratic administration of the regional states tended to replace guild jurisdictions. In the alimentary trades, for instance, there was strict regulation of supply of provisions, an important matter threatening public order as prices rose in the late sixteenth century—food riots were a potential tinderbox in the city. In Florence, the ducal government maintained storehouses of grain and controlled food prices (which limited the profits of landowners), and ordered bakers to produce 'ducal bread' in years of scarcity. In Rome, besides grain, the sale of meat by butchers was strictly regulated. Beef cattle could be slaughtered only between the feast of St John (24 June) and the beginning of Lent of the following year; pork became available in November; lamb between Easter and 23 June. It is often argued that guild regulation instilled a conservative routine-mindedness into artisan industrial producers that furthered the seventeenth-century economic stagnation, although increasingly in this period entrepreneurs attempted to introduce new products and expand production into the countryside, beyond the urban control of guild regulations. In the eighteenth century patrician landowners often supported the movement to end guild and other trade restrictions. The guilds disappeared in Florence (1786), in Milan (1787), generally during the French occupation of Italy in the Napoleonic period, and then finally, where they had been restored after the fall of the Napoleonic kingdoms, in Naples (1821) and Turin (1844).

Artisans and the working class

At the bottom of the social hierarchy, below the guild masters, was the large general population of artisan craftsmen, who were subordinate members of guilds or unorganized small-service providers, servants, day workers, peddlers, and the drifting population of semi-indigent people. Comparisons are difficult, since circumstances differed from place to place and from one decade to another. In Florence, according to a household census of 1632, a year of plague when the late sixteenth-century prosperity of the urban textile industry had declined, 30 per cent of households reporting occupations (3,128 out of 10,458) still described themselves as employed in textiles (wool, silk, or linen), and a third of these (1,114) were weavers, a group dependent on the masters of cloth shops, and often indebted. The next largest industrial group (9 per cent) were in the clothing trades, most conspicuously tailors and shoemakers. Next came households engaged in food selling. As industrial employment declined, the luxury of patrician landowners living from landed income maintained the demand for urban services. Small-service providers accounted for another 10 per cent of Florentine households, including 107 barbers, 149 coachmen, and 224 households listed as providing services to the ducal court. In Venice in 1642, also a year following economic downturn and plague, 25 per cent of households reporting occupations (3,823 out of 15,114) were employed in textiles or clothing trades, 14 per cent in food selling, while 19 per cent (more than in Florence) lived by renting out lodgings or were engaged in small service trades. Servants did not appear as household heads because they were recorded as subordinate members in their masters' households, but they became a significant part of the working class. They accounted for 11 per cent of the general population of Bologna in 1631, 10 per cent of the population of Florence in 1632, and 8 per cent of the population of Venice in 1642. In Florence, only 19 per cent of households had any servants, and half of these had only one, while a tiny minority among nobles and patricians of the Medici court (2 per cent of the households with 12 per cent of the servants) had ten servants or more; the most opulent noble household employed 40.

Women had an important role in the urban economy. Single and married women were subordinate household members, although the subdivision of housing in the city, and their care of children, often led widows to head their own small households. Women were employed as outworkers at home chiefly in the textile and dress industries. This could make their work different from that of their husbands. One might find a baker whose wife knitted stockings, a butcher whose wife made ribbons, or a stonemason whose wife reeled silk for thread. In a survey of the Florentine silk industry in 1663, 78 per cent of adult weavers were women, as were 65 per cent of throwsters, and apparently all 8,004 reelers of silk for thread, including 3,288 girls under the age of 15.

The working class was partly a drifting population that affirmed the still close relationship between city and countryside. About two-thirds of servants were women, some of them young country girls who hoped to earn enough for a tiny dowry and then return to marry in their native villages. Among men, manual workers in the building trades were often seasonal migrants who flocked into the cities during the warmer months. Peasants hawking produce, shepherds (the *zampognari* of Rome), and the huge drifting population of Naples also moved between countryside and city to escape even harsher rural conditions. Considering the high urban mortality rates, the cities would have shrunk in size without them. Rural population began to grow again throughout Italy at the end of the seventeenth century, a prelude to the resumption of urban population growth through in-migration in the first decades, but especially in the mid-to late eighteenth century.

The population of Turin, after growing slowly in the second half of the seventeenth century and suffering a crisis at the time of the French siege of the city in 1705, grew by nearly a quarter, from 46,278 to 58,125, between 1714 and 1750. The growth resulted from migration, mostly from the surrounding region, and this was a migration of the relatively poor, which also increased the number of beggars, especially during the summer months and among not easily employable people: women with children, the elderly, vagabond children, and the sick and maimed, who were rounded up and looked after to some extent by the Turin Ospizio di Carità, reorganized for this purpose in 1716–17. Much the same was true of other urban centres. The destitute depended on begging, soup kitchens run by monks and nuns, and alms distributed by guilds, confraternities, and urban hospitals. The civil authorities and the zeal of Counter-Reformation charity founded new large institutions for assistance. In Rome, the chief hospital for those sick with fevers was the Ospedale dello Spirito Santo, founded in the twelfth century, which had 150–400 beds in 1601. It was expanded under Pope Alexander VI in the 1660s, and again by Popes Benedict XIV and Pius VI in the eighteenth century. But each district of Rome had a hospital, and there were hospitals for pilgrims, lying-in hospitals, hospitals for convalescents. Other cities had hospitals, and new poorhouses were built in Milan in 1570, in Florence in 1621, in Genoa in 1664, in Naples in 1667 and then again with the great Neapolitan Albergo dei Poveri founded by Charles of Bourbon in 1751. These helped to mitigate the problems that resulted from the new wave of urban growth: the population of Venice remained stable with 138,000 in 1800, below its sixteenth-century maximum of 158,000, but Genoa grew by 13 per cent between 1750 and 1800 to 91,000, Milan by 9 per cent to 135,000, Florence by 12 per cent to 81,000, Rome by 18 per cent to 163,000, and Palermo by nearly

30 per cent to 139,000, while the population of Naples grew by 40 per cent between 1750 and 1800, from 305,000 to 427,000.

The religious hierarchy

The Catholic Church absolutely predominated, but some small enclaves of minority religious groups still deserve notice. Small communities of Protestants remained among Waldensians in the high valleys of the Alps north of Turin (despite the attempt of the duke of Savoy to eliminate them in the 1680s), among merchants at the free port of Livorno, and among a few foreigners established elsewhere. The Jewish communities were more conspicuous. Enclosed in ghettos in the sixteenth century, and largely self-governing under their Massai, there were some 3,000 at Livorno in the mid-eighteenth century, 1,000 at Florence, communities of 200–300 at Siena and Pisa, some 1,300 scattered among different communities in Piedmont, 1,700 in Venice, and about 3,000 in Rome.

Throughout these centuries the Catholic clergy remained a large but quite varied order in the urban scene, certainly more important than the mere numbers of clergy indicate, although these distinguish between the secular parochial (and non-parochial) clergy and the regular clergy of male religious (monks and friars in monasteries and friaries) and female religious (nuns in convents). The number of male and female religious grew during the sixteenth and seventeenth centuries, but then levelled off in the eighteenth century, even before the secular state began new efforts to erode clerical immunities. In Rome itself in 1592, clergy accounted for 4–5 per cent of the total population, counting bishops, secular priests, monks and friars, nuns, seminarians, and the courts of cardinals. Here the number of secular priests about equalled the number of religious, and the number of male religious was not much less than the number of nuns. Elsewhere the number in monasteries or convents predominated more clearly, and the number of nuns in convents could be twice or more the number of monks and friars. In Venice, in 1586, secular priests were about 12 per cent of the total clergy, monks and friars were about 30 per cent, and nuns nearly 60 per cent. In Florence in 1632, among religious alone, the number of nuns was three times the number of monks or friars, a testimony to the limited opportunities available for single women.

Through the mid-seventeenth century the regular clergy of the religious orders tended to gain territory with respect to parishes, and they assumed administration of parishes in many cases. There were many disputes between established orders (Benedictines, Dominicans, Franciscans) and new arrivals in the religious scene (Jesuits, Oratorians, Carmelites, and others). Religious disputes could erupt about the possession of a church, the possession of bits of urban territory coveted to expand churches, processions, and disputed installations of priests, and sometimes both the religious and civil authorities intervened to remove a particularly troublesome, or even subversive, congregation of monks. Criminals sought sanctuary from the police in church buildings. In the eighteenth century the attraction of the religious orders somewhat diminished, but in the second half of the century the total of clergy was still about 5 per cent in Rome, 5 per cent in Florence, 5 per cent in Milan, 4 per cent in Venice, 3 per cent in Turin, and 3 per cent in Naples. At the very end of the century the number of religious decreased in some places, due to the closing of monasteries and convents by the state, as happened in Tuscany and Lombardy. In Florence, while the number of secular priests increased slightly, the number of monks and friars decreased from 1,123 in 1738 to 917 in 1766 and to 665 in 1806, while the number of nuns decreased from 2,201 to 2,130 to 1,769.

Among the lay population, confraternities were an important source of devotional association, mutual aid, and charitable assistance to the poor. Sixteenth-century artisans were normally members of a guild along with others who practised their trade, but also of a confraternity that met in a particular church or monastery under the protection of a chosen saint. Other groups also formed confraternities. Confraternities tended to replace guilds in formal processions. These associations had appeared in the late Middle Ages when the mendicant orders (Franciscans and Dominicans) had encouraged their formation to strengthen lay piety, and they grew further in number under the Counter Reformation when, however, the city-wide associations of particular trades of the Renaissance city tended to become more controlled by individual parishes which sponsored confraternities of the Holy Sacrament. Some eighty new confraternities were founded in the city of Rome during the sixteenth century and thirty-four more during the seventeenth century; in seventeenth-century Perugia about 10 per cent of the population was involved. In Venice, before the plague of 1575–77 the six major confraternities alone (the *Scuole Grandi*) had 5,000–6,000 members, and in 1732 there were reported to have been 357 Venetian confraternities of different types. Some had quite significant endowments. A confraternity of the Holy Spirit in seventeenth-century Naples had some 6,000 members and supported a boarding school for 400 indigent girls. In Florence in 1783, when many were suppressed by the state for having insufficient resources or members, there were some 256 confraternities, more than two-thirds of them founded since 1500. But by this time nineteen no longer had any members, half had less than 100, a third 100–300, 10 per cent 300–800, and one had 1,500 members. The Florentine confraternities had also become more stratified socially; besides clergy, some had members chiefly among nobles and citizens, a few admitted women, a very few had only women, but most recruited their members among male artisans.

Public life: ceremonies and crises

The social hierarchy of different orders and strata was affirmed in all aspects of the ceremonial and ritual life of the city, although there were also rituals of protest. The rhythm of life was punctuated by the ceremonies that accompanied the coronations, marriages, births, and deaths of princes, by entertainment offered to foreign dignitaries, and by the celebration of the cycle of religious feasts. In all these ceremonies, the place of participants from different orders was well understood, from the prince and his court with standard-bearers, guards, and musicians to the upper clergy, the members of different religious orders, the members of civic councils, patrician magistrates, the members of guilds, parishes, and confraternities, down to the general populace, which was likely to introduce a significant element of drunken disorder.

The installation of a Venetian doge was always proceeded by a progress through the Piazza San Marco, where he threw out coins to the assembled, and often unruly, crowd before retiring to the *palazzo ducale* for his coronation by representatives of the senate. The doge as symbol of the state participated in numerous ritual observances through the year: the ritual marriage with the sea at the Lido on Ascension day (a spring festival in which all orders participated), the great Corpus Christi procession of clergy through the Piazza San Marco, and processions for other feast days, saints' days, and commemorations. Republican Venice tolerated a broad spectrum of popular observances, even the ferocious bridge battles that occurred through the sixteenth and seventeenth centuries between workers in the Arsenal (Castellani) at one end of the city and fishermen (Nicolotti) at the other, along canals in the centre of the city where their two territories met. The police of the Council of Ten eventually succeeded in suppressing them in the first years of the eighteenth century.

In Florence, ritual observances were more tightly controlled by the secular state, and the assertion of dominance by the Medici dukes over the hierarchy of orders reached a crescendo of magnificence in the second half of the sixteenth century. The funeral for Grand Duke Cosimo I in 1574 evoked a huge procession of Knights of St Stephen, feudal nobles, clergy, and religious orders that wound its way throughout the city. The feast of S. Giovanni Battista in June, the yearly Florentine civic spectacle, again involved a huge procession of nobles, representatives of the provincial towns, magistrates, clergy, guilds, and confraternities. For the entry into the city of the bride of the ducal heir in 1608, there were nobles, patricians, clergy, troops, and elaborately staged court spectacles. The lower orders tended to become lost in the ceremonial of the Medici court. There were bridge battles in Tuscany too (at Pisa through the eighteenth century), but those of Florence became staged appendages to court spectacles. The popular festive societies of the Renaissance republic (the *potenze*), although still active in the 1580s, disappeared entirely in the seventeenth century.

In Rome, beyond the yearly cycle of religious observances and entries of foreign dignitaries, a papal coronation, accompanied by the great procession of the *possessio* from St Peter's to the Basilica of St John Lateran, concluded a period of general disorder in the city during the interregnum between one pope and another. Crowds, and even members of the papal curia, sacked the possessions of the outgoing pope and his family. A Bernini statue of Pope Urban VIII was barely saved from destruction in 1644. With its rival and semi-independent colonies of foreigners accredited to the papal see, Rome was particularly subject to popular disturbances. In the 1730s serious disorder resulted there from recruitment among the Roman populace for the army of Charles Bourbon, the successful Spanish pretender to the crown of Naples.

Outbreaks of plague strained the social hierarchy and evoked extraordinary measures that were beginning to gradually shift from religious to more secular responses. During the plague of 1575–7 the Venetian senate decreed construction of the monumental church of the Redentore on the Giudecca, and instituted an annual penitential procession of thousands that proceeded to the church from S. Marco over a temporary bridge of boats, a procession that proceeded further to the church of S. Maria della Salute after the plague of 1630–32 (some 46,000 deaths). In Florence, the plague of 1630 chiefly affected crowded neighbourhoods of the poor (some 12,000 deaths); there was little mortality among courtiers or patricians. A state magistracy of health (*sanità*) had been instituted in the 1520s, which ordered and attempted to inforce a universal quarantine. The religious response culminated in April 1633 with a great procession heralded by church bells to welcome the image of S. Maria dell'Impruneta which was carried to the major churches, while at the same time the secular authorities fired off cannons from the fortress to warn the Florentine populace to remain indoors. Florence escaped the plague of 1656–7 entirely, partly through timely action of the secular authorities to block any commerce with the infected regions of Genoa and the South. From Naples (some 150,000 deaths) the horrified Tuscan agent wrote in June 1656: 'the pest houses are filled with the dying . . . multitudes die at home [or] in the streets.'[5]

Scarcity of foodstuffs was one cause of seventeenth-century revolts (at Milan in 1628 and Palermo in 1647); taxation was another (the protracted *Guerra del Sale*—salt-tax war—in Piedmont during the 1680s and 1690s). The most serious popular uprising was the revolt of Naples in 1647–8. Here, misgovernment by the Spanish viceroy, the duke of Arcos, rural discontent, growing urban population, food scarcity, the weak Spanish military presence, and a new tax imposed on fresh fruit in July 1647 set off nine months of turmoil. The initial

---

[5] Vincenzo de Medici, quoted in L. Dal Panto, *Le epidemie nella storia demografica italiana (secoli XIV–XIX)* (Turin, 1980), 171.

popular leader, the fishmonger Tommaso Aniello (Masaniello), survived for only ten days; he was assassinated by agents of the nobility loyal to the viceroy. His followers among the populace hailed him as a saint. Some groups in the establishment of lawyers (Togati) pressed for constitutional reforms. Others among patricians sought to install a republic under the protection of the French Henry of Lorraine, duke of Guise. Disunity among the orders that divided Neapolitan society frustrated a decisive outcome. A negotiated settlement in April 1648 reduced some taxes, while Spanish troops re-entered the city.

Emergence of a modern public sphere

In the eighteenth century the outlook of some groups in the upper and middle classes began to evolve in a new direction. With the realignment of dynasties in the first decades of the century the regional courts began to fade as the chief focus of urban civil society, and academies, newspapers, and reading clubs gained in importance. Some academies dated back to the sixteenth century, such as the *Accademia Fiorentina* and *Accademia della Crusca* in Florence. Short-lived scientific societies followed in the seventeenth century (the Roman *Lincei* of 1603 and the Florentine *Cimento* of 1657). The Roman *Arcadia*, a literary society founded in 1690 under the protection of the exiled Queen Christine of Sweden, is indicative of the membership: the *Arcadia* attracted 1,163 members between 1690 and 1710, half of them laymen, and in 1723 it had 2,619 members, mostly in the Papal States, the kingdom of Naples, and the grand duchy of Tuscany. Masonic lodges, although condemned by the Church, began to spread in the 1730s; they first appeared in Florence, Milan, Venice, and Naples. The short-lived Milanese *Accademia dei Pugni* gave birth to Pietro and Alessandro Verri's journal *Il Caffè* of 1764–6. In Naples Abbé Ferdinando Galiani organized an *Accademia delle Scienze*; the *Accademia delle Scienze* of Turin appeared in 1783. Florence produced the first agrarian academy in Europe in 1753, the *Accademia dei Georgofili*. It is possible to discover the social status of the 941 members of the four Florentine academies in 1783. Besides foreign corresponding members, about half were local Tuscan patricians or nobles, and half were non-nobles. Many were priests, who accounted for a fifth of the noble members and for two-fifths of the non-nobles. An important group among lay non-nobles consisted of lawyers and doctors.

Italy contained important centres of publishing, especially Florence and Venice, where there were strong traditions of book production and censorship was relatively mild. Ephemeral gazettes of the mid- to late seventeenth century gave way to literary journals and newspapers. By the last quarter of the eighteenth century nearly every capital in the north and centre, and also Rome and Naples, had experienced a journal or gazette of some kind, at least temporarily. Gazettes, such as the Florentine *Gazetta universale* (1773–1811), which appeared in some 2,500 copies twice weekly, provided news of the world. The older Florentine gazette, the *Notizie del mondo* (1769–91) (where Filippo Mazzei published reports of the American Revolution) also appeared twice weekly in some 1,700 copies. It was not to be confused with the Venetian *Notizie del mondo* (1778–1812), one of several Venetian gazettes. Such journals were instrumental in forming a nucleus of public opinion. Translation of foreign books became common. At Livorno, the printer Giuseppe Aubert published works of Rousseau, and in 1770 an edition of the French *Encyclopédie*.

From this reading public emerged many of the *Giacobini* who welcomed the French army of Napoleon Bonaparte's first Italian campaign in 1796, and who rallied with Phrygian caps and newly planted liberty trees into the political clubs of the Cisalpine republic (Milan, 1797), the Ligurian republic (Genoa, 1797), the Roman republic (1798), and the short-lived Parthenopean republic (Naples, 1799). But the institutional changes of the Napoleonic period, which further dismembered the society of orders, had already begun in the 1760s–80s, especially through the reforms undertaken in Lombardy and Tuscany under Habsburg rule. In Florence and Milan, entails of noble estates were curtailed, the old magistracies staffed by patricians disappeared, guilds were abolished, monastic property was secularized, clerical immunities were challenged, and legal reform began. Under Napoleon the privileges of patricians in Venice and Genoa ended, and the first tentative efforts were made (realized only much later) to end the feudal system in the kingdom of Naples. But the dawn of the Risorgimento involved only an urban minority. When the French were temporarily forced out of Italy in 1799, the clerical and rural reaction against the urban sister-republics was significant and violent: the Sanfedist crusade of Cardinal Ruffo and Calabrian peasants to retake the city of Naples, and the *Viva Maria!* in Tuscany directed against the French and their supporters in Florence. A world of cultural difference still separated city and countryside. Under the restored regional states in 1815 much remained to be accomplished beyond the tentative and uneven social evolution of early modern Italy.

6

The political world of the absolutist state in the seventeenth and eighteenth centuries

Geoffrey Symcox

Italy's fragmented political geography, enshrined in the peace treaty of Cateau-Cambrésis in 1559, persisted through the Old Regime. On the eve of the Napoleonic invasion in 1796 the political map still looked much as it had two centuries earlier. Apart from the Habsburg—first Spanish, later Austrian—imperial possessions (Lombardy, and the kingdom of Naples and Sicily until 1734), most states were ruled by autonomous princes aspiring to absolute author-ity. The old and increasingly inert city-republics of Venice, Genoa, and Lucca coexisted with the rising dynamic of princely absolutism. 'Italy' was in fact a system of regional states, republican or princely, competing for territory and status.

Until the middle of the seventeenth century the Italian states still possessed the capacity to prosecute their quarrels in the narrow arena of peninsular politics, but the so-called 'War of Castro' in the 1640s, pitting the papacy against a league of rival states, was the last conflict between them as independent belligerents. Thereafter they fought, if they fought at all, as auxiliaries of bigger powers outside the peninsula, for by then it was clear that they were incapable of independent action on the wider European stage. Even the largest—Venice and its Terraferma, with 1.8 million inhabitants in 1700, or the twin viceroyalties of Naples and Sicily, with a combined population of 3.3 million—could not match the demographic and economic strength of the monarchies beyond the Alps. The one Italian state to pursue a successful policy of military expansion, Piedmont, did so only by acting as the paid satellite of the great powers.[1] Foreign subsidies compensated the Savoyard state for its slender resources: a population of about 1.4 million souls in 1700, many of them inhabiting unproductive Alpine uplands. And for the Savoyard state, military adventurism brought only limited gains; the human and financial costs, however, were high.

During the two centuries covered by this chapter the Italian state-system went through two great cycles of warfare, followed by periods of peace and reconstruction. The first began when Charles Emanuel I of Savoy invaded the duchy of Monferrato in 1613, unleashing a chain reaction of conflict until 1659. Three decades of tranquillity followed, until in 1690 the peninsula was plunged into a second round of warfare until 1748. Peace then returned, providing the opportunity for some states to launch programmes of reform, until the irruption of the French revolutionary armies in 1796 overthrew the political structures of the Old Regime once and for all.

Widening war, 1613–27

In April 1613 Duke Charles Emanuel I of Savoy (1580–1630) invaded the neighbouring duchy of Monferrato, a possession of the Gonzaga dukes of Mantua. His pretext was to uphold the rights of his daughter, the widow of Duke Francesco II of Mantua, who had died in December 1612, to this portion of the Gonzaga inheritance. Charles Emanuel's attack was a challenge to the *pax hispanica* in Italy. Spanish

---

[1] Piedmont formed the nucleus of the territories ruled by the Savoyard dynasty, along with the duchy of Savoy, the duchy of Aosta, and the county of Nice, plus Sardinia after 1720. 'Piedmont' and 'Savoy' will be used interchangeably to designate the territories of the House of Savoy.

hegemony rested on possession of the duchy of Milan (or Lombardy), the viceroyalties of Naples and Sicily, the tiny state of the Presidi on the Tuscan coast, and Sardinia. Spain's interest was to maintain the status quo: any insurrection, any conflict had to be suppressed, since it raised the spectre of foreign—more specifically French—intervention. Charles Emanuel's invasion of Monferrato posed a threat not merely to Spain's protégé, the duke of Mantua, but to the entire edifice of Spanish power in Italy. Spanish troops from Milan therefore invaded Piedmont in defence of the duke of Mantua's rights, which allowed the opportunistic Charles Emanuel to pose as the champion of Italian liberty against foreign domination. But the other Italian states distrusted him and offered no support.

Venice's stance soon changed, however. In 1615 the republic's conflict with the Uskok pirates of Dalmatia escalated into war with their protector, the Habsburg emperor. When the king of Spain intervened to aid his Austrian cousin, Venice subsidized Charles Emanuel's war in Monferrato as a diversion of Spanish strength. France, plunged into a turbulent regency since the murder of Henri IV in 1610, joined Venice in supporting Charles Emanuel. But the Spanish army captured Vercelli in the summer of 1617, forcing him to make peace. His claims to Monferrato were not recognized. Spanish dominance over the Italian peninsula was unshaken. But the conflict had reawakened French interest in Italy, and in 1619 a dynastic marriage was concluded between Charles Emanuel's heir and Louis XIII's sister. Thus began a Franco-Savoyard alliance destined to endure, off and on, until 1690.

The outbreak of the Thirty Years War in 1618, and the resumption of hostilities between Spain and the Dutch republic in 1621, made northern Italy a theatre of paramount significance for the major powers. Milan formed the pivot of the Spanish military power: Spanish troops were ferried from Spain or Naples via Genoa to Milan, then up the 'Spanish Road' through the Valtelline pass northwards into Germany, or north-west towards the Netherlands. In July 1620 the governor of Milan fomented an uprising by the valley's Catholic population, who massacred their Protestant overlords, the Grisons, thus securing the Spaniards' route to the north. Severing this military lifeline became a high priority for the Habsburgs' enemies, led by France. But it was no easy task.

Beset by aristocratic rebellions and Huguenot insurgency, Louis

XIII of France was at first unable to counter the Spanish hegemony in Italy. But with the advent of Cardinal Richelieu in 1624 French policy became more aggressive. Richelieu sent a force to interdict the Valtelline, with Venetian support, and coordinated an attack on Genoa with Charles Emanuel I. The city was not only a vital staging post on the Spanish Road but, even more importantly, the financial heart of the Spanish empire: loans from the great Genoese banking houses kept the Spanish armies fighting. Both operations failed, so Richelieu abandoned his Italian allies and came to terms with Spain in March 1626. The Valtelline was declared a neutral zone, but Spanish troops continued to use it as before. Charles Emanuel I and the Venetians, embittered by what they regarded as Richelieu's betrayal, distanced themselves from the French alliance.

From the Mantuan succession to the War of Candia, 1627–69

In 1626 Duke Ferdinando of Mantua died, and was succeeded by his brother Vincenzo. When the latter died childless in December 1627, a dispute erupted over the Gonzaga inheritance between two collateral branches of the dynasty: the dukes of Guastalla and the dukes of Gonzaga-Nevers, the latter domiciled in France. Other interests were at stake too. The Spanish monarchy could not allow the Gonzaga duchies of Mantua and Monferrato, which flanked the duchy of Milan, to fall into unfriendly hands. The duchies were also fiefs of the holy Roman empire, and so fell under the jurisdiction of the Habsburg emperor Ferdinand II. And Charles Emanuel I renewed his claim on Monferrato.

Vincenzo Gonzaga had bequeathed the Gonzaga inheritance to Charles of Nevers, but the emperor, deeming him pro-French, sequestered it. Meanwhile Charles Emanuel arranged with the Spanish governor of Milan to partition Monferrato. In March 1628 a Spanish army besieged its key fortress of Casale, while a Piedmontese force occupied the remainder of the duchy. Early in 1629, however, a French army crossed the Alps to aid Charles of Nevers. Charles Emanuel quickly resumed his alliance with Louis XIII, and helped him relieve and garrison Casale. But the French army soon withdrew to deal with a Huguenot revolt. In August a powerful Habsburg army besieged Mantua, while a Spanish force besieged the French garrison at Casale.

Northern Italy was now a key battleground in the conflict between Bourbon and Habsburg. In May 1630, having quelled the Huguenot insurrection, Louis XIII led his army back into Italy. But before the French could reach Mantua, the imperial army took the beleaguered city in July and brutally sacked it. This was only the most dramatic episode in an unfolding tragedy. The contending armies ravaged the north Italian plains from Piedmont to the Veneto, and touched off an epidemic of plague which soon spread to regions of the peninsula unaffected by the fighting.[2]

In October 1630 French and Habsburg envoys negotiated a truce confirming Charles of Nevers as duke of Mantua, leaving the French garrison in Casale, and ceding some territory in Monferrato to the new duke of Savoy, Victor Amadeus I. In July 1631 by the treaty of Cherasco he ceded Pinerolo to France. From Pinerolo and Casale, French armies could now pass at will into northern Italy. In 1635 France, hitherto fighting as an auxiliary against the Habsburgs, entered the conflict as a full belligerent. Richelieu allied with Piedmont and the small north Italian states to attack Spain's Italian territories: Venice, Tuscany, and the Papal States remained neutral. On the death of Victor Amadeus I in 1637 this league broke up, as the Savoyard state was paralysed by civil war between his widow, the duchess-regent, and his brothers. This civil strife merged into the Franco-Spanish conflict, Richelieu backing the regent while Spain supported her adversaries, until in 1642 she and her brothers-in-law patched up a peace.

Revolts in Catalonia and Portugal in 1640, and in Naples in 1647, severely weakened Spain's military power. But France lacked the strength to exploit these opportunities, and the outbreak of the Fronde in 1648 permitted a modest Spanish recovery. In 1652 the French garrison was expelled from Casale. Stalemate then ensued, until in 1659 the two powers signed the treaty of the Pyrenees. They did not consult their respective Italian allies, and the treaty did not alter the territorial status quo.

Meanwhile in 1645 Venice had become embroiled in a long and

---

[2] This is the plague described by Manzoni in *I promessi sposi*.

costly war with the Ottoman empire. A Turkish army landed in the Venetian colony of Crete and quickly overran the island except for its main stronghold, Candia. The Venetians were able to ferry reinforcements to Candia, but they could not expel the Ottoman army. In 1669 the Turks conquered Candia—the Venetians lost 11,000 men in this year alone—and the republic made peace.[3] In 1684, after the Turkish defeat at Vienna the previous year, the republic allied with Austria and the papacy, and embarked on a war of revenge. Venice conquered the Peloponnese, which the Ottomans ceded in 1699. But in a third round of hostilities between 1715 and 1718 Venice lost this conquered territory again. The republic would now remain at peace, its maritime empire reduced to the island of Corfu and the Dalmatian coast, until its extinction in 1797.

Revolts in Naples and Sicily

The fighting in northern Italy spared the Spanish viceroyalties of Sardinia, Naples, and Sicily. They were only troubled by attacks on their coasts by Muslim raiders; in a typical incident, an Ottoman fleet sacked Manfredonia in 1620. Defence against these raids—a galley squadron at Naples, forts, and watch-towers—consumed most of the revenue in all three viceroyalties until the outbreak of the Thirty Years War. These expenditures were then dwarfed by the cost of supporting the Spanish war effort in northern Europe. The poverty-stricken viceroyalty of Sardinia contributed little, Sicily somewhat more; most of the burden fell on Naples. In 1647 punitive taxation there precipitated one of the most serious uprisings to convulse Europe in the mid-seventeenth century.

The Neapolitan revolt sprang from other, more deep-seated causes too: a sense that the Spanish crown was failing to rule justly, according to the precepts of *buon governo*, and the oppression of the feudal barons. They dominated the countryside, perverted justice, and subverted the rights of the towns and rural communes. In the city of Naples they held five out of the six *seggi* or city wards that formed the municipal council. But the barons formed the indispensable prop for

---

[3] Ludovico Antonio Muratori, *Annali d'Italia* (Rome, 1788), vol. 11, pt. 2, p. 169.

Spanish rule. As the Spanish crown's financial needs grew, it sold tax-collection rights, jurisdictional rights, and demesne lands—including royal towns—to the barons, strengthening their privileged position. And while the nobles were largely exempt from taxation, a host of new gabelles on foodstuffs, farmed out to wealthy financiers, aggravated the fiscal burden on the non-privileged.[4] Through the 1640s, a time of recurrent famines, taxation rocketed.

Rising taxation, however, could not balance the budget. The huge sums remitted from Naples to underwrite the Spanish crown's military commitments—11 million ducats between 1631 and 1643 alone—swelled the public debt, which was held by nobles, tax farmers, and speculators. In May 1647 bread riots at Palermo escalated into rebellion by the citizens, who demanded lower taxes and equal representation with the nobles in the city government. But events in Sicily were soon eclipsed by a huge revolt at Naples on 7 July, sparked by a protest against a new gabelle on fruit led by a fisherman, Tommaso Aniello—or Masaniello. The city's population took up arms, sacked the houses of tax farmers and nobles, and besieged the Spanish garrison in the city's forts. Many of the city's professionals and merchants joined the rebels. The murder of Masaniello ten days later only intensified the revolt. The rebels demanded the abolition of the new gabelles, and reforms to break the nobles' hold on the city government. Rebellion spread from Naples to the countryside. The rural population rose in revolt against the barons, who responded by mobilizing their private armies.

In October a Spanish fleet attacked Naples. The citizens repelled the assault, and proclaimed a republic, expecting help from France. But no help came, the baronial forces blockaded the city, and the rebel front began to crumble. On 6 April 1648 a negotiated settlement allowed the Spanish garrison to re-enter Naples, while in the countryside the baronial forces gained the upper hand over the peasants and rebel communes. The Spanish crown and its baronial allies had won, but things did not revert completely to the way they had been before the revolt. The viceroys now consulted representatives of the non-privileged orders on fiscal issues, and the haemorrhage of revenue to support Spain's military commitments slowed. The viceroys could

---

[4] A. Calabria, *The Cost of Empire: The Finances of the Kingdom of Naples in the Time of Spanish Rule* (Cambridge, 1991), 56–72.

not—and did not want to—enact far-reaching reforms, but their officials strove with some success to reassert the crown's juridical authority and to recover revenues and lands alienated to the nobility.

Uneasy calm descended on the viceroyalty of Naples. In Sicily, however, a serious insurrection broke out at Messina in 1672. The city's artisans rebelled against the ruling oligarchy of merchants and nobles. In July 1674 the urban oligarchy took its revenge, crushed the popular forces, expelled the Spanish governor, and called in aid from France. Louis XIV, then at war with Spain, despatched naval expeditions which kept the revolt alive. But when he made peace with Spain in 1678 he withdrew his forces and the revolt collapsed. Events at Messina showed unmistakably that French influence in Italy was growing as Spanish power waned.

Aristocracies and the state

The Neapolitan insurrection was only the most cataclysmic of many revolts that shook the Italian peninsula in the seventeenth century. Rural and urban uprisings, and persistent banditry in many places from Piedmont to the southern Papal States and the kingdom of Naples, clearly demonstrated the fragility of state structures. Rulers might aspire to absolute authority, but in practice they lacked the administrative or military means to coerce their subjects. And since the early seventeenth century war, plague, and agricultural depression had multiplied the problems of public order and left the Italian states financially exhausted. Public debt—loans contracted by governments to pay their armies, borrowing by cities and rural communities to pay their taxes—had risen alarmingly.

After 1659, peace offered a chance to return public finances to solvency. The dukes of Savoy and the Spanish governors of Lombardy abolished some wartime taxes and worked to reduce interest on their debts, recover alienated revenues and lands, and bring order to the chaotic budgets of their local communities.[5] The dukes of Mantua and Parma, the patricians of Venice, and the viceroys of Naples and

[5] D. Sella, *Crisis and Continuity: The Economy of Spanish Lombardy in the Seventeenth Century* (Cambridge, Mass., 1979), 141 ff.

Sicily responded less effectively to the emergency. But no government attempted thoroughgoing fiscal reform. The old tax systems remained in place, favouring nobles and clergy over commoners, city populations over country people, one region over another. Privilege—fiscal, judicial, social—was the cornerstone of the existing order, and contemporary rulers, whether in princely states or republics, strove to maintain it. The ideal of 'prudence' central to seventeenth-century statecraft warned them to eschew rash innovations; the ideal of *buon governo* enjoined them to balance competing social forces in the interests of stability. The ideal prince was a wise father who governed his state like a family patrimony, conserving it to hand on to his heirs. (Authority was gendered masculine; the duchesses who twice headed regencies in Piedmont faced opposition because of their sex.)

The problem of public debt and fiscal inequality highlights the dominant position enjoyed by aristocracies everywhere. Wealth, seigneurial jurisdiction, and access to high office combined to assure their ascendancy. The troubled times of the seventeenth century strengthened their position as the chief creditors of governments and local communities. In Piedmont and Naples the nobles were the principal beneficiaries from the alienations of tax revenues and demesne lands. In Tuscany, nobles owned one-third of the public debt by the end of the century. Everywhere the nobilities' fiscal immunities were on the rise, eroding state revenues. Of necessity, therefore, any solution to the problem of public indebtedness would require an assault on the fiscal privileges and economic interests of the nobility. But this no government was willing to undertake.

The issue here went beyond public finance. Princes could hardly conceive of attacking noble privilege, for they and their nobles were united by a common aristocratic culture. Their shared values found expression in the orders of chivalry headed by various rulers—like the order of Santo Stefano in Tuscany—and in the military vocation, still strong in the seventeenth century (although it would later wane), that impelled many aristocrats to serve their princes on the field of battle.[6] At court, nobles and princes took part together in chivalric entertainments and opulent ballets whose symbolic language

---

[6] G. Hanlon, *The Twilight of a Military Tradition: Italian Aristocrats and European Conflicts, 1560–1800* (London, 1998), ch. 9.

articulated the nobles' loyalty to their prince, and the code of honour to which they jointly subscribed. The court fulfilled other vital functions, too: it was the state's political and administrative nerve-centre, the apex of its clientage systems, the gateway to high office, the fountainhead of favour. Service under arms or access to the court encouraged the growth of an exclusive sense of blood and lineage separating nobles from the rest of the population.[7] This sense of caste depended for its validation on the prince, for he alone could confer noble status and adjudicate disputes over rank between his nobles. The prince thus formed the capstone on the edifice of privilege, the ultimate guarantor of the social hierarchy. Aristocratic values radiating from the court set the tone for society as a whole. Ennoblement was the goal to which ambitious commoners aspired. For them, the acquisition of an office—often by purchase—was the avenue to membership of the class that enjoyed political and cultural dominance.

But the relationship between princes and nobles was fraught with tension. To the nobles, the prince (or in the Spanish domains, his representative) was not only a partner but also a rival, any expansion of his authority a threat. They looked askance at attempts to curb duelling and vendetta, to mediate between them and their peasants, or to question their fiscal exemptions. In opposition they could be formidable. The aristocracies of Milan, Naples, and Sicily intrigued against their Spanish viceroys; in Sardinia a viceroy was murdered by dissident nobles. The rebel nobles in Piedmont posed a serious challenge to the duchess-regent's authority. But the fundamental community of interest between princes and nobles was never called into question, for the absolutist state rested on a compromise. The prince's power was limited by his obligation to uphold his nobles' prerogatives. His nobles in turn looked to him to validate their social ascendancy.

The prerogative of nobles was to command, and nobilities everywhere dominated the machineries of state. In the republics of Venice and Genoa the identification between noble status and political power was clearest: office was closed to all but the patricians. They *were* the state. And though in theory power was distributed equally

---

[7] e.g. Giovan Pietro Crescenzi, *Corona della nobiltà d'Italia* (1639), cited in Aldo Berselli, *Storia della Emilia-Romagna* (2 vols. Bologna, 1977), ii. 43–4.

within these patrician oligarchies, in practice it was restricted to an inner circle of older, richer families, to the exclusion of the more recently ennobled and the less well off. Political tensions resulted, and would grow more acute in the next century. The nobilities of the Venetian Terraferma dominated their local regions, under the eye of a governor drawn from the Venetian patriciate. Patricians too dominated the political apparatus in Milan. Spanish governors might come and go, but the patrician elite remained, ensconced in the senate and the high offices of state. Elsewhere the identification between noble rank and state office was less clear-cut. In the Papal States, the urban nobilities and feudal barons were subject, at least in name, to clerical officials appointed by their overlord the Pope. In the viceroyalty of Naples after 1647, baronial power was to some extent checked by the crown's legal officers. In Tuscany, 'new men' competed with old patrician families for places in the state bureaucracy.[8] In Piedmont, the expanding army and bureaucracy created opportunities for non-nobles to purchase offices, and then go on to acquire fiefs and titles. Members of old noble families, too, sought positions in the army or the state administration, and these two groups gradually merged into a composite elite. In Piedmont, more than in any other Italian state, the aristocracy came to define itself in terms of its service to the state and the ruling dynasty.

The Italian Wars, 1690–1713

Two factors hastened the decline of Spanish influence and destabilized the Italian state-system in the later seventeenth century. One was the power of Louis XIV's France. French support for the Messinese rebels was followed by the occupation of Casale in 1681, through a secret arrangement with the duke of Mantua, and by the bombardment of Genoa in 1684, to punish the city for aiding Spain. Caught between French garrisons at Casale and Pinerolo, Piedmont became a satellite of Louis XIV. The second factor undermining the balance of forces was the rising power of the Austrian Habsburgs. Victory over

[8] R. Burr Litchfield, *The Birth of a Bureaucracy: Florence under the Grand Dukes* (Princeton, NJ, 1988), 41–51.

the Turks in 1683 rekindled the imperial ambitions of the house of Austria, which reasserted its claim to suzerainty over Milan, and over Parma, Tuscany, and Mantua, as fiefs of the holy Roman empire. These claims alarmed the popes, who feared a revival of the medieval holy Roman empire's suzerainty in Italy.

In 1688 Louis XIV became involved in war against a coalition that included the maritime powers (England and the Dutch republic), Spain, and the Habsburg emperor Leopold I. Victor Amadeus II, duke of Savoy, joined them in order to escape French tutelage. The strategic position of his domains, commanding the Alpine passes, made him valuable to his allies. Thanks to the troops and subsidies they furnished, he withstood a French invasion, despite serious defeats in 1690 and 1693. In 1695 he and his allies expelled the French garrison from Casale, which was handed back to the duke of Mantua. Next year he abandoned his allies and came to terms with Louis XIV, in return for the cession of Pinerolo. He had liberated his state from direct French pressure, but at the cost of alienating his allies.

The war produced significant changes in the Italian state system. Piedmont was developing into an effective military-bureaucratic state. Leveraging the subsidies from his allies and tapping the resources of his domains through an efficient administrative machine, Victor Amadeus II built up his army, forging the instrument for expansion. His aim to push his frontier eastwards into Lombardy, however, meant conflict with Leopold I, who was staking out his own claims there, ready for the moment when Spain's Italian possessions would fall vacant on the death of the last Habsburg king of Spain, Charles II, his cousin.

Charles died on 1 November 1700, bequeathing his empire to Louis XIV's grandson, who ascended the Spanish throne as Philip V, founder of a new Bourbon dynasty. The Spanish governors in Italy declared allegiance to their new sovereign, and French troops reinforced them. Victor Amadeus II was bound—reluctantly—to the Bourbon cause by the marriage of his daughter to Philip V. The only other Italian prince to align with the Bourbons was the duke of Mantua. The rest temporized, for Leopold I had not accepted the transfer of the Spanish empire to the Bourbons. In April 1701 an Austrian Habsburg army invaded Lombardy, bent on conquering Milan for the archduke Charles, Leopold's second son. The war of the Spanish Succession had begun.

Unable to conquer Milan unaided, in 1703 Leopold I detached Victor Amadeus II from the Bourbon alliance with an offer of territory in Lombardy. The change of sides cost him dear. French armies overran Piedmont, and in 1706 besieged Turin. An Austrian relief army marched across Lombardy to join forces with the beleaguered duke and rout the French on 7 September. Bourbon resistance collapsed. In March 1707 the Austrians took Milan and Mantua, dispossessing its duke for siding with the Bourbons, while Piedmontese forces occupied Monferrato. In July an Austrian army occupied Naples without a struggle. The Austrian Habsburgs had replaced their Spanish cousins as the dominant power in the Italian peninsula. The treaty of Utrecht, which ended the war in 1713, ratified the Austrian conquests of Milan, Mantua, and Naples, and granted them Sardinia, conquered earlier by a British fleet. The treaty also confirmed the gains made by Victor Amadeus II. Besides Monferrato and parts of western Lombardy he received—through the intercession of the British negotiators—Sicily and the title of king that it conferred. Long-cherished Savoyard ambitions for a royal crown had been gratified, elevating the dynasty above the other Italian princely houses.

Great Power rivalries, 1713–48

The peace of Utrecht did not produce lasting stability in Italy. It could not efface the jealousy between the erstwhile allies, Piedmont-Savoy and Austria. The emperor wished to reunite Sicily with Naples; Victor Amadeus II coveted Habsburg Lombardy. Nor did it accommodate the resurgent power of Spain. Philip V had refused to make peace with the emperor, keeping open the option of recovering Spain's former Italian possessions. France, although it had lost its footholds in Italy, remained a powerful influence there, and Great Britain sought through diplomacy and naval power to maintain a balance of power in the peninsula.

Spanish ambitions posed the most direct threat to the Utrecht settlement. After the death of his first wife, Philip V in 1714 married Elizabeth Farnese, bearer of a hereditary claim to Parma and Tuscany. The two sons she bore him, Don Carlos and Don Felipe, could not inherit the Spanish throne, which would pass to Philip V's heir by his first wife, but they could lay claim to these states, whose rulers had no direct heirs. Philip V pressed these claims as part of his strategy for restoring Spanish ascendancy in Italy. In 1717 a Spanish fleet seized Sardinia, and in the following year another captured Sicily from Victor Amadeus II. Britain and France intervened, forcing Philip V in 1720 to disgorge his conquests. To pacify the emperor, and so make the settlement more durable, they obliged Victor Amadeus II to exchange Sicily for Sardinia. The kingdom of the Two Sicilies was now reunited under Austrian Habsburg sovereignty, and the house of Savoy would henceforth draw its royal title from Sardinia. But the successions to Parma and Tuscany remained to be settled. In January 1731 Duke Antonio Farnese died, and under Anglo-French pressure the emperor allowed Don Carlos to take possession of Parma. Meanwhile the aged and childless Gian Gastone de' Medici recognized him as heir to Tuscany. A peaceful settlement seemed within reach.

But events at the opposite end of Europe now precipitated war in Italy. France and Austria had backed rival candidates to the Polish throne following the death of Augustus II in February 1733. When the French candidate lost, his sponsor sought compensation by attacking the Austrian territories in Italy. In September 1733 France allied with Charles Emanuel III, the new ruler of Piedmont-Savoy and Sardinia. His reward was to be the duchy of Milan. But at the same time France allied with Spain, promising the kingdom of the Two Sicilies to Don Carlos, and allotting Parma and Mantua to the Bourbons. Charles Emanuel had his own designs on these territories, and did not relish the prospect of a strong Bourbon presence in Italy. His disquiet increased when in 1734 Don Carlos conquered Naples. In October 1735 preliminary peace terms were agreed, and the death of Gian Gastone de' Medici in 1737 led to a final agreement in March 1738. It recognized Don Carlos as King Charles of the Two Sicilies, and restored Austrian Habsburg rule in Lombardy, shorn of its western provinces of Tortona and Novara, which were ceded to Charles Emanuel III. Tuscany was assigned to Austria's ally, Duke Francis Stephen of Lorraine, whose former domains were annexed by France. He had recently married Maria Theresa, heiress to the Habsburg empire, bringing Tuscany under indirect Austrian rule.

Italy was now divided between a Habsburg bloc in the north and a Bourbon bloc in the south. Charles Emanuel III still sought territorial gains in Lombardy, and the outbreak of the war of the Austrian succession gave him that chance. In 1741 a Bourbon alliance attacked Maria Theresa's Italian territories, to win a throne for Philip V's younger son, Don Felipe. Both sides sought Charles Emanuel's aid; early in 1742, he allied with Maria Theresa in return for a promise of territory in Lombardy. In 1745 Don Felipe took Milan, but next year the Austro-Sardinian allies pushed his forces out of Lombardy and into Genoese territory. They then occupied Genoa, sparking a violent revolt by the citizens. In November 1748 peace was signed at Aix-la-Chapelle. Don Felipe obtained Parma, inaugurating a new Bourbon dynasty as Duke Philip, and Charles Emanuel III received more territory in western Lombardy. The treaty ushered in a half-century of peace by establishing Italy as a separate state system, insulated from the rivalries of the great powers. The Italian branches of the Habsburg and Bourbon dynasties were severed from their parent houses. Milan remained a province of the Habsburg empire, but Tuscany was constituted as a separate sovereignty under Maria Teresa's second son, Peter Leopold. Likewise sovereignty over the Two Sicilies and Parma was vested in the junior branches of the Bourbon dynasty.

The diplomatic calm was, however, disturbed by the continuing insurrection of Corsica against Genoese rule. In the 1760s a brilliant leader, Pasquale Paoli, united the rebels and almost expelled the Genoese. His achievements excited admiration all over Europe. But in 1768 the Genoese oligarchy cut its losses and sold the island to France. A French army drove Paoli into exile and annexed the island. (Napoleon Bonaparte, born in August 1769, was therefore a French subject.) The loss of Corsica, coming on the heels of the citizen revolt in 1746, revealed the corruption and incompetence of the Genoese oligarchy. The ruling patricians were incapable of undertaking the reforms needed to revitalize their ossified regime. Like the oligarchy ruling their sister-republic, Venice, they were untouched by the currents of reform that were now transforming many of the other Italian states.

Enlightenment and reform

Reform was not a single, uniform process: its pace and intensity varied from state to state. Some states, like the city-republics or the Papal States, were unaffected; others, like Piedmont, Tuscany, or Austrian Lombardy, underwent radical transformation. Reform everywhere was initiated from above; Enlightenment sovereigns perpetuated the paternalism of the previous century's absolutist princes. But with a crucial difference: their intent was now secular, for Enlightenment political theory instructed them to assure their subjects' wellbeing in this world rather than their salvation in the next. Privilege was now regarded as contrary to the general welfare; clerical privilege in particular became a target of the reformers, who restricted transfers of property to the Church (*manomorta*), and whittled away the tax exemptions on clerical lands. Some went further, insisting that monastic institutions serve the public through educational or charitable work, and dissolving them if they did not. The Jesuits attracted the reformers' special hostility for their wealth and influence. They were expelled from one state after another, and in 1773—under pressure from Catholic rulers inside and outside Italy— they were dissolved by papal decree.

Piedmont was the first Italian state to undergo structural reform. Building on a century of prior development, Victor Amadeus II completed the work of integrating the nobility into state service. To centralize the administration, an intendant was put in charge of each province, and in 1717 the executive bureaus of the government were reorganized. The laws were recodified in 1723, in 1729, and again in 1770. Land tax registers were revised, eliminating many exemptions claimed by the clergy and the nobility, and increasing the state's revenue, most of which went to expand the army. A concordat in 1727 (renegotiated in 1742) restricted the clergy's fiscal immunities and the jurisdiction of church courts. Education and poor relief were taken over by the government. Reform continued under Victor Amadeus' successor, Charles Emanuel III, and his minister, Bogino. They initiated the abolition of serfdom in the duchy of Savoy; in Sardinia they repressed banditry and promoted agrarian reform. But their policies—particularly their efforts to break up the Sardinian common lands—provoked resistance.[9]

The Savoyard model of reform, however, was highly specialized. Its purpose was to increase the state's military strength, a goal which most Italian governments—with the exception of the new Bourbon kingdom of the Two Sicilies—had renounced. In the realm of economics it looked back to mercantilism rather than forward to the Physiocrats. By the middle of the century more modern visions of reform were overtaking it, exemplified by the work of the Habsburg ministers in Lombardy and Grand Duke Peter Leopold in Tuscany. Benefiting from the peace after 1748, they sought to promote economic rather than military efficiency. In the kingdom of the Two Sicilies, by contrast, attempts at reform produced only limited results, despite the backing of the most important school of political economists in eighteenth-century Italy, the Neapolitan disciples of Antonio Genovesi. They urged the government to dismantle the feudal order, but baronial power obstructed the reforms of King Charles and his minister Tanucci. Under Charles's son Ferdinand IV, reform languished. The failure to break the power of the feudal order would be a central cause of the Neapolitan revolution of 1799.

After 1748 the empress Maria Teresa launched a determined effort to modernize the administration of her heterogeneous domains and increase their revenues.[10] A new land tax register (*catasto*), designed to stimulate agricultural production for the state of Milan, was completed in 1757. The reform of local and central government was carried through in the teeth of opposition from the Milanese patricians, who lost their commanding position in the state's administration. A new *Supremo Consiglio di Economia*, set up in 1765, fostered economic development according to Physiocratic principles by lowering tolls on agricultural produce and abolishing the guilds, viewed as monopolistic bodies. The Viennese authorities took advantage of the dissolution of the Jesuits to set up public schools and reorganize the university of Pavia, in order to train loyal officials, and educate clerics according to the *Reformkatholizismus* espoused by the government. As at Naples, but with far greater effect, local intellectuals, led by

---

[9] G. Ricuperati, *Le avventure di uno stato 'ben amministrato'* (Turin, 1994), 57–134.
[10] C. Capra, *La Lombardia austriaca nell'età delle riforme, 1706–1796* (Turin, 1987).

Pietro Verri and Cesare Beccaria, participated in the reforms. But the initiative came from above, and with the accession of emperor Joseph II in 1780 Vienna assumed closer control over policy by consigning the Milanese intelligentsia to a more subordinate role.

Grand Duke Peter Leopold of Tuscany provides perhaps the best example of a reforming sovereign in eighteenth-century Italy.[11] Faced by a catastrophic famine when he assumed power in 1765, he and his ministers concentrated on agrarian reform. They freed the trade in grain and abolished the traditional provisioning system (*annona*) that favoured the towns. They divided the common lands and sold off the grand-ducal estates, to raise production by creating a class of independent smallholders in place of the poor tenant farmers. But these lands were bought by the better-off landowners rather than the peasants, while the free trade in grain favoured big proprietors with a surplus to sell. Their influence was enhanced by the new constitution promulgated in 1779—the first and only one in Italy—which created local assemblies of landed proprietors but did not enfranchise the mass of the population. As in Habsburg Lombardy, the government undertook ecclesiastical reform, reducing the number of feast-days (to increase the number of working days), dissolving monasteries, and promoting an austere, Jansenist piety. These changes were highly unpopular. When further religious reforms were introduced at the synod of Pistoia in 1786, they were greeted with riots.

The vicissitudes of reform in Tuscany and Lombardy illustrate the limits of even the most advanced programmes of Enlightenment reform in Old Regime Italy. Economic policies designed to promote the general welfare in fact benefited the propertied classes, and exacerbated social tensions. Despite the reformers' best efforts, poverty was on the rise. Religious reforms provoked a backlash among the lower orders. The professional and intellectual elites felt increasingly estranged from a process of reform dictated from above, even by benevolent rulers like Peter Leopold or Joseph II. Losing faith in the customary avenues for change, they began to seek new outlets for their aspirations in masonic lodges, provincial academies, and political clubs. Some even began to contemplate the possibility of change by other means: not through the existing state machinery, but in opposition to it. The outbreak of revolution in France in 1789 seemed

[11] Litchfield, *Birth of a Bureaucracy*, ch. 14.

to offer them their chance. As the contagion of revolutionary ideas spread to Italy every government, princely or republican, strove to repress it. But the embattled little groups of intellectuals and radicals scattered throughout the peninsula, who were starting to call themselves patriots or Jacobins, welcomed the French revolution as the harbinger of change. In 1796 the defeat of the old states at the hands of Napoleon's armies seemed—for a moment—to offer them the chance they awaited, to recast Italian politics in a new mould, based on some form of popular sovereignty, and on a dawning idea—as yet inchoate—of national unity. Their hopes, however, were quickly dashed. Napoleon and the French government, on whose support the Italian patriots totally depended, had a very different vision of the new Italy waiting to arise from the ashes of the old order.

PART III

IDEOLOGIES AND PRACTICES: COMPETING LANGUAGES, CONVERGING VISIONS

7

Religion, spirituality, and the post-Tridentine Church

Anne Jacobson Schutte

Conceptual frameworks

At first sight, 1580 may seem a year of no particular significance in Italian religious history: no pope died, no ecumenical council met, no major doctrinal or disciplinary directive was promulgated, no important bureaucratic organ was established, no new religious order was founded, no famous heretic was executed, no saint was elevated to the honour of the altars. In recent historical writing, such conventional chronological markers matter less than they once did. Rather than looking for critical moments associated with persons or institutions, scholars now focus on processes. From this perspective, 1580 or thereabouts appears to mark the beginning of a distinctive phase in early modern Italian Catholicism.

Contrary to earlier assumptions, this phase did not feature a seamless continuation of initiatives begun in the fifteenth century (the 'Catholic Reformation') or of the belated offensive against Protestantism undertaken in 1542 (the 'Counter Reformation'). Nor can it be equated with 'the implementation of the decrees of the Council of Trent'. Instead, the period from c.1580 to c.1789 is best conceived as featuring a process of confessionalization and social discipline.

These twin paradigms, applied first to central Europe, have since been extended to other regions. They connote the coordinated efforts of ecclesiastical and secular authorities to make their inferiors understand and conform to directives from on high. Prelates and rulers aimed to form clerics and layfolk well-informed about the tenets of the faith adopted by their rulers, readily inclined to conduct correctly and take part regularly in all mandated religious observances, alert and willing to denounce deviations from orthodoxy. Soon, confessionalizers and social discipliners hoped, the people would become obedient subjects of their religious and secular superiors by accepting and internalizing mandates on matters ranging from settlement of disputes to behaviour consonant with one's social station.

Just as the rulers of Russia after 1917 endeavoured to create a 'new Soviet man', ecclesiastical and secular rulers in early modern Europe sought to fashion ideal types of male and female subordinates. With means of persuasion and coercion much less effective than those available to twentieth-century totalitarian dictators, they were unable fully to achieve their goals. The first part of each section that follows is devoted to their efforts and the medium-term outcomes they achieved.

Yet the paradigms of confessionalization and social discipline have certain drawbacks. They look too far forward toward nineteenth- and twentieth-century phenomena: the Church of the nineteenth and twentieth centuries, headed by a pope officially proclaimed infallible in 1870; the modern fully bureaucratic and omnicompetent national state. They present the temptation to draw unsophisticated global inferences about 'success' or 'failure'. They entail, furthermore, the dubious assumption that cultural change moves in only one direction: from top to bottom. Privileging initiatives imposed from above, scholars operating in terms of confessionalization and social discipline tend to depict ordinary people (both layfolk and low-level clerics) as an undifferentiated mass, potentially capable of following orders but more likely to exhibit stubborn, 'backward' resistance to them. In order to overcome these drawbacks, the second part of each section will concentrate on the objects of the authorities' attention. Not only, as we shall see, were they able to employ 'the weapons of the weak' against their superiors; in fact, they could and did exercise agency, thereby playing a role in the development of early modern Catholic spirituality and religious practice.

The Roman Inquisition and the Index of Prohibited Books: repression and resistance

In his bull *Licet ab initio* (1542), Paul III 'professionalized, monasti-cized and centralized'[1] the Inquisition, assigning it the clear mandate of combating Protestantism. To operate in any Italian polity, the Holy Office needed the ruler's explicit consent, easily obtained everywhere but Lucca (Sicily and Sardinia fell under the jurisdiction of the Spanish Inquisition), and enthusiastic cooperation, almost always forthcoming except in instances of jurisdictional disputes. By 1580, thanks in part to the Inquisition, the Protestant threat had receded from the peninsula. Almost all Italians attracted to northern religious ideas had died, sought refuge beyond the Alps, or made an 'internal immigration' into Nicodemism (the idea that since God knows what is in one's heart, making a show of conforming to the sole officially mandated confession by attending Mass does not jeopardize one's salvation). Small pockets of Protestants remained in the towns and villages of the north-east, but they operated perforce in such a clandestine fashion that the opportunity to enlist new recruits, even among their own children, withered away. In the early 1560s Italian Waldensians, 'heretics' with a twelfth-century pedigree aligned since the early 1530s with the Swiss Reformed, had been forcibly rooted out of Calabria; they managed to hang on only in three remote valleys of western Piedmont.

Consequently the Holy Office had to redefine its mission. During the 1580s the case-load of Roman Inquisition tribunals throughout the Italian peninsula was transformed. With almost no more native and very few foreign Protestants to prosecute, inquisitors began to target other sorts of religious 'deviants'. Most numerous among these were alleged practitioners of 'superstitious' sorcery or learned magic. (Sceptical about the classic model of diabolical witchcraft, inquisitors did not seek out and hence rarely encountered full-fledged 'witches'.) Following Gregory XV's constitution *Universi dominici gregis* (1622), priests denounced for soliciting sexual favours while administering

---

[1] R. Canosa, *Storia dell'Inquisizione in Italia dalla metà del Cinquecento alla fine del Settecento* (5 vols., Rome, 1986–90), v: 257–8.

the sacrament of confession came to constitute another major group of defendants. In the sixteenth century the Holy Office tried a small number of converts from Judaism suspected of having returned to their original faith and some practising Jews accused of committing a variety of other offences. Thereafter, prosecutions against Judaizers and Jews rapidly declined.

Recent scholarship has demolished the 'black legend' of a Holy Office relying heavily on torture to elicit confessions and frequently handing down death penalties to be carried out by the secular author-ities. On the contrary, the Roman Inquisition administered the best criminal justice available in early modern Europe. Procedures were clearly outlined in manuals, and their implementation by inquisitors in the field was closely monitored by the Congregation of the Holy Office in Rome. Those accused who chose to mount a defence had the right to counsel. Inquisitors frequently mentioned the possibility of torture in order to cow defendants, but they seldom employed it. Only a handful of recidivists and unrepentant individuals convicted of major crimes against the faith were put to death.

An accurate understanding of the Roman Inquisition's operations, however, must not entail the fabrication of a 'rose-coloured legend'.[2] Unquestionably, the Holy Office in Italy fostered a climate of conformity and disinclination to take intellectual risks. With Pius V's bull *In coena Domini* (1568), inquisitorial repression moved toward 'its culminating point and also its definitive victory':[3] the seal of the confessional (secrecy covering transactions between confessor and penitent) was seriously compromised, and the role of pastor was subordinated to that of judge. Confessors whose penitents admitted their own or divulged others' complicity in heretical beliefs and actions could no longer grant absolution from such sins; only in-quisitors had the power to do so. The line separating what priests heard in confession from what they learned in non-sacramental settings virtually disappeared. Layfolk soon realized that their pastors were fulfilling a double function: offering reassuring spiritual counsel and teaching of orthodox doctrine on the one hand, denouncing possible heresy on the other. That Inquisition records are filled

[2] A. Del Col, 'Strumenti di ricerca per le fonti inquisitoriali in Italia nell'età moderna', *Società e storia* 75 (1997), 147.

[3] E. Brambilla, *Alle origini del Sant'Uffizio. Penitenza, confessione e giustizia spirituale dal medioevo al XVI secolo* (Bologna, 2000), 550.

with so-called 'spontaneous appearances' to denounce oneself or report on others' presumed deviance is not surprising. Concealing unorthodox thoughts and actions had become almost impossible.

Close collaboration between the Holy Office and its sister Congregation of the Index served further to discourage religious nonconformity. Successive indexes of prohibited books issued throughout the period blacklisted a wide variety of titles in all languages. These included works by Protestants on theology and church history, pre-Reformation treatises advocating the primacy of councils over popes, guides for achieving unmediated contact and union with the divine through mental prayer (a position called Quietism and declared heretical in the late seventeenth century), the writings of such anticlerical and 'libertine' writers as Niccolò Machiavelli and Baldassare Castiglione (and eventually philosophes of all nationalities) and much more. A second technique, expurgation, was designed to purify some works deemed too important to suppress entirely. Implementing it soon proved too large a task for the Congregation of the Index's staff, which compiled lists of books containing words and passages deemed unorthodox, morally offensive, or politically subversive. Inquisitors were charged with using pens or blades to excise proscribed material from all the copies of offending books they could assemble. Expurgated editions of classics and newly published works, shorn of objectionable references, appeared.

Perhaps the most striking target of censorship was holy scripture. In 1596 all Italian editions of the entire Bible and its parts, as well as works containing selections from it, were placed on the Index. In the first decade of the seventeenth century, speaking to the Venetian ambassador, Paul V angrily reiterated what seemed to him the self-evident rationale for this prohibition: 'Don't you understand how so much reading of Scripture ruins the Catholic religion?'[4] Thus most Italians lost direct access to the foundational text of the Christian religion. The ban remained in place until 1769, when the first instalment of an authorized translation was issued.

Without question, inquisitorial prosecutions and the prohibition and expurgation of books significantly diminished opportunities for independent thinking within and beyond the sphere of religion. Not

---

[4] G. Fragnito, *La Bibbia al rogo. La censura ecclesiastica e i volgarizzamenti della Scrittura (1471–1606)* (Bologna, 1997), 330.

all Italians, however, resigned themselves to 'thinking with the Church'. Those in the know managed to obtain prohibited books smuggled in from the North, often disguised under innocuous titles with false publication information. Trial records reveal that some suspects challenged inquisitors' framing of their alleged crimes and resisted attempts to browbeat them into submission and silence. Like many another accused sorceress, Marietta Grimani, denounced to the Venetian Inquisition in 1666, employed ingenious legal tactics to rebut charges against her and readily described her curative techniques: herbal remedies enhanced by religious formulae. Typically, she received a very light sentence, soon revised downward.

Several lengthy trials for pretence of holiness reveal the defendants' certainty that they were in a special relationship with God, a belief they were reluctant to abandon. All were convicted, but they went down fighting; some eventually managed to gain release from confinement. Giuseppe Riccardi, a Conventual Franciscan friar from Sicily prosecuted in Venice in 1651, vigorously rebutted or tried to explain away all charges against him. To validate the orthodoxy of 'extravagant' statements he had made from the pulpit, he cited a wide variety of theological tomes. In asking permission to make an autobiographical deposition, which she hoped would exculpate her, Cecilia Ferrazzi, a laywoman who went on trial in the same tribunal in 1664, confidently addressed the members of the court as 'dear sirs'.[5] Interrogated over many months, she persisted in maintaining her innocence. With support from powerful protectors, some of whom testified in her defence, she appealed to Rome against the verdict of guilty and was eventually set free. The priest Andrea Scolari, prosecuted in 1750, adduced evidence to show that he had been framed by a mentally unstable former penitent and her Dominican accomplices. Far from being a Quietist as charged, he insisted, he had done his utmost to expose the theological errors contained in the most notorious manifesto of that antinomian movement, Miguel de Molinos' *Guida spirituale*. Somehow Scolari obtained rehabilitation: by 1757, he was in the employ of the episcopal curia of Brescia.

---

[5] C. Ferrazzi, *Autobiography of an Aspiring Saint*, ed. and trans. A. J. Schutte (Chicago, 1996), 37.

The shape of sanctity: contours of holiness

As in the past, the Church in early modern Italy endeavoured to identify and promote saints (deceased individuals who exemplified its standards of holiness). It also devoted increased attention to unmasking living persons whose claims to holiness appeared to stem from delusion, presumption, or fraud. Promoting saints was hardly a new venture, but in the early seventeenth century it assumed a novel form. In 1588, after a sixty-year hiatus in canonizations, Sixtus V put the new Congregation of Rites in charge of saint-making. The canonization of Charles Borromeo in 1610 signalled that new criteria for holiness were coming into place; the elevation in 1622 of Teresa of Avila, Ignatius Loyola, Philip Neri, and Francis Xavier confirmed it. No longer were visions and such feats as living on no food other than the Eucharist deemed sufficient for the awarding of posthumous honours. The Congregation of Rites demanded evidence of 'heroic virtues': 'the glory of grace', enabling undertakings surpassing normal human capabilities; 'heroic endurance' in withstanding pain; 'heroic resistance' against opponents ranging from obtuse spiritual advisers to enemies of the faith, which sometimes culminated in martyrdom.[6]

Saint-makers in Rome worked with materials generated on the periphery: the records of investigations conducted by bishops. In a series of decrees promulgated between 1625 and 1634, Urban VIII gave assurances that the centre would remain fully in control of the process. For holy people who survived initial scrutiny by the Congregation of Rites, he introduced the category of 'blessed'. In the interest of rendering cases historically solid, he ordered that investigators rigorously verify the heroic exploits of prospective saints, making certain that these were neither perpetrated by the protagonists nor inflated by their promoters. To prevent informal saint-making, he prohibited the initiation of local cults without explicit papal authorization. To circumvent the danger that political and personal pressure and temporary waves of enthusiasm for certain charismatic figures might

---

[6] Romeo de Maio, 'L'ideale eroico nei processi di canonizzazione della Controriforma', in his *Riforme e miti nella Chiesa del Cinquecento* (Naples, 1973), 257–8.

result in imprudent promotions to sainthood, he ruled that half a century must pass before they were canonized. After Urban VIII's successors had refined the new system, it was fully articulated in *De Servorum Dei beatificatione et beatorum canonizatione* (1734) by Prospero Lambertini, the future Benedict XIV.

Peter Burke has identified five professional profiles of holy people promoted to sainthood in this period: founder of a religious order, missionary, charitable activist, pastor, and mystic/ecstatic. Considering the requirements necessary to play these roles enables us to see how crucial social status and gender were to individuals' chances of being recognized as holy, not only after their deaths but also during their lives. To become a pastor or missionary, it was necessary to be a male from a family with the means to finance schooling, or to attract a patron who would furnish that opportunity. Charitable activism, open to both women and men, required independent means and/or help from well-heeled supporters, the latter difficult though not impossible to obtain if one came from humble origins. Only those already priests or religious stood any chance of establishing and gaining papal approval of a new order. Thus the prerequisites just outlined applied to male founders; for women to become nuns and then foundresses, the socio-economic threshold was even higher.

Two examples will show how members of elites achieved recognition for holiness, one in the role of pastor and the other as a mystic/ecstatic. Gregorio Barbarigo (1625–97) was one of several exemplary bishops in the late seventeenth century; all that distinguishes him from his contemporaries Innico Caracciolo, Antonio Pignatelli and Giacomo Cantelmo Stuart of Naples and Stefano Durazzo of Genoa is his eventual promotion to the rank of saint. The son of Venetian patricians, he was raised for a brilliant career. After studying civil law at the University of Padua, he embarked on his political apprenticeship: accompanying the Venetian ambassador to Münster to observe the negotiations concluding the Thirty Years War. Here he met the papal ambassador, Fabio Chigi, whose gift of Francis de Sales's *Introduction to the Devout Life* prompted him to reconsider his plans for the future. After returning to Venice and taking up his first elected office, he decided that a secular career was not for him. He considered joining a monastic order but was persuaded by his parish priest to enter the secular clergy. In 1655, with a degree from Padua, he was ordained to the priesthood.

Not long thereafter, Barbarigo's mentor Chigi, now pope, summoned him to Rome. In short order he was rewarded for his high birth and promise with several appointments in the papal curia. When named bishop of Bergamo in 1657, he immediately took up residence in his backward and troubled diocese. There he soon earned a reputation as a model bishop—a second Charles Borromeo, as one biographer later put it—by undertaking a visitation aimed at identifying and correcting incompetent priests and combating several varieties of heresy.

In 1660 Alexander VII elevated Barbarigo, who was only 35, to the cardinalate. He reluctantly accepted a transfer to a more prestigious but less challenging diocese, Padua, where he spent his remaining years. Among his chief concerns were the improvement of the parish priesthood, which he accomplished by frequent visitations and close attention to the diocesan seminary, and the condition of poverty-stricken women. When he died, those who knew him were certain that his soul had flown straight to heaven. Official recognition of his saintliness was long in coming—in part because no posthumous miracles complemented his concrete accomplishments. In 1761 Clement XIII approved his beatification; John XXIII canonized him in 1960.

The career of the Capuchin nun Maria Maddalena Martinengo (1687–1737), member of a prominent noble clan in Brescia, was marked by leadership in her convent and visions, on which she wrote several treatises. Somewhat atypical of spiritually ambitious people in this era, she conducted audacious experiments with penance. Far from treating her as a wilful woman whose extravagant behaviour needed to be corrected, Martinengo's male superiors, the bishop of Brescia and a Jesuit confessor, indulged her every whim. No longer content with wearing the especially prickly hair shirts she and her confessor manufactured and sticking needles into various parts of her body, she decided to etch the Most Holy Name of Jesus on her shoulder. For this purpose, she wrote in her spiritual autobiography, 'a small quantity of sulphuric acid of the most perfect kind was consigned to me',[7] probably by one of her enablers. Fellow nuns who

---

[7] Anne Jacobson Schutte, '"Orride e strane penitenze". Esperimenti con la sofferenza nell'autobiografia spirituale di Maria Maddalena Martinengo', in proceedings of conference 'I monasteri femminili come centri di cultura fra Rinascimento e Barocco' (Bologna, Dec. 2000), forthcoming.

saw the gaping wound made in her leg when she spilled the acid kept her secret. Martinengo's extreme penitential initiatives evoked little attention and no criticism during or after her lifetime. Her mystical writings and her order's promotional efforts account for her beatification in 1900; since 1987, she has been under consideration for elevation to the rank of saint.

In theory, since God is no respecter of persons, the role of mystic/ecstatic should have been open to all. In fact it was not. Those who practised 'discernment of spirits', the art and science of evaluating religious inspirations, assumed that no one lacking the advanced spiritual training available only to priests and religious could be a fit candidate for inspirations, visions, and revelations of divine provenance. If a lay person of low status presumptuously claimed to have done so, the cause must be delusion, physical illness, or conscious fraud. (The possibility of diabolic possession was rarely considered.) Such was the case with the Friulian miller Domenico Scandella, nicknamed Menocchio, denounced to the Holy Office in 1583 by his parish priest. Witnesses confirmed that for many years the miller had publicly advocated a variety of heretical beliefs concerning the origin of the universe; the nature of God, Jesus, and Mary; the authenticity of the scriptures; and the sacraments, which he called 'merchandise', human inventions designed by churchmen to fleece the poor. He was also accused of owning and reading suspect books, including a vernacular translation of the Bible.

How did Menocchio acquire these beliefs? Inquisitors were certain that a mere miller could not have arrived at them on his own but must have learned them from one or more representatives of high culture. Menocchio denied having human mentors. When first interrogated, he claimed that 'it was the evil spirit who made me believe such things, and he also instigated me to say them to others'.[8] Then he assumed sole responsibility. 'Whatever ideas I had came out of my own head,' he asserted. 'My mind was lofty and wished for a new world and way of life, that the Church should act well and that there should not be so much pomp.'[9] He acknowledged inspiration from various books (none of them Protestant); ideas encountered in them

---

[8] A. Del Col, *Domenico Scandella known as Menocchio: His Trials before the Inquisition (1583–1599)*, trans. John and Anne C. Tedeschi (Binghamton, NY, 1996), 24 (interrogation of 7 Feb. 1584).

[9] Ibid. 34, 47 (interrogations of 22 Feb. and 7 May 1584).

he processed in an idiosyncratic way. Whether, as has been con-
jectured, an ancient stratum of peasant materialism or an under-
ground current of Catharism provided the interpretive framework
for his reading cannot be determined. Menocchio's beliefs, which
attracted no support from his peers, evoked a mixture of shock and
disdain among his inquisitors. When, after a first conviction in 1586,
the stubborn miller resumed voicing his beliefs, he was brought to
trial again, sentenced to death, and executed in 1599.

More than a century later, in 1728, the absentee bishop of Brescia
ordered his vicar-general to investigate a young peasant woman,
Lucrezia Gambara of Alfianello. She was reporting visions both
divine and diabolical and appeared to have the wounds of Christ's
passion imprinted on her body. The Benedictine monk who examined her repeatedly during a four-month period concluded that she
was not bewitched but suffering from illness: her visions, he wrote
in language reminiscent of Locke, resulted from 'the effect of the
sensible impressions made on the fantasy'. This 'weak subject' had
deluded herself into believing that she was receiving divine inspirations, and had participated to some extent in publicizing her
allegedly prodigious experiences. Gambara required not a trial by the
Inquisition and a sentence, but a cure. To 'put her on a safer road to
health and liberate her from so many illusions', the monk and the
vicar general encouraged her to marry. Busy with house work, labour
in the field, and child care, they believed, she would have no time to
indulge in spiritual fantasies so inappropriate to her station.[10]

Pastors and sheep

As Charles Borromeo's and Gregorio Barbarigo's posthumous fortunes indicate, bishops' governance of their dioceses was a high-
profile, high-priority matter in the post-Tridentine era. Responding
to long-reiterated complaints, the Council of Trent had insisted
that ordinaries reside in their sees. Willingly or not, an increasing
number did so, or at least supervised tightly the operations of their

[10] A. J. Schutte, *Aspiring Saints: Pretense of Holiness, Inquisition, and Gender in the
Republic of Venice, 1618–1750* (Baltimore, 2001), 148–53; quoted passages at 151, 152.

vicars-general. Episcopal visitations, sporadic before the Council, gradually became much more frequent. From these inspections bishops gained information they could use in trying to upgrade the performance of priests and improve the religious understanding and behaviour of the laity—that is, to enforce confessionalization and social discipline.

Priests, essential transmission belts in the religious delivery system, were primary candidates for improvement. Everywhere in their dioceses, especially in the hinterland beyond the cities in which they were located, bishops on visitations encountered priests who were appallingly ignorant. Most could hardly recite the Latin words of the Mass correctly, let alone preach in Italian. All too many comported themselves exactly like laymen: hunting, gambling, eating and drinking to excess, maintaining relationships with concubines, seeking to provide for their children, and condoning or even participating in sorcery. The very worst had to be removed from office, but replacements were hard to find. Following the lead of Charles Borromeo, bishops employed two short-term means of further education for the others. In occasional diocesan synods, they harangued their clergy and issued reforming regulations. They also instituted monthly regional meetings, at which priests were instructed on preaching and handling cases of conscience in the confessional.

The Council of Trent had strongly recommended a long-term solution for priestly inadequacy: the establishment of a seminary in every diocese. In these new institutions, candidates for the priesthood were to be trained thoroughly in Latin and all relevant branches of theology, socialized into distinctively clerical behaviour, and tested before they went to work. Setting up seminaries and maintaining them in existence required considerable financial resources and consistent close attention on the ordinaries' part. In very few of Italy's more than 300 dioceses, especially the smaller ones in the south, were these available. Many seminaries opened, struggled briefly to survive, and then ceased to operate. Even at the end of the eighteenth century, by no means all dioceses were providing seminary training for prospective priests.

Bishops and their collaborators accomplished much with city dwellers, who over time became thoroughly confessionalized and disciplined. Schools of Christian doctrine, a sixteenth-century innovation, continued to impart basic religious knowledge and literacy to poor children and adults. Long-established and newly founded confraternities (notably those dedicated to the Virgin Mary) helped to ensure that their members, mainly men of elite and middling status, assiduously frequented the sacraments and provided assistance to the less fortunate; the objects of their charitable attention ranged from indigent young women requiring dowries to convicts needing spiritual consolation before they were executed. In Naples, the only diocese in which frequency of resort to the sacrament of penance has been examined closely, more and more lay people far exceeded the minimum requirement of annual confession. An increasing number of city folk, especially elite women, attached themselves to spiritual advisers, whose counsel they meticulously followed; sometimes, in a reversal of roles, a devout woman took the lead in such a relationship. As much as and perhaps more than was the case before the Council of Trent, urban people marched in or viewed religious processions and flocked to sermons delivered by famous preachers during Advent and Lent.

In contrast, rural people remained difficult for pastors to reach. Although the quality of country priests probably improved slowly, religious ignorance and 'superstition' persisted among their flocks. All over the peninsula, these problems were particularly acute in remote mountainous areas. There, bishops could do little. On visitations they spoke mainly to priests, who almost invariably assured them that all was well, and to local notables holding administrative office in parishes. They had little direct exposure to and knowledge of peasants.

Members of newer religious orders committed to evangelization— Capuchins, Jesuits, and the Fathers of the Mission, founded in the 1620s by Vincent de Paul—attempted to fill the gap. Although most of them would have preferred the opportunity to convert heathens on foreign soil, many found themselves assigned to internal missions in what they called 'our Indies'. The people they encountered there— not only on the 'savage' islands of Corsica and Sardinia but also in such mainland regions as Monferrato and Sabina—struck them as barely human. Living in poverty among their animals, these peasants, served badly if at all by local priests, desperately needed instruction in the most elementary fundamentals of the faith: the Ten Commandments, the Lord's Prayer, the Creed. They needed to be informed, often for the first time, about requirements concerning marriage, confession and the Eucharist.

Since peasants were illiterate, edifying printed materials produced in profusion for urban lay people did them no good. Missionaries could employ only oral means, confession, and above all hellfire-and-brimstone sermons. In reports to their superiors, they painted glowing pictures of the effects these initially had: weeping recipients kissed the visiting priests' hands and vowed to amend their lives. A missionary campaign, however, lasted only a few days or weeks. Soon after the fathers' departure, its effect naturally wore off, and these rural sheep reverted to their previous spiritual condition. Not until the nineteenth century would some rural areas of Italy be fully Catholicized.

In work with the laity, religious not only complemented the efforts of the secular clergy but also tended in certain ways to supplant them. Aggrandizement by friars of priests' responsibilities was not new in the early modern period. For two reasons, many lay people had long preferred friars to their designated confessors, parish priests: religious had better training than the secular clergy in administering the sacrament of penance; and knowing less about those who confessed to them, they were not so likely to become closely involved in penitents' lives. The growing popularity of spiritual advisers in this period undoubtedly enhanced the regular clergy's influence. Friars and clerks regular, furthermore, owed allegiance not to bishops but to the heads of their congregations. That Dominican and Franciscan inquisitors, who closely monitored many aspects of lay people's religious comportment, reported directly to the Congregation of the Holy Office (presided over by the Roman pontiff) placed yet another limitation on the secular clergy. Hence the post-Tridentine emphasis on the parish as the centre of spiritual life, the incumbent priest as its manager, and the bishop as his overseer was less pronounced than some recent historians have claimed.

Over one group, female religious, bishops gained more power in this era. As well as insisting on their strict enclosure, the Council of Trent placed nuns, most of whom had previously been subject to the male branches of their orders, directly under the control of the ordinaries. Bishops now visited convents and issued orders about such minute details of active and passive cloister (keeping nuns within convent walls and others out) as the size of apertures in the grate of the parlour. They required that relatives and friends, both lay and clerical, obtain written permission to visit. Evidently, however, they did not observe carefully the Council's instructions to question young women closely to make sure that they were entering religion of their own free will. At least until the end of the eighteenth century, monachization 'by force and fear'—prompted by elite and middling families' desire to preserve patrimonies—ruined the lives of many women and an even larger number of men.

'The kittens have opened their eyes':[11] conformity, protest, and reform

In the last century of this period, most urban lay Italians appear to have been believing, practising Catholics who obediently followed directions from their ecclesiastical superiors. They expressed their piety by praying, confessing, attending Mass, hearing sermons, invoking assistance from the saints to whom they were particularly devoted through prayer and revering their relics, taking advantage of opportunities to gain extraordinary remission of sins offered by the Church in 'pardons' and jubilees, aiding the less fortunate through confraternal activities, and (if literate) buying and reading spiritual books. By choice or through compulsion, many—though perhaps fewer than in the late sixteenth and seventeenth centuries— embarked on what seemed a surer path to salvation by entering monasteries and convents. Men who entered the priesthood were likely to receive more thorough training for and supervision in this role than their predecessors two centuries earlier. To a considerable degree, then, confessionalizers and social discipliners had achieved their aims.

Without questioning its genuineness, one might characterize Italian religion of the eighteenth century as normalized, routinized, and conformist. As in the past, some religious experienced and recorded mystical transports. Alfonso Maria de' Liguori (1696–1787) exemplifies a more common pattern of late early modern Italian

---

[11] *Lettera d'un cavaliere amico fiorentino al reverendissimo padre Lorenzo Ricci, generale de gesuiti esortandolo ad una riforma universale del suo ordine* (Lugano [Venice], 1762), quoted by F. Venturi, *Settecento riformatore, ii: La chiesa e la repubblica dentro i loro limiti, 1758–1774* (Turin, 1976), 20, applies the Tuscan proverb to religion.

holiness. This Neapolitan priest, founder of the Redemptorist order, wrote numerous learned tomes and vernacular manuals of moral and dogmatic theology. In his anti-Jansenist *Dogmatic Work against the Heretics Claiming to be Reformed* (1769), which posits the universal accessibility of grace through prayer, he 'does not scrutinize the mystery [of grace] but affirms and draws from it only norms for practical conduct'.[12]

In the 1720s discordant voices began to be heard. Protest assumed a new form and new names: jurisdictionalism and regalism, referring to secular governments' right to redraw boundaries between Church and state to the latter's advantage. Drawing on arguments articulated in the sixteenth century by the Florentines Machiavelli and Francesco Guicciardini and in the early seventeenth by the Venetian Servite friar Paolo Sarpi, Pietro Giannone, a lawyer in Naples, argued in his *Civil History of the Kingdom of Naples* (1723) that over many centuries the Church had practically destroyed civil government and society in southern Italy. Rightly anticipating that his book would be put on the Index, he fled to Vienna, travelled widely in northern and central Italy, and then settled briefly in Geneva. In 1736 he was lured across the border to Chambéry, where Piedmontese police arrested him. Brought before the Torinese Inquisition in 1738, Giannone recanted the errors identified in his writings. For the last ten years of his life, he remained in prison.

Giannone's name and works, along with Sarpi's, inspired successive generations of enlightened critics. From the 1720s to the 1750s a flock of erudite historians and political philosophers, most notably Ludovico Antonio Muratori of Modena and Scipione Maffei of Verona, analysed the causes of Italy's 'decadence' and fought a battle against 'superstition' that influenced even an unusually open-minded pope, Benedict XIV (in office 1740–58). In the late 1750s, prompted by developments in Portugal, Spain, and France, reformers began to focus on more specific targets. First among these were the Jesuits, whose dominance of secondary education, unscrupulous economic activities, and attempt to conceal from penitents the duty to obey their secular rulers rather than the papal prince appeared increasingly subversive of political authority. In 1773, following the expulsion of

---

[12] G. Cacciatore, 'Alfonso Maria de Liguori, santo', in *Dizionario biografico degli italiani*, ii (Rome, 1960), 347.

Jesuits from several European and Italian states, Clement XIV issued a brief suppressing the order.

For enlightened critics, the Society of Jesus was only the tip of the iceberg. Simultaneously, they highlighted other closely related problems: the immense wealth of the Church, the excessive number of its personnel (especially monks and friars), the negative consequences of its predominant influence on education and culture, the crushing weight of its legal hegemony on all aspects of life (the economy, marriage, crime and punishment). Ecclesiastical control of print media did not succeed in stemming the tide of their analyses, couched in ever more open anticlerical and anti-curial terms, which flowed from presses located all over Italy and abroad. The *Corriere letterario* and *L'Europa letteraria* (edited in Venice by, respectively, Antonio Graziosi and Domenico and Elisabetta Caminer), the *Novelle letterari* (edited by Giovanni Lami in Florence), and *Il Caffè* (edited by Pietro Verri in Milan) stand out among many short-lived periodical publications. Notable books include Carlantonio Pilati's *Di una riforma d'Italia* (Chur, 1767), Cosimo Amidei's *La chiesa e la repubblica dentro i loro limiti* ([Florence] 1769), Tommaso Antonio Contin's *Reflessioni sopra la Bolla in Coena domini* (Venice, 1769) and Salvatore Spiriti's *Dialogo dei morti* ([Naples, n.d.]). Polemical responses from the other side, such as the Dominican Tommaso Maria Mamachi's *La pretesa filosofia de' moderni increduli* (Rome, 1767), exerted little influence outside circles sympathetic to the papal curia.

Far from being armchair utopians, jurisdictionalist and regalist writers collaborated with statesmen to bring about reform. In the 1760s, for instance, Antonio Genovesi collaborated with Bernardo Tanucci, chief minister of the kingdom of Naples, in the campaign against the Jesuits, the attack on ecclesiastical property, and the reform of the university. Not all the critical intellectuals were laymen. In the duchy of Parma, a group of enlightened jurists and ecclesiastics supported the reforming activities of prime minister Guillaume Du Tillot. Nor did they all operate from a base in the secular administration. In the late 1770s and early 1780s, Scipione de' Ricci, bishop of Pistoia and Prato, sought to turn his diocese into a 'national' church subject to the reformist secular ruler, Grand Duke Pietro Leopoldo.

Finally, enlightened governments in the last quarter of the eighteenth century curtailed the powers of the Roman Inquisition and then did away with it. Abolished in Milan in 1775, Modena in 1780, and Tuscany in 1782, it disappeared during the years of revolutionary tumult in the 1790s from Venice, Genoa, and Piedmont. But the Holy Office was not dead. Resuscitated in the early nineteenth century, it continues in operation to this day, since 1988 under a new name, Congregation for the Doctrine of the Faith. From a long-term point of view, therefore, the tumultuous changes in Italian religion at the end of the early modern period mark not the dawn of a new era but merely a caesura.

8

Mare magnum: the arts in the early modern age

Jon R. Snyder

Introduction

Italian art, architecture, literature, and music were never more influential abroad than during the years 1550–1796. The first truly international aesthetic, which is conventionally called the 'baroque', was born in Italy as Renaissance culture metamorphosed by the mid-sixteenth century. This new aesthetic—especially in art, architecture, and music—spread quickly across a large swath of the planet, from Rome to St Petersburg, from Madrid to Lima, from Manila to Mexico City, from Goa to Salvador (Bahia). The internationalization of Italian culture between the sixteenth and eighteenth centuries had its basis in the equivalence of the concepts of 'Italy' and 'universal values' in the eyes of the rest of Europe. Italian culture was adopted as the international standard of the age because its values—thanks to the prestigious achievements of antiquity and the Renaissance—were identified with those of culture itself.

I will not, however, employ the term 'baroque' here; it has been used too often to denigrate the culture of those years, especially its literature. I will instead use 'early modern' to denote the culture of Italy under absolutism, an era which runs at least from the Sack of

In memoriam H. Stuart Hughes

Rome in 1527 to the invasion of Italy by Napoleon's army in 1796. Within this vast time frame are found numerous cultural cross-currents linking the aesthetic products of the era to one another. Italy spawned the new international aesthetic, but eventually lost its cultural primacy in Europe as the national cultures of France, England, and Holland emerged, along with prosperous cosmopolitan capitals such as Vienna. However, the culture of the peninsula continued to be a primary point of reference for painters, poets, architects, and musicians everywhere in Europe. Many of their Italian counterparts worked outside Italy, thus creating an interpenetration of cultures and perspectives that was unparalleled in the history of the west.

These developments occurred while early modern Italy was a patchwork of absolutist states collectively known as the Old Regime. The elite culture of absolutism relied on spectacle to maintain and enhance its legitimacy and its hold on power over an evolving public sphere. Most artists in Italy depended on the patronage networks of church, nobility, and state far into the eighteenth century, although there were important exceptions (the painter-writer Salvator Rosa (1615–73), for example). This does not mean, however, that artists, composers, and writers worked only to further the interests of the powerful. Much of the fascination of early modern art, literature, and music lies in the double-edged nature of their aesthetic.

On the one hand, early modern Italy witnessed a proliferation of new techniques of representation that transgressed against earlier, more mimetic ways of seeing and listening. Anamorphosis, metalepsis, dissonance, and infinite regress, among many other devices, were used to shock, disorient, and ultimately overwhelm the senses of the spectator, reader, or listener.[1] For this new aesthetic, the only truth of the object was that it was irrevocably altered, rather than repeated, in the act of representation. Thus all representations—political, social, religious—with claims to permanence and foundational truth could now be potentially questioned by a critical gaze able to resist the shock force of the new art.

---

[1] Anamorphic pictures may be viewed only when reflected in a cylindrical or convex mirror, or from an extreme angle; otherwise they appear as formless, inchoate blotches of paint. Metalepsis is a rhetorical figure that takes metaphor to an extreme by substituting metonymically one term with another one that is already a metaphor. Infinite regress may be likened to the effect created by two mirrors facing one another, in which the object represented appears as an endless chain of identical but receding images.

On the other hand, this same aesthetic was a key component of what José Antonio Maravall calls the 'lyrical engineering of the human world' in the early modern era. The Tridentine reforms instituted a new proselytizing role for religious art, and ultimately the functions of secular art were affected as well. Artistic products were part of a highly sensitive communicative apparatus that sought to further social discipline through its special power of persuasion. The agenda of early modern artistic patronage was to control the growing ranks of individuals who felt increasingly autonomous, thanks to the circulation of books, letters, and other cultural goods, by reintegrating them into what was an essentially conservative social and political system of hereditary privilege.[2] A powerfully persuasive and seductive art that could overcome the resistance of the individual was needed to face this challenge. The search for new modes for the deployment of power through aesthetic innovation in early modern Italian culture explains in part the stunning intensity and variety of its artistic output. The resulting paradox—a transgressive aesthetic supporting a conservative social and political status quo—would endure until the end of the Old Regime.

Art and architecture

Painting and sculpture

The category of the visual was central to early modern culture. Experiments, often radical, with the representation of space and figure constitute the core of early modern visual aesthetics in Italy. These range from Pietro da Cortona's great *macchine* or ceiling paintings to the vogue for anamorphic paintings, from Caravaggio's chiaroscuro pictures to Giacomo Torelli's painted stage backdrops and sliding wings generating illusions of infinite regress, and from the stunning spatial transgressions of Borromini's buildings to sculptures that appear to move with every change in the spectator's position, thus creating an infinite search for meaning. The goal, set by the

---

[2] J. A. Maravall, *Culture of the Baroque: Analysis of a Historical Structure*, trans. T. Cochran (Minneapolis, 1986 [1975]), 263.

Tridentine reforms, was to generate a supreme aesthetic and spiritual experience that would 'exceed every expression of words'.[3] Exemplary was Bernini's (1598–1680) project for St Peter's Square, begun in 1656, with its curved colonnades as an icon of the universal Church's irresistible embrace of the world: '[the colonnades] reach out with open arms to embrace Catholics in order to reaffirm their belief, heretics to be reunited with the Church, and agnostics to be enlightened with the true faith'.[4] In both Italian cities and courts, patrons displayed their wealth, status, and faith through cultural investment, especially in art and architecture, throughout the Old Regime period. Recent research has gone beyond patronage studies, however, in placing new emphasis on the complex role played by both art markets and the broad sociocultural horizons (from production to reception) of artists and their communities in the making of the new art.

In an era of mixed-media and multimedia artist-entrepreneurs such as Bernini, it was increasingly difficult to separate the traditional triad of painting, sculpture, and architecture. There were of course sculptors like Bernini's precursor, the virtuoso Flemish-born Giambologna (1529–1608), a Medici favourite in Florence for nearly half a century, who was admired for extraordinarily complex three-dimensional figures that violated the rules of ancient and 'Renaissance' sculpture. Giambologna directed a workshop specializing in high-quality small bronzes that could be transported easily, thus favouring the rapid spread of the new aesthetic beyond the borders of Tuscany. Painting too remained prominent, especially in Venice and Rome, where wealthy patrons vied with one another in the decoration of new palaces and churches (a great many more churches were built in Italy after, rather than before, 1550, in accordance with the Tridentine programme). Influential academies concerned with painting, such as the Accademia di San Luca in Rome, appeared in the second half of the sixteenth century, lending further prominence to the field. The painter and architect Vasari (1511–74) published his *Lives* in 1550 (revised edition 1568). In this first critical history of

---

[3] C. F. Black, '"Exceeding Every Expression of Words": Bernini's Rome and the Religious Background', in A. Weston-Lewis (ed.), *Effigies and Ecstasies: Roman Baroque Sculpture and Design in the Age of Bernini*, exhibition catalogue (Edinburgh, 1998), 21.

[4] From Bernini's 1659 memorandum, cited in E. Sladek, 'The Colonnade of the Piazza San Pietro, 1659', in Weston-Lewis, *Effigies and Ecstasies*, 109.

Italian art, Vasari codified the tradition of Italian painting from its origins to the present. Painters from across Europe continued to pour into Italy to study its artistic treasures, and many Italian painters were recruited to work for foreign rulers.

The complex interdependency of painting and sculpture was, however, central to the work of Bernini, the quintessential artist of the seventeenth century. His genius as a sculptor was unrivalled; Bernini's astonishing technical prowess, and that of his assistants, allowed him to produce in a five-year period (1618–23) a series of masterpieces in marble, including *Apollo and Daphne* and *Pluto Abducting Proserpina*. Among the greatest works of western art, these sculptures drew on Bernini's knowledge of antiquity and Michelangelo. The young artist sought to challenge painting on its own ground by establishing a single privileged viewpoint for his sculpture (not necessarily the front of the work), thus enabling direct comparison—and competition— with painting and urging sculptors to manipulate space, colour, and motion even better than painters. Success was to be measured by the *meraviglia* (wonder) created by the work in the mind of the viewer, who could only believe that these lifelike works were actually meant to be seen from an infinite sequence of viewpoints. Bernini's sculpture used the illusion of perspective to create another illusion, that of continuously renewed three-dimensionality; his art was the illusion of an illusion, the defining trait of the new aesthetic.[5]

At the close of the sixteenth century, two artists came to Rome and began to paint in dramatically different ways, setting off a controversy that would echo throughout the seventeenth century. Caravaggio (1573–1610) started to represent biblical scenes with extreme naturalism and dramatic contrasts of light and shadow ('chiaroscuro') that suggested spiritual turmoil. Annibale Carracci (1560–1609) instead developed a serenely idealized style, drawing on the work of past masters such as Raphael, that was to become the hallmark of European 'academic' painting. Caravaggio's brooding work in the Contarelli chapel in S. Luigi dei Francesi in Rome (1599–1602) stood in pointed contrast to the classicized purity of Carracci's gallery in the Palazzo Farnese (1597–1600). The Cerasi chapel in S. Maria del

---

[5] I draw here on the essay by Anna Coliva, 'Apollo e Dafne', in A. Coliva and S. Schütze (eds.), *Bernini scultore. La nascita del barocco in casa Borghese*, exhibition catalogue (Rome, 1998), 270–4. For an opposing point of view, see J. Kenseth, 'Bernini's Borghese Sculptures: Another View', *Art Bulletin* (Mar. 1981), 191–211.

Popolo in Rome, on which both artists worked near the turn of the century, was a study in divergent practices of pictorial representation, each of which would attract followers, detractors, and synthesizers for generations in Europe. Carracci's followers were legion, including the 'divine' Guido Reni (1575–1642), Domenichino (1581–1641), Guercino (1591–1666), and Poussin (1594–1665), but his influence extended to many other artists, including Rubens (1577–1640). Rubens, who was in Italy from 1600 to 1608, subsequently transformed his experience of Italian art into a personal style that could be understood everywhere in Europe, making him the harbinger of the new international aesthetic.

Caravaggio, whose violent life and enigmatic work have seen a resurgence in interest over the past few decades, was the consummate anti-academician, attracting fewer followers. The most important of these were Orazio Gentileschi (1563–1639) and his daughter Artemisia (1593–1653). Artemisia, one of the most successful early modern female artists, has also been the focus of much scholarly debate and public interest in recent years. After being raped in Rome in 1611 and braving the trial that followed, she became an accomplished artist whose paintings of female figures were much sought after by collectors. The rediscovery of her long-neglected work has become emblematic of the project of contemporary feminist art historians to redefine the 'powerful feminist message' of women in western art and culture.[6]

The most prominent Italian painter of the seventeenth century, however, was Pietro da Cortona (1596–1669). Cortona developed a highly original technique of monumental ceiling painting that initiated a long tradition in European art. His large-scale works, or *macchine*, were carefully organized through the use of bright colours, complex, energetic crowds of figures, and multiple perspectives. These allegorical works were commissioned by powerful patrons, usually princes or popes, to glorify absolutism and the Catholic faith. Cortona's most famous work, the ceiling fresco cycle in the Palazzo Pitti in Florence, was begun in 1637, in the same period in which he was completing the renowned ceiling fresco *The Triumph of Divine Providence* for the Palazzo Barberini in Rome. Both of these created the illusion of an infinite depth of space and hence of the infinite power of those figures that were exalted in them. Well into the nineteenth century, Cortona's imitators were legion across Europe.

[6] M. D. Garrard, *Artemisia Gentileschi: The Image of the Female Hero in Italian Baroque Art* (Princeton, NJ, 1989), 8.

Although his most important follower on the peninsula was Luca Giordano (1634–1705), Cortona also left his mark on Venetian art, which produced the leading Italian painter of the eighteenth century, Giambattista Tiepolo (1696–1770).

Tiepolo executed frescos, decorative cycles and ceiling paintings with luminous chromatic schemes and virtuoso optical illusions that drew on Cortona's work, making figures seem to float in an ethereal space stretching far beyond the boundaries of the building that housed them. Acclaimed the 'universal painter' of the age by contemporaries, he was commissioned to decorate royal palaces in Würzburg and Madrid. Another Venetian painter of international stature, Canaletto (1697–1768), supplied the booming international art market with views of the city and the lagoon. Piranesi (1720–78), who ranks as a printmaker with Dürer and Rembrandt, also relied extensively on the international tourist trade to sell his views of Rome and its antiquities. The success of Canaletto and Piranesi in the international commerce of artworks signalled the impending end of the system of Old Regime patronage and the universal pre-eminence of Italian painting. Although the 'Rococo' movement—the so-called 'second wave'—was not important for eighteenth-century Italian art, it was left to foreign-born artists and theorists such as Adolph Mengs (1728–79) and Johann Winckelmann (1717–68) to introduce 'neoclassicism' into Italy, thus reversing the outflow of aesthetic innovations that had distinguished early modern Italian visual culture for so long.

Architecture

The major figure of late sixteenth-century Italian architecture was Palladio (1508–80). His great international stature remained unchallenged throughout the eighteenth century. The official architect of the Venetian republic, Palladio published his famous treatise, *Four Books of Architecture*, in 1570; two centuries later, Thomas Jefferson called it 'the Bible' of all architects.[7] Palladio's architecture was a 'reading' of antiquity in modern terms; his buildings did not

---

[7] R. Tavernor, 'Palladio's "Corpus": *I quattro libri dell'architettura*', in V. Hart and P. Hicks (eds.), *Paper Palaces: The Rise of the Renaissance Architectural Treatise* (New Haven, Conn., 1998), 233.

resemble ancient Roman structures, but displayed their formal proportions, spatial organization, and ornamentation. From the Basilica in Vicenza to country villas and the Venetian churches of the Redentore and S. Giorgio Maggiore, Palladio sought to express the classical lexicon, grammar, and syntax of ancient architecture with modern means. In the wake of Giulio Romano (1499–1546) and Sebastiano Serlio (c.1475–1554/5), Palladio insisted upon complex decorative schemes—statuary, frescos, etc.—for his buildings, thus creating an interpenetration of functional and figural elements that did much to found the early modern architectural aesthetic.

Rome, expanding capital of early modern Catholicism, was the true epicentre of Italian architecture and, between the sixteenth and eighteenth centuries, provided the basic repertory of all European architecture. The two greatest architects of Catholic Rome were Bernini and Borromini (1599–1667). Borromini was the more radically innovative of the two. From S. Carlo alle Quattro Fontane to S. Ivo alla Sapienza, he built daring sacred structures whose designs collapsed the difference between sculpture and architecture. The serpentine façade of S. Carlo, with its interplay of concave and convex spaces, exemplifies Borromini's efforts to represent the complex emotional force of religious faith. Favoured by great patrons, Bernini instead helped to transform Rome with his doctrine of the *bel composto* or 'total work' that synthesized all the arts. From the Cornaro chapel in Santa Maria della Vittoria, with its statue of Santa Teresa writhing in ecstasy, to the triumphant Scala Regia linking the Vatican to St Peter's, Bernini blended sculpture, architecture, and even painting in an overpowering manipulation of space and light meant to enrapture and sway viewers, drawing them toward transcendent Catholic spirituality. The third great Roman architect of the age was Cortona, whose S. Maria della Pace redefined the urban piazza, street(s), and church façade as a single theatrical set, once again transgressing the boundaries between the arts.

Further north, the Venetian architect Longhena (1598–1682) built the gravity-defying church of S. Maria della Salute on the Grand Canal between 1631 and 1638. In Turin, Guarini (1624–83) followed in Borromini's footsteps with intricate geometrical designs for the domes of S. Lorenzo and the Chapel of the Holy Shroud that made reason and faith appear to belong to the same universal plan. Juvarra

(1678–1736)—the greatest Italian architect of the eighteenth century—worked in Turin for the Savoy court. A gifted synthesizer of classical and modern, he built the Superga religious complex and the hunting lodge ('la Palazzina di Caccia') in Stupinigi before being called to Madrid by Philip V. Theatrical architects such as Antonio Bibiena (1700–74) built theatres so modern that, with modifications, they are still in use today. Finally, in 1751 Luigi Vanvitelli (1700–73) began to construct the immense palace of Charles III at Caserta. The epitome of the architecture of the centralized Old Regime state, the 'Reggia' was built along a three-kilometre perspective axis connecting city, palace, and park like a giant theatrical set.[8] This was to prove to be the last project of its kind in Italy before the traumatic Napoleonic years, when the early modern aesthetic—the language of European architecture for centuries—was swept away on the tide of revolution.

Collectors, tourists, ruins

The early modern Italian courts saw the creation of some of Europe's foremost collections of works of art. Eventually some of these formed the basis of the first public museums: the Capitoline Museum opened in Rome in 1734, the Uffizi Gallery in Florence in 1769. Although antiquarian fashions came and went throughout the early modern period, only in the eighteenth century were systematic archaeological excavations undertaken in the 'dead cities' of Herculaneum (1738) and Pompei (1748) near Naples. The Bourbon rulers of the kingdom of the Two Sicilies provided royal sponsorship for the excavations. Later on, the Greek temples at Paestum, to the south of Salerno, and the ancient city of Syracuse in south-eastern Sicily were also excavated by Bourbon archaeologists.

These discoveries, along with numerous others across the peninsula, fired the imagination of Europe. Throughout the Old Regime period, Italy remained not only a major exporter of art and artists but a magnet for foreign artists, intellectuals, and tourists. By the eighteenth century Italy was the centre of the world's first full-scale tourist industry. Well-heeled northerners, especially the

---

[8] C. de Seta, 'The Royal Palace of Caserta by Luigi Vanvitelli: The Genesis and Development of the Project', in H. A. Millon (ed.), *The Triumph of the Baroque: Architecture in Europe, 1600–1750*, exhibition catalogue, 2nd rev. edn. (New York, 1999), 371.

British, came in droves on the Grand Tour to visit its cities, ruins, and artworks. Italian art was further disseminated by tourists who acquired either originals (such as Piranesi's prints or Canaletto's views) or reproductions, and new markets for these products were created when the tourists returned home. Because they participated actively in this economy, Italians should be thought of as actors and agents on the scene of the Grand Tour, rather than mere figures in the landscape. Internationalization made Italian the universal language of European art until the end of the eighteenth century—if not for the present, then for its unmatched past.

Music

Italy was the unquestioned leader in musical innovation in Europe from c.1500 to 1650. Italian was the *lingua franca* of musical Europe, and imported Italian musicians were to be found throughout Europe at courts and in cities. Even the court composer of Louis XIV was a Florentine, Giovanni Battista Lulli, alias Jean-Baptiste Lully (1632–87). Well into the eighteenth century, Italy influenced greatly the direction of European music, not only in terms of composition, but also in terms of performance, theatrical design, instrument-making, and language (Italian seemed the most 'musical' of languages, best suited for song). The centres of musical life on the peninsula were many: each city or court developed its own school, attracting a flow of musicians from beyond the Alps (such as Schütz and Handel) who sought to learn from the Italian masters or to work with them. Although it is difficult to generalize about 'Italian' music, for each city or court had its own particular interests and practices, recent scholarship has revalued the seventeenth-century music of the peninsula for its complex, highly expressive aesthetic of contrasts.[9] I will limit myself here to the 'concerto' style, in which a combination of disparate and discontinuous elements (voices and instruments, solos and larger ensembles, dissonance and harmony, different tempos

---

[9] L. Bianconi, *Music in the Seventeenth Century*, trans. D. Bryant (Cambridge, 1987 [1982]), argues cogently that the rise of musical publishing around 1600 made possible the codification of this aesthetic, whose components may be found originally in earlier musical practices (p. 1).

and/or musical moods (*affetti*)) was intended to surprise and sway the listener, provoking a powerful sense of *meraviglia*.[10]

The premier composer of the second half of the sixteenth century, Giovanni Pierluigi da Palestrina (*c*.1525–94), was a former choirboy who rose to become the Vatican's *maestro di cappella*. A peerless composer of sacred polyphonic choral music, and influential well into the eighteenth century, Palestrina was one of the first professional musicians and an early member of the Vertuosa Compagnia dei Musici, a musical guild that today exists in Rome as the Accademia di Santa Cecilia. His fellow guild member Luca Marenzio (1553/4–99) wrote madrigals that placed a new emphasis on the words of the text. This was linked to current developments in Italian poetry, in which new modes of intense emotional expression were starting to appear. Composers, who felt close affinities with poets, also began to try to recapture some of music's former expressive force. In Venice, the polyphonic sacred music of Andrea and Giovanni Gabrieli (*c*.1510–86; *c*.1557–1612) pushed the use of *cori spezzati*—multiple choirs and instruments scattered around St Mark's—to new heights. The dominance of contrapuntal music or the 'first practice' was, however, already threatened by developments occurring elsewhere on the peninsula. In Florence the Camerata society, led by Giovanni de' Bardi (1534–1612), met regularly in the 1570s and 1580s to discuss the revival of ancient Greek music. From these discussions emerged the first codified use of the *basso continuo* (in the music of Caccini, *c*.1585), a technique that was to alter the history of European music.

The *basso continuo*, an abbreviated chordal notation, called for one or more singers to be accompanied by a single chordal instrument, while allowing for variation and improvisation in the accompanying instrumental harmonies. Thus an instrument effectively took the place of another singer, freeing the words in the song from the rhythmic constraints of counterpoint. This in turn gave the singer(s) greater expressive and vocal range in declaiming the poetic text, including the use of dissonance, and created new possibilities for composers seeking a style somewhere between speech and song. Such accompaniment, as a way of adding texture to madrigals or filling in for missing singers' parts, was certainly known to musicians before

[10] I wish to thank Professor Andrew Dell'Antonio of the University of Texas, to whom I am indebted for the formulation of my argument here.

the Camerata showed interest in it. Bardi's group set the practice into discourse, however, thus giving new authority to the *basso continuo* technique, which was seen as the distinguishing trait of the *nuove musiche* ('new music'), a style of non-contrapuntal music that privileged text.[11] A similar concern for matching music and language was found in Claudio Monteverdi's (1567–1643) *seconda prattica* ('second practice'), which rejected a 'first practice' solely concerned with music in favour of a fusion of musical and textual expression. Others, such as Sigismondo d'India (*c.*1582–*c.*1629), became skilled at composing according to the rules of either the 'first' or 'second practice', depending upon the requirements of patrons.

In Florence, however, experiments with voice and text led to even more radical kinds of composition. The Medici dukes and their courtiers sponsored large-scale musical pageants for the court on festive occasions. Recent research has shown that the 1589 *intermedi*, staged during the performance of Girolamo Bargagli's play *The Female Pilgrim* in the Teatro Mediceo for the wedding of Ferdinando I, were a synthesis of music, poetry, dance, art, and architecture. For carnival 1598 the first full-length opera was produced in Florence in the palace of Jacopo Corsi, and was presented in subsequent years for the Medici court. With its music (now largely lost) by Jacopo Peri (1561–1633), *Dafne* displayed the representational potential of the new recitative style. Soon afterward, Peri's *Euridice* (1600), also with a libretto by Ottavio Rinuccini, was performed at court, and became the first opera whose printed score has survived intact.[12] Monteverdi's first operatic masterpiece, *Orfeo* (produced at the Gonzaga court in Mantua in 1607), drew heavily on Peri's path-breaking achievements with the new style of musical drama in Florence. Instrumental music, unconcerned with text, instead either continued to pursue the 'first practice' far into the seventeenth century, accompanying dances, or to follow the innovations of the 'new music', most notably in the expressive intensity of Girolomo Frescobaldi's (1583–1643) toccatas for keyboards.

Only in 1637 did the first public opera production take place at the Teatro San Cassiano in Venice. Prior to that date, opera was performed sporadically in various northern Italian courts on ceremonial

[11] J. W. Hill, 'Florence: Musical Drama and Spectacle, 1570–1650', in C. Price (ed.), *The Early Baroque Era: From the Late 16th Century to the 1660s* (London, 1993), 128–37.

[12] Ibid. 134–8.

occasions. The musically sophisticated Venetian public accepted the operatic convention of recitative, or sung (rather than spoken) dialogue, as well as the genre's stylistic multiplicity and mythological/ pastoral subject matter, and was swept away by spectacular new theatrical production technologies that could 'set the entire stage into simultaneous motion'.[13] The public thus endorsed an aesthetic of vivid contrasts between the visual and aural fields, and further forceful contrasts within those respective fields (dissonance, etc.). Although box-office revenues were important, Venetian aristocrats underwrote much of the enormous costs of operatic organizations and productions. In becoming a musical institution, Venetian opera also legitimated the stage presence of professional female singers, who could command large sums for performances of roles requiring virtuoso skills (*castrati* singers, trained in sacred music, would gravitate to the opera stage later in the century). Travelling companies of singers known as *febiarmonici* took Venetian opera to other Italian cities, where it was quickly embraced by the urban elites.

From the outset, rulers throughout Italy recognized the propagandistic power of operatic spectacle, and sought through patronage to exploit it as a vehicle for dynastic and absolutist interests, whether at court or in theatres.[14] Venice—the only important exception to absolutism—remained, however, the undisputed centre of opera in Europe for many years. In 1642 alone, four opera houses produced seven different operas, and between 1637 and 1678 more than 150 operas were produced in the city.[15] Monteverdi wrote his final two operatic masterpieces, *Il ritorno d'Ulisse in patria* (1640) and *L'incoronazione di Poppea* (1643), for the Venetian theatre. The latter was a libertine opera, the first to represent historical rather than mythological characters. It retold the chilling story of Nero and his lover Poppea, employing 'Neostoic' and Tacitean themes to depict ambiguously for republican Venetian audiences the amorality of

[13] E. Rosand, *Opera in Seventeenth-Century Venice: The Creation of a Genre* (Berkeley, Calif., 1991), 106.

[14] Bianconi, *Music in the Seventeenth Century*, 72–3, notes: 'source of glory and prestige, sonorous device of an institution, collective entertainment for a community, adornment for ceremonial occasions, instrument of worship, demonstration of power: these are the ideologically oriented functions which dominate the horizons of seventeenth-century musical consumption.'

[15] E. Rosand, *Opera in Seventeenth-Century Venice*, 3.

absolute power.[16] A jarring multimedia synthesis of text, music, and art, *L'incoronazione di Poppea* displayed the narrative and emotional force of the genre as few operatic works have ever done. The opera boom—new theatres, impresarios, composers, writers, singers, and works—continued in Venice until the late 1670s, and the city had more theatres than any other in Europe well into the eighteenth century. Only after 1700 would Naples begin to rival Venice for its operatic productions; by then opera was the Italian 'national' art form, and Italian opera the cosmopolitan model in London, Paris, and Vienna.

Sacred music had a significant role to play in early modern Italian culture. In Rome, where opera was performed only intermittently, oratorios and cantatas flourished, thus adhering to the early modern paradigm privileging vocal music. Alessandro Scarlatti (1660–1725) spent parts of his prolific career in Rome while composing more than 700 cantatas, both sacred and secular (*da camera*). Starting in the late seventeenth century, however, secular music was given new momentum as orchestras were created throughout Europe and operas became less innovative. Northern Italian master craftsmen such as Stradivari perfected the making of stringed instruments, whose sound could match or surpass that of the human voice. Arcangelo Corelli (1653–1713) helped to popularize string music with his instrumental works for solo violin and ensemble concertos, but Antonio Vivaldi (1678–1741)—a virtuoso violinist as well as composer-conductor at the Pietà orphanage in Venice—made the purely instrumental concerto the benchmark for the music of his age. There was enough complexity in the sound of instruments, including many recently invented or perfected wind instruments, to rival opera's expressivity and pathos.

By the early eighteenth century, operatic juxtapositions (aria versus recitative, for instance) came to be seen as part of a standard order of representation, weakening the original shock-effect of the genre. Vivaldi's music—which featured patterns of structural repetitions along with passages of great inventiveness—also sought to respect the notion of 'order'. The operatic reforms of Apostolo Zeno (1668–1750) and Pietro Metastasio (1698–1782) were extremely successful with the public, and subsequently led to a lessening of interest in the aesthetic

---

[16] I draw here on the controversial interpretation of *Poppea* as a 'Neostoic' opera by I. Fenlon and P. N. Miller, *The Song of the Soul: Understanding 'Poppea'* (London, 1992), ch. 4–5.

of contrast, surprise, and wonder. One of the last original musical genres to appear in Italy, the comic opera poked fun at the *opera seria* and its austere rules, while giving new publicity to music among the masses.[17] Italian musicians continued to be in demand across the continent, and the conservatories flourished, but by mid-century the centres of musical innovation were elsewhere. There was, however, one last key musical contribution to be made by early modern Italy. Some time around 1750, quite possibly in Milan, the orchestral 'sinfonia' that introduced the opera was performed independently, and the symphony was born. Thus European culture was indebted— and would remain so until the twentieth century—to Italian musicians, composers, and artisans for virtually every aspect of what is today called 'classical' music.

Literature

The shift toward visual and musical modes of representation in early modern culture transformed Italian literature. Poetry, fiction, and drama attempted to replicate by linguistic means the visual and aural effects of the new art. Theatrical texts, for instance, were 'seen' and 'heard' by the public through performance. Composers set countless lyrics to music, and opera depended upon the poetry of the libretto. Marino's (1569–1625) *Poems* (1602) and *Adonis* (1623), which were frequently set to music, in turn aspired to musicality at the level of language. The famous episode in *Adonis* concerning the song of the nightingale was paradigmatic for early modern literature. An amorous (but unhappy) singer consoling himself with music was challenged by the bird to a contest, and, after virtuoso passages of onomatopoeic effects, the nightingale collapsed and died, unable to overcome the power of love. In this episode, Marino also mentioned new anatomical discoveries concerning the ear, and praised contemporary Italian singers such as Adriana Basile, all in the same virtuoso fashion. Painters, musicians, sculptors, writers, and architects adopted the 'Marinist' aesthetics of *meraviglia*, which offered a forceful critique of

[17] See C. Gianturco, 'Naples: A City of Entertainment', in G. J. Buelow (ed.), *The Late Baroque Era: From the 1680s to 1740* (Englewood Cliffs, NJ, 1993), 105–7, 118–22, on Metastasio and the *opera buffa*.

poetic mimesis, calling instead for the seduction of the public through witty concepts and surprising metaphors that would astound and delight with their artifice. Marino's poetic practice constituted the extreme limit of literary classicism in the Old Regime period.

Humanism was gradually replaced by a new international literary culture—'classicism'—that recirculated and recycled an encyclopedic repertory of classical texts, mythologies, epigrams, and common-places. This virtually inexhaustible supply of thematic material underlay the entire early modern universe of representation.[18] The repertory of classicism formed a sort of cultural capital; to write and to read meant to take possession of it and to reuse it creatively, thus generating fresh value for it, as Marino did in *Adonis*. This was far from a static process, often producing innovative results in neo-Latin or in the vernacular, yet it conferred continuity to the literary culture of Italy over a very long period. The poets Guarini (born in 1538) and Alfieri (born in 1749) would likely have had little difficulty conversing with one another, for they both possessed much of the same cultural capital of classicism, while employing it to very different ends.

Most members of the European elites could detect references to and decipher the meaning of this repertory, allowing them to participate in an international cultural exchange. This was the literary culture of 'civility' or 'civil conversation'. Whether in the courts or in the cities, it contributed an aesthetic dimension to sociability by giving a clearly defined shape to the fluid domain of intersubjective communication. The culture of civility was constructed around three early modern Italian treatises on conduct—Castiglione's *Book of the Courtier* (1528), Della Casa's *Galateo* (1558), and Guazzo's *On Civil Conversation* (1574), all literary masterpieces and foundational texts of classicism—together with the corpus of Petrarchism. These three treatises ran through so many editions and translations, and were so widely cited, admired, and imitated, that they were truly the first contemporary pan-European books.

The second half of the sixteenth century saw dramatic changes in the material conditions of Italian literary culture. The market for printed books continued to expand rapidly, despite the establishment of the Index of Forbidden Books (1559), with which the Church

---

[18] A. Quondam, 'Introduzione', in S. Guazzo, *La civil conversazione*, ed. A. Quondam (2 vols, Modena, 1993), i. xi.

hoped to control the circulation of unorthodox texts. Because of the political fragmentation of the peninsula, however, there was no uniform enforcement of censorship. Publishers took risks to print banned works, sometimes attributing them to fictitious or foreign presses. Venice was the centre of Italian publishing, although printers and bookshops were to be found in cities from Sicily to the Alps. Professional writers supplied a steady stream of texts for the bookmen, who also printed translations, editions, anthologies, and collections. Only widespread illiteracy, demographic collapse due to epidemics, and economic decline in the seventeenth century slowed the diffusion of print culture.

A far-flung network of literary academies emerged: between 1550 and 1600, 203 literary academies were established in Italy, and at least 568 more were created in the seventeenth century.[19] Although they often had whimsical names and frivolous regulations, the academies played a key role in the spread of literary culture beyond the courts. In the absence of a more prominent public sphere, they created new forms of sociability and channels of communication for members. The academies were infrequently reserved for the nobility alone. Indeed, the notoriously libertine Accademia degli Incogniti in Venice, which at one time could boast nearly 300 members, had only a slim majority of aristocrats by 1647.[20] The 'republic of letters' formed by the academies, in which ideas could be circulated and contested, stood in counterpoint to the absolutist politics of the peninsula, although there was considerable osmosis between court and academy. Moreover, the latter was central to the intense interchange between creative writing and criticism that distinguished Italian literature between the mid-sixteenth and early eighteenth centuries. The works of Tasso (1544–95), Guarini (1538–1612), and Marino were hotly debated by their contemporaries in the academies, and these writers were keenly aware of the criticism directed at them. The Accademia degli Arcadi ('Arcadia'), founded in Rome in 1690, was the first national literary academy, present in every city and region, and set the standard in taste for nearly fifty years. Only in the eighteenth century did the spread of academies slow.

[19] A. Quondam, 'L'Accademia', in A. Asor Rosa (ed.), *Letteratura italiana* (8 vols., Turin, 1982–91), i. 872.

[20] M. Miato, *L'Accademia degli Incogniti di Giovan Francesco Loredan, Venezia (1630–1661)* (Florence, 1998), 61.

The revival of Aristotle's *Poetics* in the sixteenth century gave support to the widespread literary critical revolt against the tenets of humanism. With the uncontrolled proliferation of print culture, the new criticism sought the discipline of 'Aristotelian' critical rules in order to make writers work within recognizable genres. Castelvetro (1505–71), for example, proposed the internationally influential theory of the 'three unities' (time, place, and action) of the mimetic text. Tasso's haunting Christian epic about the First Crusade, the *Gerusalemme liberata* (written 1565–75), offered a single unified plot ('illustrious, great, and perfect') with multiple episodes, in adherence to current interpretations of Aristotle. Critical controversy over Ariosto and Tasso—romance versus epic—raged on and off in Italy until the end of the eighteenth century. Cross-fertilization between genres nevertheless occurred, as in Guarini's 'tragicomic' *The Faithful Shepherd* (written 1580–83) or in literary-philosophical dialogue, triggering bitter critical quarrels.[21] More hybrid forms, including the novel, followed in the seventeenth century, ensuring an enduring critical debate.

Patronage for writers at the absolutist courts was often unreliable. Many, unable to obtain patronage or become courtiers, took up the post of secretary to the powerful, with a consequent loss of economic and intellectual autonomy. Much poetry—the most prestigious of the verbal arts—continued to be produced for courts, from Tasso's epic masterpiece to Marino's *Adonis*, but much more was written for academies and book markets. The great number of women poets included such figures as the courtesan-poetess Veronica Franco (1546–91) and the actress-poetess Isabella Andreini (1562–1604). The figure of Tasso loomed large for all those who came after him, but Marino may well have been more important for the direction of poetry in the seventeenth century. Although the Petrarchan vein was still popular, no one could avoid confronting Marino's influential poetics of metamorphosis and hybrid textual polyphony.

Only the Arcadians were able seriously to weaken Marinism, substituting new conventions of naturality and conversational spontaneity for Marino's doctrine of metalepsis and other extreme poetic figures, while still relying on classicist thematics. By then Italian poetry had

---

[21] On the controversy concerning dialogue, see J. R. Snyder, *Writing the Scene of Speaking: Theories of Dialogue in the Late Italian Renaissance* (Stanford, Calif., 1989), 134–80.

lost its prominent position in European culture with the development of the national literatures of England and France, which no longer needed it as an exclusive point of reference. Indeed, the process of internationalization began to reverse direction in the eighteenth century. The influence of Enlightenment currents from abroad was felt strongly by Parini (1729–99), whose verse satire *The Day* (1763–5, parts 1 and 2) scathingly criticized the social codes of the aristocracy. Although still indebted to classicism, the protoromantic *Poems* (1789) of Alfieri (1749–1803), with their expressive violence, and stark, unmusical verse, both of which drew on other European literatures, were the final chapter in the history of Italian poetry during the Old Regime, as the reading public, including ever-larger numbers of women, welcomed new poetic trends and themes from beyond the Alps.

Perhaps the most successful form of early modern Italian narrative fiction was the novella. This short genre was used in collections widely translated and imitated across Europe, and provided source material for Shakespeare and others. Bandello's (1485–1561) *Four Books of Novellas* (1554) broke new ground by sometimes using local dialects and emphasizing scenes of pathos. Giraldi Cinzio's (1504–73) novellas, also a source for Shakespeare, instead incorporated scenes of brutality for shock effect. Both were highly popular among European readers. Many plots and characters in novellas were drawn from popular culture, effecting an interpenetration of 'high' and 'low' voices that was attuned to the new aesthetic. By the early seventeenth century, however, prose fiction had evolved beyond the limits of the novella. In Naples, Giambattista Basile (1575–1632) abandoned the tradition in favour of a new genre destined to become wildly successful for the next four centuries: the literary fairy tale. Many of the most beloved of all European fairy tales—Sleeping Beauty, Cinderella, Puss in Boots, etc.—appeared, sometimes for the first time, in his collection *Pentameron* (1634–36). Jettisoning the laws of verisimilitude, Basile's prose fables, written in Neapolitan dialect, followed the new Marinist poetics, seeking to generate wonder in readers through imaginative thematic and linguistic play. Basile's experimental fairy tales led the reader into a labyrinth of unlimited metamorphosis, an infinity of possible worlds, that paralleled the discoveries of seventeenth-century science.[22]

---

[22] See N. L. Canepa, *From Court to Forest: Giambattista Basile's 'Lo cunto de li cunti' and the Birth of the Literary Fairy Tale* (Detroit, 1999), 60.

The novel was not a popular literary genre in early modern Italy, although Marini (*c*.1594–*c*.1662), Algarotti (1712–64), and many others wrote novels. Memoirs, autobiographies, journals, and letters were instead well received by the public; and who knew where the truth of these ended, or the fiction began? The most remarkable of all eighteenth-century autobiographies was Casanova's (1725–98) *Story of My Life* (composed 1791–8 in French). The Venetian libertine examined in his highly embellished work the infinite possibilities of personal freedom, both philosophical and sexual, turning existence into an aesthetic event that supplanted the rule of religion. Far superior to any Italian novelistic fiction of the era, Casanova's twelve-volume autobiography documents the degree to which freethinking penetrated the Italian elites prior to the French Revolution, helping to prepare the demise of the Old Regime.

The *mare magnum* of Italian treatises constitutes one of the most distinctive traits of early modern classicism. Adrift in this 'sea' of ink that circulated throughout Europe were many memorable literary texts, such as Della Porta's (1535–1615) *On the Physiognomy of Man* (1st edn. 1586), which helped to revive the art of 'reading the body' like a text; Tasso's *Dialogues* (written 1578–95), which display the poet's profound grasp of Tridentine culture; Moderata Fonte's (1555–92) *The Worth of Women* (1600), an impassioned defence of female equality; Campanella's (1568–1639) *The City of the Sun* (1602), probably the greatest work of early modern utopian fiction; Malvezzi's (1595–1654) *Proud Tarquin* (1634), whose elegantly laconic prose attracted the admiration of Europe; Accetto's (*c*.1590–*c*.1641) *On Honest Dissimulation* (1641), a probing study of the secret codes of dissimulation; Tesauro's (1592–1675) *The Aristotelian Telescope* (1st edn. 1654), one of the most important statements of seventeenth-century poetics in Europe; Tarabotti's *Defence of Women* (1651), with its condemnation of misogyny; Muratori's (1672–1750) *On Perfect Poetry* (1706), a call to reform Italian poetry in accordance with the new Arcadian poetics; Vico's (1668–1744) *Principles of the New Science* (1st edn. 1725), with its brilliantly idiosyncratic theory of poetic language; and Girolamo Tiraboschi's (1731–94) immensely erudite *History of Italian Literature* (1772–82), which attempted to map out all of Italian literature and culture from the Etruscans to the present day. All of these works can be comfortably situated within, or in the orbit of, classicist culture.

The theatre attracted many of the premier literary talents of early modern Italy. In an age of increasing prestige for products exploiting art's capacity for illusion, nothing could compete with the theatre. The 'erudite comedy' (*commedia erudita*) of humanist origin, with its frank representations of sexuality and contemporary urban life, continued to be in demand after 1550, reaching a new level of comic intensity with Bruno's (1548–1600) *The Candle-Bearer* (1582). Despite critical reservations, modern tragedies were composed by Giraldi Cinzio and others, and ancient tragedies by Sophocles and Seneca were revived. Hybrid forms that combined genres, such as the 'serious comedy' (Bargagli, *The Female Pilgrim*), the pastoral comedy (Tasso, *Aminta*), and pastoral tragicomedy (Guarini, *The Faithful Shepherd*) were nevertheless on the rise. Not only were Italian plays widely translated and imitated abroad, but Italian settings and characters often took centre stage. Machiavelli himself, author of groundbreaking comedies such as the *Mandragola* (*c*.1518), became a proverbial figure of evil on the Elizabethan and Jacobean stage. In most of Italy, however, courts, palaces, and academies continued to be the most prestigious venues for theatrical performances, largely by amateurs, at least until the decade 1570–80, when stable professional theatres were established in Venice, Florence, and Naples.[23]

The first itinerant professional troupes of comedians existed by 1545. Using masks and dialects, they performed improvisational comic theatre, now known as *commedia dell'arte*. Emerging out of the folk tradition of carnival, the 'Arte' troupes used temporary stages, rudimentary plots (*canovacci* or *scenari*), stock characters and repartees, slapstick farce, sight-gags, and (in some cases) female players, such as Vincenza Armani and Isabella Andreini. These anti-humanist comedies were wildly popular throughout Italy, and were quickly exported to France, where Italian comic actors set the standard for many decades (Molière studied with the actor Tiberio Fiorilli, who played Scaramouche). The juxtaposition of 'high' (the lovers) and 'low' (the servant Harlequin) characters, mutually incomprehensible dialects, or masked and unmasked actors, together with simultaneity of action and fragmentary multiple plots: these contrasts and

---

[23] S. Ferrone, *Attori mercanti corsari. La commedia dell'arte in Europa tra Cinque e Seicento* (Turin, 1993), 56.

dissonances, freed from a strictly representational function and held together by a slender thread of illusion, helped to make the theatre a central metaphor of early modern Italian culture.

The theatre continued to develop in the seventeenth century in accordance with the new aesthetic of surprise and wonder. Spectators, once they had paid to enter theatres, found familiar social hierarchies weakened: the most important distinction was now between performers and public. The experience of theatre-going thus became a discovery of an unknown 'other' social world. The most prominent seventeenth-century Italian playwright, G. B. Andreini (c.1578–1654), wrote a series of brilliant comedies pushing 'Arte' concepts to extremes of illusionism, such as *Love in the Mirror* (1622)—which starred two great actresses, Virginia Ramponi and Virginia Rotari, as lovers—and *Two Comedies in One* (1623), with its double play-within-a-play. New 'Arte' masks and zany stock plots appeared in the course of the seventeenth century, as the theatrical system was professionalized and institutionalized throughout the peninsula. The end of the century, however, saw a marked weakening in the appeal of the 'Arte', although troupes of Italian comedians continued to be invited to perform in Paris and elsewhere.

Goldoni (1707–93) worked much of his life for theatres in Venice, producing realistic comedies laced with acute social commentary. From *The Inn-Keeper* (1752) to *The Lovers* (1758) and beyond, Goldoni broke away from the 'Arte' tradition, of which he was a master, emphasizing satire, psychology, and Enlightenment ideas instead, and attracting the attention of Europe. Although Goldoni spent the last thirty years of his life in France and drew a French royal pension, Italian theatre shifted from the centre to the periphery of European drama in the eighteenth century, even as its actors, technicians, and designers were still in vogue. The tradition was not, however, extinguished all in one breath. Gozzi (1720–1806), a Venetian nobleman, wrote a series of bitter-sweet fables for the theatre, such as *The Love for Three Oranges* (1761) and *Turandot* (1762), that drew on both fairy tales and the 'Arte' repertory in open defiance of Goldoni's reforms. Inspired by developments abroad, Alfieri's tragedies (*Saul*, 1782; *Mirra*, 1784–86) marked the final contradictory phase of early modern Italian theatre, rejecting the comic heritage of Old Regime culture while clinging to the conventions of theatrical illusion which that culture had perfected.

Even after political, social, and economic reforms and revolutions had left the Old Regime in ruins, the achievements of the early modern arts were destined to remain powerfully present in the aesthetic life of Italy and Europe, like the roar of the sea in an empty shell.

Science and society

Paula Findlen

The renaissance of science

In the middle of the sixteenth century, the Italian peninsula could easily lay claim to being the centre of the scientific world in western Europe. Home to the oldest and most venerable universities, nascent Jesuit colleges, a thriving print industry, and academies where learned men congregated to discuss books and present their own work, Italy was institutionally and intellectually fertile ground in which ideas could thrive. Northern European scholars routinely made the pilgrimage to Italy to benefit from its unique intellectual resources. Nicolaus Copernicus' decision to dedicate *On the Revolutions of the Heavenly Spheres* (1543) to the Farnese pope Paul III, for example, was the culmination of his long association with the Italian tradition of mathematics and astronomy that began with four years at the University of Bologna in 1496–1500, a brief stint in Rome and Padua, and his 1503 degree from Ferrara. Sent to Italy by his uncle to study law, Copernicus enjoyed the tutelage of Bologna's astronomy professor, Domenico Maria Novara, whose early criticisms of Ptolemy provided an important point of departure for Copernicus' decision to reject geocentrism in favour of a heliocentric universe.

1543, the year that Copernicus' *On the Revolutions* appeared, was an especially fertile moment in the history of science. That same year the mathematician Niccolò Tartaglia's Italian translations of Euclid and Archimedes appeared, following his work on the dynamics of projectiles that demonstrated how the new warfare and weaponry of Renaissance Italy inspired the pursuit of mathematics. In Urbino, more learned mathematicians such as Federico Commandino were digging into the ancient and medieval manuscripts housed in the duke of

Urbino's library in order to produce definitive Latin editions of the entire Greek corpus of mathematical writings. While tentative discussions of calendar reform in Rome in the 1510s contributed to the transformation of astronomy as the divine calculating science, the battlefields, fortified towns, water management, and land reclamation projects of northern and central Italy provided an environment in which practical mathematics flourished.[1] At the same time, humanist collecting and translation projects demonstrated how incomplete knowledge of ancient mathematical sciences was and inspired humanists to make a fuller understanding of past science the basis for improving the state of knowledge in the present.

Medicine and the natural sciences were also undergoing similar transformations. In 1543 the physician Girolamo Cardano, who would be well known by the 1550s for his writings on astrology, medicine, natural philosophy, and mathematics, finally won a coveted professorship in medicine at the University of Pavia. Cardano's fame grew in relationship to his publishing, but his acerbic criticisms of traditional Galenic medicine and his bold readings of the horoscopes of famous and powerful individuals alienated him from many of his fellow physicians. Cardano eventually received a coveted professorship at Bologna, but he was not on the list of professors that Duke Cosimo I de' Medici planned to invite to the University of Pisa. In 1543 Cosimo decided to revitalize Tuscany's somewhat lacklustre university, paying particular attention to medicine and the natural sciences. While he failed to persuade the German naturalist Leonhart Fuchs to join the Pisan faculty, the following year he succeeded in wooing Luca Ghini away from the University of Bologna by promising him not only a chair in medicinal botany but also the funds to create a university botanical garden—one of the first in Europe, along with the botanical garden of Padua which opened in 1545.

Cosimo I briefly persuaded the anatomist Andreas Vesalius to lecture and dissect at Pisa in the winter of 1544, supplying cadavers from the hospital of S. Maria Nuova in Florence by floating them down the Arno. But he was unable to get Vesalius to move permanently to Tuscany. With the publication of *On the Fabric of the*

---

[1] Gregory XIII authorized the Gregorian calendar in a papal bull of 1582, subtracting 10 days from October that year.

Human Body (1543), his challenge to Galen's account of the human body, Vesalius won the coveted title of imperial physician and left Italy to join his patron, the holy Roman emperor Charles V. But Vesalius, even more than Copernicus, can justly be said to have benefited from the flourishing of science in the Italian peninsula, since his magisterial work of anatomy was filled with beautifully engraved images from Titian's workshop that suggested the unique intersection of two different aspects of Renaissance medicine: more plentiful access to cadavers in Italy than in other parts of Europe, and the emergence of an artistic community that paid special attention to the anatomical depiction of the human body in the wake of great artists of the previous century such as Leonardo da Vinci.

During the 1540s, achieving a deeper understanding of the natural world was not simply a project for a handful of university professors, but a widespread preoccupation of society. In 1543 the d'Este dukes of Ferrara established a chair in medicinal simples at their university, reminding all of Europe that Ferrara had been an important centre for debates about Pliny the Elder's *Natural History* at the end of the fifteenth century. In his inaugural lecture, the first professor, Giuseppe Gabrieli, remarked that natural history was not just a subject for lowly herbalists, but for 'people coming from every social class conspicuous for political power, wealth, nobility and knowledge'.[2] Addressing himself specifically to Ercole II, Gabrieli praised his patron for understanding that knowledge of nature was important to a Renaissance city-state. He was not alone in this belief. Just as scholars in northern and central Italy made the reconstitution of mathematics and medicine a collective and often contentious project, the new appetite for botany created a community of patrons and practitioners.

North of Ferrara, in the city of Gorizia, the physician Pier Andrea Mattioli was on the verge of completing his 1544 Italian translation of Dioscorides' *On Medical Material*, an ancient pharmacopoeia. His commentary on Dioscorides became one of the most important natural histories of the sixteenth century. Its success was due in no

---

[2] Gaspare Gabrieli, *Oratio habita Ferrariae in principio lectionum de simplicium medicamentarum facultatibus* (1543), in F. Gioelli, 'Gaspare Gabrieli. Primo Lettore dei Semplici nello Studio di Ferrara (1543)', *Atti e memorie della Deputazione Provinciale Ferrarese di Storia Patria*, ser. 3, 10 (1970), 33–4.

small part to the fact that Mattioli relied upon physicians, apothecaries, university professors, and custodians of botanical gardens to
supply him with new specimens and information for each subsequent
edition of the book. Mattioli's book became a repository of all the
new knowledge that flowed into Europe. It was more widely read
than natural histories such as Ulisse Aldrovandi's *Ornithologies*
(1599–1603) because Mattioli astutely recognized that his work would
be even more successful in Italian than in Latin, publishing it in both
languages in order to reach audiences in his native region as well as in
northern Europe.

The renaissance of science in the sixteenth century was both an
intellectual transformation of specific sciences and a political investment in the idea of natural knowledge and technical expertise. Popes,
princes, and republican governments competed for the best scholars
and engineers that Italy's schools produced. The growing demand for
scientific and technical expertise in late Renaissance Italy directly
reflected the complexity of the built environment in a highly urbanized society and the continuation of long-standing projects to control
and transform the natural world. In addition, scientific activities
gradually became an important point for social life and cultural
exchange. Baldassare Castiglione's *Book of the Courtier* (1528) did not
place special emphasis on scientific knowledge, preferring that the
perfect courtier be well versed in arts and letters. Yet by the end of the
century, nobles and patricians considered a basic understanding
of mathematics and an appreciation of nature fundamental to their
identity.

'Cabinets of curiosities' exemplified the intersection between
science and cultural life at the end of the Renaissance. In virtually
every Italian city, men of learning filled their studies with natural
objects, scientific instruments, books, antiquities, and paintings. They
visited naturalists such as Bologna's famous professor Aldrovandi,
whose museum, filled with thousands of natural objects, was
described by many as the 'eighth wonder of the world'.[3] The cabinet
of curiosities brought together the many different kinds of scientific

---

[3] G. Olmi, *L'inventario del mondo. Catalogazione della natura e luoghi del sapere
nella prima età moderna* (Bologna, 1992); C. Scappini and M. P. Torricelli, *Lo Studio
Aldrovandi in Palazzo Pubblico (1617–1742)*, ed. S. Tugnoli Pattaro (Bologna, 1993);
and P. Findlen, *Possessing Nature: Museums, Collecting, and Scientific Culture in Early
Modern Italy* (Berkeley, Calif., 1994).

activities. It contained the fruits of humanistic learning in the form of new editions and translations of key texts by ancient authors that inspired new books by Renaissance authors. It housed compasses, surveying tools, astrolabes, and armillary spheres that evoked the world of Copernicus and Tartaglia. It displayed dried plants, for scientific study as well as for making medicines, exotic animals, figured stones, and other artefacts that brought the Indies to Italy for those who could not travel halfway around the globe. The cabinet of curiosities reflected a universal aspiration for knowledge that did not separate the sciences from each other, or divide ancient and modern learning, but emphasized their points of intersection. It was a tactile encyclopedia that made the world comprehensible through representative objects and their interpretation.

The new world of knowledge, in short, was a new material world. Taking possession of this world was as much a political as an intellectual project. When the Venetian republic built a permanent anatomical theatre in Padua in 1594, where the learned Aristotelian anatomist Hieronymus Fabricius taught a young William Harvey, to complement their botanical garden, they reminded their citizens that scientific knowledge was not simply a bookish pursuit, locked inside ancient writings for learned professors to decipher, but a dynamic enterprise whose advancement depended on new resources for learning and new ways of looking at the world. At the end of the sixteenth century, Padua exemplified the sort of climate in which physicians, philosophers, and mathematicians could continue the critical reassessment of knowledge initiated in the works of late Renaissance humanists.

This image of science was not lost on a 30-year-old Galileo, then a young mathematics professor eking out a living on a less than spectacular salary. In 1592 Galileo moved from Pisa to Padua because the Venetian republic was known to support learning and reward enterprising inventors. Equally important, Venice was known for its willingness to defy the authority of Rome. For philosophers increasingly interested in exploring the less orthodox aspects of the new scientific learning, the political climate in the Venetian republic was perhaps as attractive as its material resources. In 1611, for example, the Aristotelian philosophy professor Cesare Cremonini expressed disbelief that Galileo would 'leave behind Paduan liberty' to accept a position as chief mathematician and philosopher to the grand duke of Tuscany, Cosimo II.[4] This brings us to another facet of scientific life in Italy, for the rich institutional and cultural climate that Italy offered was also a complex religious world. In an age defined by the reformation of Catholicism at the Council of Trent (1545–63), what constituted good knowledge was as much a religious as a philosophical question.

Philosophical liberties

The year that ushered in Copernicus' and Vesalius' important publications also saw the establishment of the Index of Prohibited Books, though it did not take any concrete form until the 1559 Roman Index of Paul IV. In 1543 the Roman Inquisition was only a year old and the Society of Jesus, only 3 years old, had barely more than its ten original members. While the implications of Copernicus' *On the Revolutions* seem to have been debated in Rome by the master of the sacred palace, the figure eventually responsible for the authorization of printed books in Catholic lands, the Catholic Church as a whole remained relatively uninterested. The state of knowledge was not a priority when there were fundamental issues of church doctrine to be discussed and souls to be saved from the pernicious influence of Protestantism.

By the 1570s, however, the problem of controlling knowledge had become a more pressing issue. Pius V established the Congregation of the Index in 1571, making the inspection of books a more important part of reformed Catholicism. At the same time, the local Inquisitions in various cities, both Spanish and Roman, became more active in their prosecution of heresies that concerned the interpretation of the natural world. In 1570, for example, the Bologna Inquisition arrested the physician Cardano on suspicion of heresy. His unorthodox intellectual practices included casting the horoscope of Christ, arguing for the natural causes of supernatural events, and advocating the value of dreams in foretelling the future. By February 1571, the Inquisition had accepted Cardano's private abjuration, extracting a promise from

---

[4] In A. Poppi, *Cremonini e Galileo inquisiti a Padova nel 1604. Nuovi documenti d'archivio* (Padua, 1992), 27.

him never to teach or publish in the Papal States again. That same year the Bologna Inquisition called the naturalist Aldrovandi before them for the second time. Aldrovandi's first encounter had led to his imprisonment in Rome in 1549, after publicly abjuring his heresies in the church of San Petronio in Bologna, under grave suspicion of being a *luterano*, or at the very least a highly unorthodox Catholic.[5] The Holy Office continued to monitor the books in his library, suspicious of his contacts with Protestant naturalists and the wide range of his reading.

One of Aldrovandi's correspondents found himself in deeper trouble with the Inquisition. Between 1574 and 1580, Giovan Battista della Porta, whose *Natural Magic* (1558, but vastly expanded in 1589) made him famous throughout Europe as a learned magus, was called twice before the Neapolitan Inquisition, which suppressed his scientific academy because it was believed to be heretical. Among other things, della Porta denied the diabolical power of 'witch's salve', arguing that it was a hallucinogenic drug that induced an altered state through natural rather than diabolic means. Just as Cardano claimed too much for his powers of foretelling the future, della Porta overstepped the boundaries of natural magic by arguing that certain elements of the supernatural could be explained away. Both of them were good examples of the kinds of natural philosopher whom Sixtus V had in mind when his 1586 papal bull *Coeli et terrae* banned works of magic, divination, and any astrology not used for practical purposes in agriculture, medicine, and navigation. When della Porta circumvented the increasingly restrictive rules for publication in 1592 by attempting to print an Italian translation of his *Human Physiognomy* (1586) in Venice without Rome's permission, the Inquisition intervened, holding up the presses until the Holy Office finally granted permission for the edition published in Naples in 1598.

The careful inspection of della Porta's activities came in the midst of a growing controversy about Renaissance naturalism. In 1565 Bernardino Telesio published his influential *The Nature of Things According to Their Own Principles*. He continued to revise and republish this work until his death in 1588, teaching his new philosophy of sense experience at an academy in Cosenza. Telesio's

[5] A. Biondi, 'Ulisse Aldrovandi e l'eresia a Bologna', *Annali dell'Istituto Storico Italo-Germanico in Trento* 17 (1991), 77–89.

critique of Aristotelian philosophy, and his argument that all sciences were founded directly in nature and made manifest through the senses, offered an influential account of Renaissance naturalism. His work was not placed on the Index until 1593, but it exemplified the growing tendency towards more radical readings of ancient philosophies. Controversial figures such as Giordano Bruno and Tommaso Campanella, both famous victims of the Inquisition, counted themselves among Telesio's followers.

While Cardano, della Porta, and Telesio argued for a more powerful place for natural observation in the realm of philosophy, other scholars found themselves in trouble with the Holy Office for rejecting outright the idea that a good Catholic education should be based in the writings of Aristotle. In the very years that the Society of Jesus made Aristotle and his great medieval interpreter, Thomas Aquinas, the foundation of the Jesuit college curriculum, Francesco Patrizi declared that Platonic thought was better suited to Catholicism. In 1578, Duke Alfonso II d'Este made Patrizi professor of Platonic philosophy in Ferrara. His *New Philosophy of the Universe* (1591), dedicated to Gregory XIV, connected Platonism to the rise of the mathematical sciences and rejected Aristotle's traditional concept of the four elements in favour of the four principles of space, light, heat, and humidity. Clement VIII was so intrigued by Patrizi's Platonic revolution that in 1592 he invited him to teach at Rome's university, La Sapienza. Papal patronage did not protect Patrizi from a brush with the Roman Inquisition. The Congregation of the Index was less concerned with Patrizi's defence of Plato over Aristotle than with the theological implications of his idea of a world soul. Patrizi's efforts to correct his errors in the second edition of his book led to its prohibition. Upon his death in 1597, Patrizi's book had been on the Clementine Index *donec corrigitur* (until corrected) for a year.

The year of 1597 was a grim one for the community of scholars committed to the freedom to philosophize. In Rome, Bruno languished in the Inquisition's prison, where he had been moved in 1593 over the protests of the Venetian Inquisition that had brought him in on suspicion of teaching the diabolic arts of memory, denying the Trinity, and attempting to start his own sect in Germany. Since 1594, Inquisitors had been trying to read Bruno's difficult, often impenetrable books. His ecstatic advocacy of an infinite, eternal world and his argument for a new metaphysics to accompany a new understanding of the cosmos ushered in by Copernicus' astronomy and Telesio's naturalism struck godly readers such as the Jesuit Robert Bellarmine as the height of impiety. It was not Bruno's heliocentrism that offended, but his conviction that a new philosophy would be the basis for a new theology. But what could one expect from a former Dominican whose own provincial had begun heresy proceedings against him in Naples in 1576?

'The Nolan ... has freed the human mind,' Bruno declared triumphantly in *The Ash Wednesday Supper* (1584).[6] If Patrizi's relatively light treatment at the hands of the Inquisition made Bruno optimistic about the possibilities of philosophizing freely, then the fate of two other contemporaries reminded him that philosophers without powerful patrons in Rome did not fare as well. On 5 July 1597, the Florentine Francesco Pucci was beheaded in Rome. Pucci had travelled all over Europe, aligning himself with various religious groups and philosophical projects while he worked towards the reunification of Christianity. Kicked out of Oxford, Basle, and just about every other city that he visited, he found himself in the company of the English magus John Dee. Pucci deeply alarmed Dee when he suggested that the best place for him to conjure angels and explain their interpretation of the end of the world would be in Rome before the pope. In 1587 Pucci renewed his allegiance to Catholicism and left Dee and his assistant, Edward Kelley, behind in Prague. He did not return to Rome willingly, but soon found himself in the company of Bruno and his fellow Dominican Tommaso Campanella, who spent three months in the same cell as Pucci in the spring of 1597.

This was not the first time that Campanella was suspected of heresy. In August 1592, the Neapolitan Inquisition imprisoned Campanella in San Domenico for his adherence to Telesian natural philosophy. The 24-year-old monk had also participated in della Porta's philosophical circle. In the next few years Campanella found himself in trouble with the Venetian and Roman Inquisitions, abjuring his heresies in Rome in May 1594. Three years later, he was placed under house arrest in the Dominican convent in his home town of Stilo in Calabria. By 1599 he was imprisoned on suspicion of inciting

---

[6] Giordano Bruno, *The Ash Wednesday Supper*, ed. and trans. E. A. Lerner and L. S. Gosselin (Hamden, Conn., 1977), 89. 'Nolan' was Bruno's way of referring to himself in the third person, since he was from the town of Nola, near Naples.

a revolt against the Spanish rulers of the kingdom and of relapsing into heresy. Tortured repeatedly, Campanella presented himself as a madman in order to escape the death sentence that a twice-convicted heretic of his stature would have received. His madness earned him life imprisonment in Naples in 1603, though Urban VIII would have him brought to Rome and released some twenty-five years later. Unlike Bruno, who was executed by the Inquisition by being burned at the stake in Campo dei Fiori on 17 February 1600, Campanella survived the difficult years at the end of the sixteenth century and lived to see Galileo condemned for openly advocating heliocentrism before his own death in self-imposed exile in Paris in 1639.

It is hardly surprising that outspoken, unorthodox philosophers such as Pucci and Bruno, who clearly subsumed their philosophy within a theological framework that was decidedly pantheistic, should suffer a harsh fate. The small number of individuals who ended up in prison, or worse, reminds us that the Inquisition, by and large, did not actively seek to multiply the number of heretics. A respected professor such as Patrizi was given a fair amount of latitude to condemn the educational system of his day and debate the problems of inventing a new philosophy. He inspired a younger generation of scholars to take the same measured approach to the problem of remaining faithful to the Church while advancing new knowledge.

One especially important pupil of Patrizi's, Cesare Cremonini, endured the irony of appearing repeatedly before the Venetian Inquisition between 1599 and 1626 to address concerns about his teaching and writing of Aristotelian philosophy. In 1608, for example, he was accused of arguing that the soul was mortal rather than immortal. Other complaints revolved around his strict allegiance to equally impious Aristotelian ideas such as the eternity of the world. Cremonini argued that such statements were not a matter of personal belief, but philosophical competence. In order to teach Aristotelian philosophy, he had to teach it as Aristotle had written it. This was precisely the opposite of the medieval synthesis of faith and knowledge that Aquinas had effected and the Jesuits were in the process of institutionalizing.

The unique situation of Padua emboldened Cremonini to declare to his Inquisitors in July 1619:

But as for changing my manner of speaking, I don't know how I can promise to transform myself. Some do it one way, some another. I cannot and will not retract the expositions of Aristotle, because I understand him this way and I am paid to declare what I understand. If I don't do this, I'll be obliged to offer a refund.[7]

Cremonini did not land in prison for strongly stating his convictions. His younger colleague Galileo no doubt admired Cremonini's sense of moral rectitude, even if he was ultimately unable to replicate it in 1633. But Cremonini was arguing for the right to offer an accurate account of the ideas of the west's most revered philosopher. Galileo instead found himself in the nether world between the terrain demarcated by the heretical philosophers of the late sixteenth century, many of whom argued that a new philosophy was the basis for a renewal of faith, and the technical world of mathematical and physical astronomy, which was slowly coming to terms with the implications of Copernican astronomy.

The politics of the Italian peninsula offered a complex arena in which to advocate new ideas. Each region dealt with its heretics differently. Campanella in Naples was imprisoned for life, but he wrote poetry and philosophy from his cell, received visitors, and corresponded with the world. Bruno might burn in Rome, but three years later the founders of the Accademia dei Lincei (1603–30), headed by a young Roman noble, Federico Cesi, would make the freedom to philosophize one of the cornerstones of their academy. They boldly invited an ageing della Porta to become their first distinguished member in 1610, before admitting Galileo in 1611. The most active Linceans, among them Cesi, espoused a philosophy that recalled Telesio's naturalism and sanitized the more ecstatic reading of the 'book of nature' offered by the German physician and prophet Paracelsus, whose works were banned outright by the Index. Della Porta, much more than Galileo, reflected the intellectual direction of the group. Their one collective project, in fact, was not a work of astronomy but the publication of Francisco Hernández's natural history of Mexico. Yet they were willing to support Galileo's mathematical philosophy and astronomy simply as a matter of principle. 'We profess ourselves as one only in the freedom to philosophise

---

[7] See C. Schmitt, 'Cesare Cremonini', in *Dizionario biografico degli italiani*, xxx (Rome, 1984), 620.

about physical matters,' remarked Cesi in a letter to Galileo in March 1615.[8] One did not have to be an avowed Copernican to support the advancement of learning.

The legacy of Galileo

When Cesi met Galileo in Rome in 1611, the latter was the most celebrated natural philosopher in Italy. Galileo's *Sidereal Messenger* (1610) made the telescope the arbiter of the new astronomy. His bold declaration that the moon was not a perfect celestial body, that the Milky Way was a mass of stars, and that Jupiter was a planet with four moons provided further evidence against traditional cosmology. The great Jesuit astronomer Christopher Clavius, who had taught at the Collegio Romano since 1563, confirmed what Galileo had seen in the heavens, but was reluctant to draw conclusions about what this meant for astronomy. But advocates of Copernicanism did not hesitate to use the telescope to develop new arguments in favour of a sun-centred universe. Galileo quickly emerged as the most public defender of Copernicanism in Italy.

Galileo's career reflects well the fusion of science and politics in the early seventeenth century. His intellectual ambitions led him from one university position to another, and inspired him to create inventions that suited the practical demands of the patrons he served. Presenting the Venetians with his telescope, Galileo argued that it would be an invaluable military device for a seafaring empire. Galileo may have misrepresented the uniqueness of his gift, but he was right about its use. Overwhelmingly the telescope was a terrestrial instrument in the first decades of its existence, aptly called a 'spyglass'. Galileo presented it simultaneously to the Venetians and the Florentines as a different kind of instrument that mirrored the interests of each society.

Galileo thought that leaving Padua for the Medici court in Florence in 1610 would free him from the cares of teaching so that he might pursue his research. He did not anticipate how much his work

[8] In S. Drake, 'The Accademia dei Lincei', in his *Galileo Studies: Personality, Tradition, and Revolution* (Ann Arbor, Mich., 1970), 92. Translation slightly modified.

would reawaken arguments about the relationship between faith and knowledge. In 1613 his close associate Benedetto Castelli told him about a debate he had with a philosophy professor from Pisa, before the grand duchess Christina of Lorraine, regarding the potential incompatibility of heliocentrism with scripture. Galileo's initial response echoed the words of Bruno in the 1580s. 'Who wants to fix a limit for the human mind? Who wants to assert that everything which is knowable in the world is already known?'[9] His famous *Letter to the Grand Duchess Christina* (1615) argued passionately that the Bible could not be taken as a literal description of the natural world. It circulated in manuscript the same year that a Carmelite priest from Calabria, Paolo Antonio Foscarini, published his *Letter on the Opinion of the Pythagoreans and Copernicus*, in which he argued that heliocentrism was compatible with the Bible's account of the movements of the heavens.

On 26 February 1616, after two months in Rome dealing with accusations of heresy by Dominicans in Florence, Galileo found himself in the home of Cardinal Robert Bellarmine, who had been sent by the pope to warn the mathematician personally that Copernicanism was about to be condemned as a heretical proposition and that he should neither teach nor defend it. On 5 March 1616, Copernicus' *On the Revolutions* was placed on the Index *donec corrigitur*; Foscarini's *Letter* was prohibited entirely. None of Galileo's works was banned. His own *Letter* did not appear in print until 1636, and was not published in Italy until 1710.

From prison that year, Campanella wrote his *Defence of Galileo*. While it remained unpublished until 1622, the timing was not coincidental. As the debate over Copernicanism became a public controversy, Campanella felt compelled to defend Galileo not for proving that the universe was heliocentric, but for producing some of the clearest signs that the world was about to undergo a religious and intellectual renewal. While a handful of specialists concerned themselves with the technical details of astronomy and their relationship to scripture, Campanella reflected the more dangerous implications of Galileo's project for the institutional Church: its ability to attract followers who might draw conclusions from the new astronomy, such

---

[9] M. A. Finocchiaro (ed.), *The Galileo Affair: A Documentary History* (Berkeley, Calif., 1989), 51 (Galileo to Castelli, 14 Dec. 1613).

as the idea that understanding the book of nature lay beyond the authority of the professional interpreters of God's other book, Scripture.

If Paul V and Cardinal Bellarmine had been alarmed about the implications of Copernicanism in 1616, the situation seemed quite different by August 1623, when Maffeo Barberini became Urban VIII. An admirer of Galileo, Urban was a particular fan of *The Assayer* (1623), Galileo's important work on scientific methodology that contained traces of his interest in the ancient theory of atomism, which argued that the universe was composed of infinitely small, indivisible particles of matter. At the urging of Galileo's fellow Linceans, the book was dedicated to the new pope. By the time Galileo visited Rome in 1624, he felt reasonably confident that the freedom to philosophize had been restored.

Galileo's decision to publish his *Dialogue Concerning the Two Chief World Systems* (1632) reflected his optimism about the changed intellectual climate. In July 1626, Urban VIII persuaded Spanish officials in Naples to send Campanella to Rome, where he consulted with him frequently on the papal horoscope. By 1629, Campanella was released from prison and living in the Dominican convent of S. Maria sopra Minerva, where the Holy Office would conduct Galileo's trial. Urban's favour towards him waned, since papal astrology turned out to be a very delicate business, but the pope allowed him to remain at liberty. Indeed, it was Campanella who told Galileo's associate Benedetto Castelli in March 1630 that the pope had declared that Copernicanism should never have been prohibited. Galileo completed his *Dialogue* the following month and travelled to Rome to get permission to publish it.

The untimely death of Federico Cesi, the appearance of plague, and the hesitation of the Roman censor to approve a work that discussed Copernicanism delayed the publication for almost two years. By the time the *Dialogue* appeared in Florence in February 1632, it had the approval of the Florentine Inquisition but had not been seen in its final form in Rome. But the instructions from Rome were quite explicit, since they asked him to discuss heliocentrism only hypothetically and not present it as a better explanation than geocentrism. Galileo's witty and aggressive attack on Aristotelian physics and Ptolemaic astronomy, and his final jest at the pope and the Jesuits' idea to take up Tycho Brahe's compromise, led to the pope's decision to prohibit distribution of the book.[10] In September 1632 a special commission examined its content and the Holy Office called Galileo to Rome.

Galileo's condemnation on 22 June 1633 for holding beliefs that were 'philosophically absurd and false, and formally heretical', and his public abjuration of those beliefs, is the most famous and controversial moment in the history of Italian science.[11] Scholars who praised Italy for the strength of its institutions of learning and the generosity of its patrons now discussed the problems of having institutionalized faith play such a decisive role in the pursuit of knowledge. Many Catholic scholars, among them a number of Jesuits who had given up the Ptolemaic system in its purest form, had not anticipated that the Church would intervene to this degree. When Galileo wrote to a friend in 1635 that he had felt it prudent 'to succumb and remain silent', he expressed his own frustration at a papacy that did not reflect the views of many figures within its own ranks.[12]

It would be misleading, however, to think that Galileo's only legacy lay in his failed attempt to persuade the Catholic Church that heliocentrism offered a better physical account of the universe. One decision on a single theory did not undo the work of the previous century. Observational astronomy continued to thrive in Italy. The Jesuit Giambattista Riccioli drew upon the global resources of his order to collect heavenly data for his *New Almagest* (1651). Four years later, Giovanni Domenico Cassini, invited everyone to see his newly refurbished meridian line in the church of San Petronio in 1655: 'Most illustrious nobles of Bologna, the kingdom of astronomy is now yours.'[13] Prior to the early eighteenth century, many of the best observatories in Europe were found inside the cavernous vaulted domes of Italy's great churches, including a meridian line in S. Maria degli Angeli in Rome built by Francesco Bianchini for Clement XI. The trial of Galileo, in other words, did not impede the pursuit of science, even in key areas of astronomy, though it did restrict discussions of one particularly important subject, cosmology.

---

[10] Geoheliocentrism, in which the earth and moon orbited around the sun, while all other planets orbited around the earth.

[11] Finnochiaro, *Galileo Affair*, 288.

[12] In P. Redondi, *Galileo Heretic*, trans. R. Rosenthal (Princeton, NJ, 1987), 24 (Galileo to Peiresc, 21 Feb. 1635).

[13] In J. L. Heilbron, *The Sun in the Church: Cathedrals as Solar Observatories* (Cambridge, Mass., 1999), p. 93.

Galileo played an important cultural role in the development of Italian science. He convinced Italian scholars that the language of science need not always be Latin. By choosing to write the majority of his works in his native Tuscan, including his great work of mechanics, the *Two New Sciences* (1638), he made his learning accessible to virtually anyone who was literate. This had been part of the problem in 1633. Yet by 1710, the naturalist Antonio Vallisneri made Galileo's choice a programme for intellectual renewal when he insisted that all scholarly communication among Italians should be in Italian. In stating this principle, he declared himself an heir to such figures as Francesco Redi, whose numerous publications on such subjects as the refutation of spontaneous generation and the efficacy of snakestones in drawing off poison explicitly imitated Galileo's lively accessible prose. Many scholars continued to write in Latin, among them Bologna's great anatomist Marcello Malpighi, who became the first Italian member of the Royal Society in 1669 and who believed that Latin was the best means of communicating his ideas to an international community of experts. But the increased number of important scientific works appearing in Italian suggests that science was indeed a cultural pursuit of broad interest to society.

Galileo also left behind a few disciples who continued his work in mathematics and mechanics, and sought to institutionalize a 'Galileian' approach to science. Foremost among these efforts was the Accademia del Cimento (1657–67), which included such noteworthy members as Giovanni Alfonso Borelli, whose *On the Motion of Animals* (1680) combined insights from anatomy and physics to offer a mechanical account of motion. Patronized by Leopoldo de' Medici, the academy met sporadically at court with the purpose of conducting and collectively recording the results of their experiments. By the appearance in 1667 of the *Essays on Natural Experiments Made by the Accademia del Cimento*, an unusual book that attributed the work to no single author, the academy no longer existed. Leopoldo had become a cardinal, Borelli returned to Messina, the philosopher Carlo Rinaldini accepted a position in Padua, the court physician Redi had his own experiments to do in the grand ducal pharmacy, and it was unclear to what degree other participants in the academy had a strong commitment to science. Vincenzo Viviani, Galileo's sole living disciple, continued to craft his *Life of Galileo*, published posthumously in 1717, and to urge the Medici to commemorate Galileo with a public monument. Finally despairing that it would ever happen in his own lifetime, he placed a bust of Galileo over the door of his own palace in Florence in 1693.

Academies and experimenters

While the Cimento did not survive, it appeared at a crucial moment in the development of early modern science. Readers of the 1655–6 Bolognese edition of Galileo's works, minus of course the offensive *Dialogue*, examined his natural philosophy in light of the writings of Francis Bacon, René Descartes, Pierre Gassendi, and many other important northern European philosophers whose works were becoming better known in Italy. The decade of the Cimento's existence saw the foundation of the Royal Society of London (1662) and the Paris Academy of Sciences (1666), both institutions that would count many important Italian natural philosophers and mathematicians among their members and spawn imitations in cities such as Venice and Bologna.[14] In Naples, the Accademia degli Investiganti, led by the Cartesian Tommaso Cornelio, began to meet at the palace of the marquis of Arena in 1663—appropriately enough, the same year that Descartes ended up on the Index. Their contact with the Cimento suggests that the idea of a scientific academy had changed somewhat since the days of the Accademia dei Lincei, when Cesi had hoped to found colonies throughout the world in imitation of the Jesuit colleges. Experimenting with instruments, such as Evangelista Torricelli's famous tube that produced a vacuum when inverted, had become a central part of the definition of a scientific academy. The growth of scholarly journals also created new means of disseminating this new kind of knowledge.

The Investiganti fought the Aristotelian philosophers, Galenic physicians, and just about every other form of traditional learning

---

[14] In 1681 Paolo and Giovanni Antonio Sarotti attempted to create their own version of a Royal Society in Venice. Similarly, the structure of the Bologna Istituto delle Scienze founded by Luigi Ferdinando Marsigli in 1711 drew inspiration from London and Paris. See C. Pighetti, *L'influsso scientifico di Robert Boyle nel tardo '600 italiano* (Milan, 1988); and M. Cavazza, *Settecento inquieto. Alle origini dell'Istituto delle Scienze di Bologna* (Bologna, 1990).

they could attack, bringing their disciples under strong suspicion of atheism between 1688 and 1697. Malpighi blamed the 'impudence and lack of prudence of some hot-headed Neapolitans' for almost making the issue of atomism another trial of Galileo.[15] In Rome in 1693, there was some discussion in the Holy Office of banning modern physics in its totality, but fortunately this did not occur. The papacy had no desire to repeat the mistakes of the past, and Rome in the 1690s was a less conservative city than Naples, or even Pisa, where Cosimo III prohibited the teaching of atomism in 1691.

Other academies were more circumspect in their goals, preferring the model of intellectual neutrality that the Cimento offered by experimenting without drawing hasty (or sometimes any) conclusions. In Bologna, the mathematician Geminaro Montanari's Accademia della Traccia gathered together some of his most promising students between 1665 and his departure for Padua in 1678. Generally, the Bolognese exhibited less of a taste for metaphysical and philosophical issues than the Neapolitans, preferring to address concrete problems in specific fields such as anatomy, astronomy, mathematics, and hydraulics. Malpighi, one of the members of the Traccia, was in the process of examining the anatomy of the tongue after describing the structure of the lungs. Montanari spent a great deal of his time putting his expertise in the service of various water management projects. Cassini was trying to confirm Christian Huygens' 1659 description of the rings of Saturn with the help of the best telescopes in Rome. The problem for Bologna was trying to keep these talented individuals at the university, since other cities offered enticements that their under funded institution could not match.

During the same period that the Cimento flourished, the Jesuit Athanasius Kircher's spectacular museum at the Collegio Romano, filled with marvellous machines, natural objects, antiquities, and curiosities, became a meeting ground for scholars and travellers. Kircher's endlessly erudite encyclopedias, which seem to have appeared almost yearly until his death in 1680, incorporated just about everything of importance that had happened in science in the previous century. While presenting himself as an advocate of traditional learning, Kircher, like many of his fellow Jesuits, was hardly a

---

[15] M. Torrini, *Dopo Galileo. Una polemica scientifica (1684–1711)* (Florence, 1979), 28; and L. Osbat, *L'Inquisizione a Napoli. Il processo agli ateisti 1688–97* (Rome, 1974).

strict Aristotelian. Younger Jesuits in Rome participated in the Accademia Fisicomatematica, founded by Monsignor Giovanni Giustino Ciampini in 1677. Less successful than the Cimento in producing concrete results, it nonetheless provided a forum in which traditional and modern philosophy could find common meeting ground in the discussion of ideas and the witnessing of experiments. No less a participant than the Jesuit mathematician Antonio Baldigiani, a regular correspondent with members of the Cimento, felt free to declare that he considered himself a follower of Galileo.

As the seventeenth century came to a close, the most pressing problem that Italian science faced was not the absence of lively discussions of knowledge, but the striking fact that too much of the conversation focused on intellectual developments beyond the Alps. In 1709 Luigi Ferdinando Marsigli exhorted the senate of Bologna to improve the state of learning in its famous university. He did so in a language that transcended local political allegiances: 'Now Italy has been sent into oblivion by foreigners when it comes to the sciences.'[16] Marsigli agreed with the librarian Ludovico Antonio Muratori, who had urged that science be part of the cultural revival of the republic of letters. The former soldier and student of Malpighi persuaded the senate of his city to found Bologna's Istituto delle Scienze (Academy of Sciences) in 1711.

Marsigli's idea of an academy, however, added a new dimension to the role such cultural institutions should play in society. He proposed the establishment of professorships in subjects such as physics, chemistry, astronomy, natural history, cartography, and military science that Bologna's university curriculum did not cover adequately. The Academy professors taught during hours designed to complement rather than compete with university classes. Marsigli argued that a scientific academy could be not only a place for the exchange of ideas among scholars, but also an alternative educational institution as well as a civic project rather than an act of independent patronage. The fact that his academy still exists today, in contrast to the many ephemeral academies of the seventeenth and early eighteenth centuries that tended to die with their creator, suggests that he understood

---

[16] Luigi Ferdinando Marsigli, *Parallelo dello Stato moderno della Università di Bologna con l'altre di là de' Monti* (1709), in L. Boehm and E. Raimondi (eds.), *Università, accademie e società scientifiche in Italia e in Germania dal Cinquecento al Settecento* (Bologna, 1984), 234.

well the importance of institutions in effecting real change. Royal academies flourished in cities such as Naples and Turin in the second half of the eighteenth century, and there was even a failed attempt to create an academy in imitation of the Cimento in Milan in the 1720s.[17] But Bologna was the only major city to offer a civic model of a scientific society.

During the eighteenth century Italian scholars debated the new philosophical systems that replaced the Aristotelian world view, though they circumspectly offered none of their own. They accepted the philosophies of Leibniz and Newton with considerably less controversy than those of Galileo and Descartes, even neglecting to place Newton on the Index, though Francesco Algarotti's *Newtonianism for Ladies* (1737), a popularization of Newton's optics written in the form of a dialogue between a philosopher and a noblewoman, was prohibited in its original version. Gradually the universities introduced new subjects into their curriculum, making the experimental physics cabinet a mainstay of scientific life by the middle of the century. Physicists such as Giambattista Beccaria in Turin and physicians such as Giuseppe Veratti in Bologna played an early role in developing the implications of electricity, arguing vociferously in favour of Benjamin Franklin's theory of electricity by the 1760s, revising it in the laboratory, and installing lightning rods on church spires and towers to prove the practical benefit of understanding this terrifying force of nature.

It was an enlightened pope, Benedict XIV, who did his best to encourage Italy to put the Galileo affair behind them when he authorized the publication of Galileo's *Dialogue* in 1744, 'improved and expanded from an author's copy', as part of the first official Italian edition of Galileo's complete works.[18] In the final year of his papacy, Benedict persuaded the Congregation of the Index to remove the prohibition against all books teaching heliocentrism on 16 April 1757. Galileo's *Dialogue* symbolically remained on the Index, but it was to

---

[17] In Milan, Clelia del Grillo Borromeo collaborated with Antonio Vallisneri and others to create the Accademia Clelia de' Vigilanti. Celestino Galiani helped to found the Accademia delle Scienze in Naples in 1732–44, which was reincarnated as a royal academy by the end of the 1770s. The Accademia Reale delle Scienze of Turin was founded by Count Angelo Saluzzo in 1783.

[18] Galileo Galilei, *Dialogo ... sopra I due massimi sistemi del mondo Tolemaico, e Copernicano ... In questa impressione migliorato ed accresciuto sopra l'esemplare dell'autore stesso* (Padua, 1744). An unauthorized version appeared in Naples in 1710.

all intents and purposes thoroughly vindicated. So modern did the Italians feel in the middle of the century that they celebrated their revival of learning by encouraging a handful of women philosophers to take university degrees and teach subjects such as physics, mathematics, and anatomy. The physicist Laura Bassi's 1732 degree in Bologna, and the forty-six years she subsequently spent as a university professor and member of the Bologna Academy of Sciences, reflected the optimism that many Italians felt about their capacity to enter the modern world ushered in by the important scientific work of Isaac Newton.

If Italian scholars at the beginning of the eighteenth century confessed their frustration in attempting to understand Newton's *Principia* (1687), by the end of the century they could point to numerous Italian contributions to the mathematical and physical sciences as well as the important research in medicine and natural history that had been a continued strength of Italian science from the age of Malpighi to the era of Lazzaro Spallanzani, Felice Fontana, and Luigi Galvani. Visitors to Bologna and Florence gazed in awe at the startlingly lifelike wax anatomies that were a speciality of Italian anatomists in the second half of the eighteenth century. They admired the empirical work of Italy's naturalists in areas such as fossil theory and animal regeneration, and debated the different interpretations of animal electricity—a product of the physical forces of attraction or a specific fluid conducted via the nervous system— offered by the physicist Alessandro Volta and the physician Galvani in the late 1770s. In every city, there was ample proof that scientific activities thrived in the Italian peninsula and did so in self-conscious relation to the intellectual developments in northern Europe that had eclipsed Italy's cultural primacy. Italian scholars did not cease to remind themselves, however, that science had thrived first in Italy. Works such as the mathematician Paolo Frisi's *Elegy of Galileo Galilei and Bonaventura Cavalieri* (1778), the botanist Giovanni Targioni Tozzetti's *Report on the Growth of the Physical Sciences in Tuscany* (1780), and Giovanni Battista Clemente Nelli's *Life and Learned Commerce of Galileo Galilei* (1793) inaugurated the history of science in Italy.

The increasingly complicated politics of the Italian peninsula in the era of Austrian and Bourbon rule meant that institutionalizing Muratori's idea of an Italian republic of letters was still a remote reality. But intellectual life was conducted across multiple boundaries. If there was no single issue or institution unifying the scientific community at the end of the century, it was partly because science itself had become more specialized, more institutionalized, and, to some degree, more professionalized. Academies continued to provide a common meeting ground for many different kinds of expertise. The Church gradually ceased to play as important a role in shaping interpretations of the natural world. In June 1737 Galileo finally enjoyed a proper burial in Santa Croce, where all but three fingers, a vertebra, and a tooth, removed by relic-hungry philosophers during the reburial, remain to this day under a marble stone.

10

The ethnography of everyday life

David Gentilcore

The title for this chapter suggests both an approach and a subject matter. The intention is to explore how the approaches and methodologies of sociocultural anthropology have been applied to the study of the everyday phenomena of social life in early modern Italy. The use of such approaches, beginning in the 1970s, reflected a desire among historians to reach where other approaches did not: to explore the social relationships and interactions among historical persons, people who actually existed and experienced life as a series of events. It was made all the more attractive for Italian historians by the existence of a strong, often quite historically minded, Italian ethnographic tradition. At the same time, it implied a whole new range of theoretical concepts, as well as a new way of going about research, analysis, and presentation. As one anthropologist put it: 'My own approach has been to enter into the historical material—both secondary and primary—much as an anthropologist in the field: beginning with a survey of the terrain and then looking for key informants and key clusters of events, evaluating information as I would evaluate it if it came from living informants, following clues, and relying a good deal on a fieldworker's intuition.'[1] Could historians turn to their subject from the viewpoint of anthropologists without ceasing to be historians? Historians certainly recognized a good thing when they saw it, borrowing both the expression 'historical anthropology' and the

[1] S. Silverman, 'At the Intersection of Anthropology and History: Territorial Festivity in Siena', in R. Trexler (ed.), *Persons in Groups: Social Behavior as Identity Formation in Medieval and Renaissance Europe* (Binghamton, NY, 1985), 36.

approach from anthropologists, for many of whom it was synonymous with ethnohistory. Indeed, the label 'anthropological history' might be a more accurate description of what the historian does (although which discipline is nominal and which adjectival varies with the practitioner). As we shall see, when historians talked about their use of 'anthropology', they frequently meant one specific form of it—symbolic or interpretive anthropology, especially as advocated by Clifford Geertz. His insights appeared to be applicable to the documents Italian historians had available. The label 'thick description' became a totem. When Geertz said that exploring culture meant exploring context, 'something within which social events, behaviours, institutions or processes can be intelligibly—that is thickly—described', he was speaking a language historians could understand.[2]

The historiographical form most amenable to this was 'microhistory'. Microhistory evolved during the 1970s and 1980s, in Italy. It shared with Geertzian anthropology the choice of the small scale as the object of investigation, the use of thick description, and the importance attributed to narrative in the presentation. Its practitioners proposed that a new kind of research would create an ethnographic history of everyday life by devoting itself to extremely circumscribed phenomena. 'Ethnographic' sources suggested themselves, first and foremost written records of oral speech. The judge in a long-distant criminal trial might stand in for the ethnographer, eliciting testimony from witnesses that might approach information supplied by anthropological informants. Microhistory sought to use this evidence in an anthropological way, working from 'actor's categories'. The underlying assumption was the alienness of the past to the present. Practitioners of microhistory also aimed to present their findings in a way that was novel for historians. The stress was on suggesting possibilities, on exploring the complexity of reality, rather than providing complete and straightforward answers. Microhistory was not the only way of practising anthropological history, but the two approaches are so closely related for historians of early modern Italy as to be virtually synonymous. Indeed, much of what follows is based on studies that might be labelled 'microhistories'.

---

[2] C. Geertz, *The Interpretation of Culture* (New York, 1973), 3–30.

Orality and literacy in a composite society

From an ethnographic point of view, early modern Italian culture was neither completely oral nor completely literate but a mixture of the two. This is evident in Carlo Ginzburg's classic contribution to the microhistorical genre, his study of the sixteenth-century Friulian miller Domenico (Menocchio) Scandella. Ginzburg's analysis suggested that Menocchio was an active reader, shaping what he read according to his own world-view, rooted in ancient popular tradition. It tells us as much about that tradition as it does about Menocchio's reading strategies. The work has been criticized for seeking to explore Menocchio's own unique, rather curious cosmology, while at the same time adopting him as a spokesman for an entire culture, otherwise hidden from view—this despite the fact that the evidence of the oral tradition came largely from Menocchio's own ideas. Yet the study remains significant for its exploration of the interface between orality and literacy within a traditional society.

The majority of early modern Italians were illiterate. Historians have shown, however, that their oral culture was every bit as vibrant as the written culture of the elites, and of prime importance in the lives of ordinary people. It has been characterized in various ways: customary, repetitive, communal, group-oriented, local. It has been adopted as one of the defining characteristics of 'popular culture'. Historians believed that this popular culture could be 'read' in much the same way as learned culture, even if the sources might not be quite as direct. They turned to the mass of cheap literature produced during the period as a guide to popular values and opinions. Much of this was supplied by itinerant book-pedlars, selling chapbooks and pamphlets, often the works of itinerant *cantastorie*.

Historians have also studied literate writers who were assumed to be part of popular culture, despite their literacy. This was Piero Camporesi's great contribution. Camporesi revived the fortunes of a little-known seventeenth-century Bolognese writer, Giulio Cesare Croce, in an early study of Croce's *Bertoldo*. Bertoldo is the astute peasant who becomes the king's favourite, only to succumb to the riches of the courtly diet which overwhelms his rustic constitution. In the tradition of Mikhail Bakhtin's exploration of the carnivalesque,

Camporesi used Bertoldo to explore the figure of the peasant through time by mixing literary sources with oral tradition. Camporesi overwhelms our senses with a succession of vibrant and perplexing images conjured up from the past. He used written sources to explore a common oral culture—archaic forms that were at the roots of both. The interpenetration of oral and literate were implicit in his approach. Writing and reading had an important role at all levels of Italian society, which increased with the advent of printing. Thus historians have turned to an investigation of how different forms of communication—writing, reading, speaking—were used and how they interacted in actual situations. There is no doubt that, at the beginning of our period, literacy was on the increase, though it soon reached a plateau (where it more or less remained until Unification). The connection between writing and the 'state' was becoming a closer one. Italian states drew up official reports, the *relazioni*; they developed tax censuses (the *catasto*, *anagrafo*), which required high literacy and numeracy; they relied on secret, written denunciations to initiate legal proceedings; they printed health passes (*bollette di sanità*) to allow uninfected people and goods to move during time of plague; they posted official notices—edicts and proclamations—in prominent public places. In Milan these were known as *gride* ('cries' or 'shouts'), which reminds us that they were not only posted in order to be read (or to intimidate), but were also read out for the benefit of the illiterate.

It is possible that by the sixteenth century a limited ability to read and write for practical purposes was attained by a majority of the urban working population, especially among males. In Venice some male artisans read for instruction and pleasure; few were completely illiterate. Roman labourers seem to have had functional elementary literacy, although their Neapolitan counterparts often did not (due in part to the constant influx of migrants from the provinces, where formal education was more haphazard). Literacy was sometimes suspect. Literate peasants might find themselves on trial as much for their ability to read and write as for the uses to which they put this knowledge. Such was the case in the 1606 trial against Giacomo Baldacci, a peasant from Roversano (near Cesena) suspected of magical practices. How did he learn to read and write? the court wanted to know. Baldacci knew the symbolic and practical value of writing, going so far as to rent a house in Cesena so that his sons could learn to be scribes. This latter point serves as a reminder that, whatever the cultural tensions may have been, we should not regard literacy as a convenient dividing line between two cultures. Writing was certainly a source of power, but it does not follow that the illiterate majority was cut off or helpless. The mayors and aldermen of the Calabrian village of Pentidattilo may have been largely illiterate, but this did not prevent them from engaging in frequent written communication with the royal authorities, via a range of scribes, and so protecting the village's interests.

Although literacy skills varied, the entire peninsula belonged to what has been called a notarial culture. This stemmed from a Roman law tradition which stressed the registration of legal documents (wills, contracts, agreements). When the sick engaged a medical practitioner, for example, they might have a notary stipulate the precise terms, nature, and duration of the treatment. Notaries were often hired by trade guilds to record their (largely oral) deliberations. In this way, guild members revealed quite a sophisticated understanding of how the legal system could serve them. Historians have repeatedly been struck by the competence, indeed confidence, with which people from all walks of life were able to use a complex judicial system to protect or further their own self-interests. From individual Sienese before their own medical magistracy (the *Protomedicato*) to an entire town in the Papal States confronting the authority of the governor's court in Rome, from Turinese before the city's mercantile tribunal to inhabitants the length and breadth of Italy before their local ecclesiastical courts, negotiation was the order of the day.

Ritual behaviour

The historian has to be thankful that everyone at all levels of society did negotiate, and that their words and actions were recorded for posterity. The words and actions set down in judicial proceedings have allowed historians to reconstruct witchcraft beliefs. The concerns of the Counter-Reformation Church to eradicate what it regarded as diabolical apostasy and heresy meant that witchcraft and magic became subjects of choice for a while. Tracing the nature of the judicial encounter, where two mentalities or worlds met—official and unofficial, clerical and lay, urban and rural—became the objective. From the *benandanti* of Friuli (good witches walking the fields in night battles) to the *donne di fuori* of Sicily ('the ladies from outside'), historians focused on how witchcraft beliefs were shaped by the encounter with the courts, sometimes utterly transformed in the process.

Anthropology taught historians that witchcraft and magic did not inhabit a separate sphere from religion. They could be part of the same world-view. The concept of actors' categories was a useful tool in investigating the responses of traditional culture to early modern Catholicism. It reveals how the 'faithful' could be pious in their devotions to saints and yet make use of invocations and spells; how they could choose to be healed by a local physician, living saint, exorcist, or wise woman; and how elements of this 'system of the sacred' could be marginalized over time. The focus on ritual behaviour allows the historian to observe how people coped with the problems of everyday life and how they attached value to these activities. When disease, drought, or sterility threatened individuals and groups, rituals provided a way of bringing 'cosmic order' into daily life. In the sense first advocated by Émile Durkheim, rituals allowed people to tap the powers of the sacred. At the same time, by bringing the participants in them together as a group, they reinforced social dependence. Church-sponsored rites of passage—birth, marriage, death—are obvious examples. Births, necessary for the survival of family and community, were surrounded by official rites of the Church: baptism, the choice of godparents, the 'churching' of the mother. While rituals gain their very force from being repeated, they are not unchanging. The annual cycle of local and ecclesiastical rituals was affected by changes in the structures of social life. These changes made themselves felt with the Counter-Reformation and then again in the latter half of the eighteenth century.

A broader definition of ritual saw it in many forms of repeated, formalized human activity. The study of carnival and carnivalesque festivals—with their temporary overturning of established norms— have been used to focus on practice and the power of different interpretations of rituals. Carnival was centred on the body. It invoked bodily pleasure, but also violent social conflict and protest. This is especially apparent in the ritual combats and dangerous sports of early modern Italy, like the Palio of Siena or the 'bridge battles' of

Venice. On most occasions the disruption was temporary, and things returned to 'normal' after the event. Ritualized rebellion took things a step further, expressing particular aims according to a calendar of its own. The Neapolitan revolt of July 1647 has been interpreted as just such a social drama, whose outbreak was linked to the feast of the Virgin of the Carmine, where a mock battle turned first into a spontaneous riot and then into an organized revolt.

The applicability of the anthropological notion of ritual is perhaps more apparent with regard to government. The governments of the city-states, principalities, republics, and monarchies of early modern Italy adopted, borrowed, and invented an extraordinarily rich repertoire of rituals. The repeated enactment of rituals created the idea of the state as something that transcended the particular individuals who inhabited and governed it. The point was to create a centre of harmony, unity, and continuity, where power was in fact unequally distributed. These functions are evident in Venetian civic rituals, which had the avowed purpose of sanctifying the ruling regime and representing government authority. The absolutist courts, at least until the beginning of the eighteenth century, had their own rituals. They were directed at sacralizing the figure of the prince. His elevated status was expressed in gestures and symbols borrowed from religious liturgical practice. This mixing of secular and religious practices is perhaps most evident in the ritual of papal Rome, where court usage took on increasingly monarchical forms.

Community: place or process?

Attempts to unify the inhabitants of large cities like Venice through ritual belied the very real differences within them. Early modern Italian cities were composed of smaller, distinct communities with their own subcultures. Such were the working-class shipbuilders who lived around the Venetian Arsenale and engaged in the bridge battles mentioned above, or the Neapolitan labourers around the Piazza del Mercato who rioted with Masaniello. In some cities, like Florence and Genoa, neighbourhoods became the power bases of influential families. Historians borrowed from the 'community study', the tradition in the social sciences of basing research on what could in some sense be treated as a bounded group of people, culturally homogeneous and resident in one locality.

The 'communities' anthropologists conventionally studied were villages, tribes, islands. Italian historians privileged the first of these. The closed, local, peasant community—the village—was considered a primary group. It acted as the central economic, ritual, cultural, and social control unit. But how 'closed' was it? Trial records from Pentidattilo suggest the importance of individual honour and reputation, the network of links between men and women, the respective position of insiders and outsiders, the expectations placed on men and women, and the fluidity, vibrancy, and relative egalitarian character of community life within the village. While it was remote and poor, Pentidattilo engaged in frequent and diverse contacts with the outside world. Insider/outsider disputes might manifest themselves in the fraught relations between the community and its immediate hinterland, as in the Ligurian seaside community of Cervo. Inhabitants had a strong sense of 'our place' as opposed to the outside world; they were all 'of the village' (*paesani*). For the South in particular, there has been a tendency to stress the unchanging monotony of peasant life, determined as it was by nature, the terrain, the seasons, religious rhythms. Buildings were similar to one another, shaped by local materials, technical skills, and finances into an 'ostentatious anonymity'.[3] Village toponomy, in the naming of gates, streets, and quarters, reflected the villagers' unchanging mental map of their surroundings. It is easy to exaggerate this inward-looking immobility, however. From an economic point of view, peasant production may have been oriented first and foremost towards household reproduction rather than individual profit, but a knowledge of the wider economic picture was nevertheless essential. Peasants specialized or diversified production, bought and sold land, regulated family size, or migrated back and forth according to changing commercial pressures and opportunities. From a political point of view, when we look at the internal organization of village communities, we find that they could be quite complex and not at all the sites of communal consensus which is sometimes assumed. We also find, looking at their external relations, that villages were far from being either

---

[3] G. Labrot, *Quand l'histoire murmure. Villages et campagnes du royaume de Naples (XVIe–XVIIIe siècle)* (Paris, 1995), 362.

autonomous and self-sufficient or isolated and forgotten (depending on one's point of view).

Anthropologists and historians alike have studied community at a symbolic level: how 'community' is elicited as a feature of social life, how membership is marked and attributed, and how notions of community are given cultural meaning. From this perspective, community can be as much a process as a place, constantly negotiated and contested. It can change according to time and circumstance. From the late sixteenth century, Siena's *contrade*—the administrative districts into which the city is still divided—appear primarily as festival organizations. The Palio was the major function of the *contrade*—a focus for their identity and a stimulus to their formal organization. The parish, as another level of community in Italian towns and cities, was not a constant, unchanging factor. Parish sensibilities ebbed and flowed according to a range of political, economic, social, and religious factors. While communities were systems of social structures and institutions, they were also worlds of meaning in the minds of their members. Through them people expressed the importance of attachment to a common body of symbols: in other words, their identity.

Identity, or 'steering by two rudders'

Like community, identity in early modern Italy was ambiguous. It sustained boundaries by both expressing commonality and sustaining diversity. The study of identity has a long pedigree in Italian historiography, dating back to Jacob Burckhardt's notion of Renaissance individualism. We might define individualism more anthropologically, as the capacity to reflect and to choose among obligations, as part of a process of defining and protecting the self. We could configure the personal identity of the man or woman of early modern Italy through their social networks and personal bonds, as revealed in family memoirs, account books, and diaries. History and anthropology have often been at odds over the weight they ascribe to individuals and groups in society, but there may finally be some convergence in the notion of the 'complex individual'. Such a person, John Martin has written, 'was self-conscious about the degree to which the inner self . . . directed the outer, public self in its daily interactions with one's fellow citizens, subjects, or courtiers'.[4] The self has regained a history (alas, still to be written).

Current notions of the self focus on agency: the ability to act on one's own account, although with reference to others. Agency is involved in the self's management of identity. While the self is experienced as one, identities can be experienced as a plurality. Nowhere is this more evident than in those individuals labelled 'Marranos'. According to one witness testifying in Venice in 1580, a Marrano was 'one who steers by two rudders: that is, he is neither Christian or Jew.' The phenomenon of Marranism puts us squarely in the realm of the individual. Suspects accused before the Venetian Inquisition conjure up the spectre of agency: individual choice, life experiences, cultural and religious ambivalence.

The historian—like the ethnographer—is unable to get at the self directly, in an unmediated fashion. Even the most direct testimonies we can only get as close as their own representations of who they were. And yet this narrative self can be very revealing, offering voyages of discovery, within the self and around the world. For contemporaries, 'Marrano' was synonymous with insincerity. Paradoxically, the Counter-Reformation Church went so far as to encourage such duplicity (or, if you prefer, agency) in the individual in certain circumstances. Catholics who had converted to Islam were given lighter sentences by the Roman Inquisition upon their return, if they could show that their conversions had been only 'external' and not 'from the heart'. What we have are individuals trying to reconcile opposing cultures. The lucky ones were able to carve out a role for themselves as cultural mediators. The Venetian merchant Giovanni Battista Flaminio, captured in Persia, where he converted to Islam (1597), was able to set himself up as factor for the Turks and Persians upon his return to Venice several years later. However, his reconversion to Catholicism was not enough to allay suspicions caused by his continuing friendship with Muslims, and he was denounced to the Inquisition in 1627. In a society of orders, what occasioned the most difficulty were those individuals and groups who inhabited two worlds at once. The resulting cultural promiscuity was regarded as

---

[4] J. Martin, 'Inventing Sincerity, Refashioning Prudence: The Discovery of the Individual in Renaissance Europe', *American Historical Review* 102 (1997), 1340.

dangerous. Of the presence of the Greek rite in his diocese, one bishop lamented that the inhabitants 'are neither good Greeks nor good Latins, because they practise first one thing and then another, according to what is most convenient'.

Group membership was obviously a source of identity: how one saw oneself and how one was seen by others. In addition to protection and security, such groups offered companionship, mutual aid, and a shared life. Occupation had an important role in individual identity formation. Each trade had its own tools and techniques, its own traditions and social practices, and its own corporation to represent it. Work is thus a key site for understanding material and cultural reproduction. But the relationship between work and identity is an indirect one, influenced by a wide range of other social variables: the place the practice of a trade had in an individual's life, the role of different spheres of belonging (sex, age, geographical origin, religion), and the role played by guild classifications and hierarchies in the larger processes of social differentiation. Demarcation disputes between different crafts, or within different levels of the same craft, can reveal relations between the world of work and the other spheres of social life. In a highly segmented society, not all groups will 'belong' to the same extent; each negotiated its status and identity as workers with the centre (the civic authorities) in different ways.

The nature of identity as a process involving notions of commonality and distinction among individuals and groups is perhaps most evident in terms of ethnic identity. For our purposes, ethnicity can be seen as a process of determining and maintaining (or losing) identity in different contexts. How this is done can be observed in terms of the boundary mechanisms between groups—between host and guest, majority and minority cultures. One can see intra- and inter-ethnic encounters as contexts where cultural differences were expressed. Clearly things were very different for the well-placed Spanish 'nation' in Rome than for the Jewish community there. The Spanish made up a fluid and constantly changing group, lacking formal organization, but all linked in some way to the Spanish monarch. From the late sixteenth to the early seventeenth century a group dynamic was at work: in their practices of collective representation, self-constitution, and imagining, immigrants from the historically diverse Iberian kingdoms began to forge a common 'Spanish' identity in Rome. The wealth and power of the Spanish 'nation' contrasted with the changing fortunes of the city's Jewish community. Although it was the oldest such community in Europe, it walked the fine line between protection and persecution. A minor prank perpetrated by a group of young Jewish men in 1551, during Purim—'one evening during the week of our carnival', as one of them called it—suggests a sense of belonging to a shared community. They were all taken as Roman, speaking Roman dialect, and the carnivalesque bound them together, at least temporarily, with the host community in a common morality. At the same time, they could pepper their speech with Hebrew words so as not to be understood. This remains a snapshot, a moment frozen in time. Did the nature of this culture contact change over the centuries? And, adopting the opposite vantage point, did the guest culture have any impact on the dominant host culture? We need more studies over several generations to determine the cultural dynamics of identity formation, maintenance, and conflict over time. Identity was not fixed and passive; it was 'a conscious, reflective process'.[5]

Consumption

A key element in the construction of identity was consumption. Simply put, consumption is the meaningful use people make of the objects that are associated with them. However, this use can be mental or material; the objects can be things, ideas, or relationships; the association can range from ownership to contemplation. Need and demand reflect the ways objects facilitate social relationships and define social identities. This is evident in the conspicuous consumption of the elites. Italian noble families built prominent palaces, furnished them lavishly, relied on liveried carriages, sedan chairs, or gondolas to get them around (depending on the city), wore elaborate but often impractical clothes, held memorable marriages and funerals, and so on. The point was to distinguish a given individual or family from others—whether equals (and therefore rivals) or social inferiors. Such behaviour may have been irrational and wasteful in

[5] R. Weissman, 'The Importance of Being Ambiguous: Social Relations, Individualism, and Identity in Renaissance Florence', in S. Zimmerman and R. Weissman (eds.), *Urban Life in the Renaissance* (Newark, Del., 1989), 271.

purely economic terms, but it was regarded as a duty, even a burden, necessary in order to sustain the honour of the house.

The opposite of honour was shame. If honour meant wearing a great ruff around the neck (whose cumbersome nature signified a detachment from everyday concerns), shame meant being denuded. When the scion of a great princely family, Giacobo Malatesta, wanted to shame a man in his service who had cheated him out of money, he met him on the road and there forced him to undress, having his clothes deposited with the local governor. As a ritual of affront it was like the charivaris (*mattinate*) used to ridicule and demean people suspected of infringing community norms. Clothing was central to social definition, defining one's gender, social rank, occupation, age, marital status, or ethnic identity. It is no surprise to learn that Italian elites possessed large arrays of apparel; but so, too, did certain Venetian dockyard workers. In part, this may be explained by the large market in second-hand clothes. But, clothes, like many other goods, could also be obtained in a variety of ways beyond strictly commercial exchanges. They might be received as gifts or as bribes, they might be hired or borrowed, they might be received in the form of poor relief, they might be given in place of salary or to guarantee a loan, and they might be stolen.

Food was, likewise, a crucial item of social exchange. Indeed, it was perhaps the most powerful instrument for expressing and shaping interactions between people. Any food system has multiple dimensions—material, socio-cultural, nutritional, medical—and all of these interrelate. Early modern Italy was no exception. Take bread, for example. Nothing secured or threatened socio-political stability so frequently as the operations of market arrangements for the selling of grain stuffs and bread. Bread also had immense symbolic importance. Making, breaking, and distributing bread carried profound connotations of friendship, communion, giving, sharing, justice. Within Christian symbolism, bread stood for the body of Christ. It marked the divide between life and death; and this could be quite literally the case, if bread was in short supply or absent (as it so often was). The folklore and mythologies of the time were haunted by the fear and threat of famine, seeking to exorcize them by imaginary flights into Lands of Cockaigne. Real celebrations, like the carnivalesque 'gnocchi bacchanal' in Verona, performed similar functions. By studying the reality and metaphor of bread, Camporesi has shown how hunger and satiation, eating and drinking, digesting and defecating, in all their aspects, dominated both private and public, official and unofficial cultures.

The patterns and meanings of consumption are evident, finally, in gift exchange. Gifts cannot be understood in terms of their market value alone. First of all, they were closely identified with the giver. When Florentine grooms gave presents of jewels and clothes to their brides, they expected to retain or reappropriate the use of them at a later date, sometimes lending or pawning them. This was all conducted in the public gaze; gift-giving was not a private matter between giver and recipient. Nor were gifts disinterested. When the mathematician-astronomer Galileo presented a telescope to the grand duke of Tuscany, it was part of a strategy geared at gaining himself a place at court and a permanent salary. Gifts, along with other services and privileges, underpinned patron–client relations. Through these, clients gained access to political, economic, or cultural resources by manipulating the personal relationships of reciprocity and exchange, honouring their patrons. As a category, 'patronage' has been used for the analysis of ritual interaction in Italian civic life, sense of heritage and identity, kinship and friendship bonds, and political and economic activity. It has helped to understand the culture, politics, and structure of early modern courts, especially when studied alongside forms of courtly etiquette and self-fashioning.

Borrowing the patron–client relations model from anthropology should not mean accepting it as a timeless given. The nature of the relationship varied with the historical context. In early modern Italy, princes tended to value the contributions of potential artist, writer, and architect clients more than those of a natural philosopher. And this is to say nothing of the individuality of each relationship, its place in the survival strategies of a given historical actor. Why was Galileo so successful in his bid for support and prestige, where others failed? The same risks are inherent in the use of 'honour' by historians. Rather than exploring a thing, we are looking at a process: how people acquired, maintained, lost, even regained it. The traditional anthropology of the Mediterranean held that male honour was linked to the reputation of the household, and to the reputation of the women who lived there. As honour was an index of the male reputation, shame was an index of the female reputation. More recent studies, anthropological and historical, have suggested that women have a much more active role in the creation of society and morality. For example, they often controlled the evaluation of an individual's public reputation (*fama*), through the all-important mechanism of gossip. And although often victims, women were not helpless. The deflowering of virgins under pretext of marriage offers an idea of the possibilities open to them to restore their honour and that of their families. They could have recourse to love magic to bring back, ensnare, or harm the 'suitor'. Even the *threat* of magic might have the desired effect. The involvement of Church and state in issues that impinged upon honour also opened up several possibilities: the only reparation considered appropriate was that the man marry the woman, or at least provide her with a dowry. If this failed, there was always one of the charitable institutions for 'fallen' women: from the victims of rape or marital crises, to women forced into prostitution. Such places were a common feature of Italian cities and towns. As in Bologna's Casa di San Paolo, women who had lost their honour could regain it.

The body: parts, processes, products

The body can likewise be a source for the study of meaning and action. We tend to take our use of our own bodies for granted; yet, if we think about it, we are well aware that people in different cultures use their bodies in different ways. The peculiarity of certain Italian gestures—like biting the finger as an insult—struck foreign travellers enough for them to record them. Indeed, the very stereotype of the gesticulating Italian, as held by northern Europeans, may have come into being in the early modern period. But the wider language or repertoire of gesture in early modern Italy can be traced just as well through contemporary judicial records. The point is that culture and society influence how we perceive and use the body.

Early modern Italians were preoccupied with enforcing distinctions between the sacred and the secular, and this manifested itself in the body. At the same time, the distinctions they made are very different from our own. They had no qualms about using various parts of the body for medicinal purposes. Fat was extracted from the corpses of executed criminals, refined, and sold as a painkiller. It was considered natural, given man's place in the cosmos, that the very body that was subject to disease should also provide remedies for it. Nor did they worry overly about carrying out anatomical dissections for the benefit of medical students, as long as proper procedures were respected. Sacred and profane came together in the body, and it was the Catholic saints of the period who took the body to its limits. While human bodies were subject to hunger and pain, prey to a wide range of diseases and, eventually, decay, those of the saints remained impassable and incorruptible, in Camporesi's memorable formulation. Their corpses exuded a heavenly scent—the 'odour of sanctity' was quite literal—which provided the faithful with a reflected image of paradise and countered their fear of hell.

Like Camporesi, anthropologists have been concerned about the cultural and symbolic elaboration of body parts, processes, and products, and about the dimensions of bodily experience in relation to certain practices or institutions. Historians have applied this to various themes: possession, disease and healing, magic, and reproduction, to name but four. They all illustrate long-standing knowledge shared by natural philosophy and theology about the interaction between the human body and the cosmos—knowledge that was itself subject to change during the early modern period. This interaction and integration is evident in demonic possession. It was associated with the female body, which would exhibit the external symptoms of dementia, frenzy, trances, and convulsions. For a phenomenon so 'other', historical studies have sought to discover a logical basis for it, such as a form of folk psychiatry or as status compensation. They have also adopted a conflict model, exploring attempts by the Counter-Reformation Church to combat a perceived proliferation of demoniacs, mostly female, with a proliferation of exorcist manuals, rituals, and practitioners. They have explored the fine line between possession and sanctity, especially within the space of the convent. At the same time, from the sufferer's viewpoint, possession was part of daily experience, embodying personal experience, historical moments, and the sufferer's relationship to the world. In this context, possession can be seen as a form of cultural knowledge, a means of knowing, which takes us out of the individual body.

Forms of healing and classifications of disease do the same thing.

Attempts by historians to explore conceptualizations of sickness and health as part of a particular world-view have been influenced by medical anthropology. One of its notions has been that of medical pluralism: the coexistence of a variety of different medical traditions within a particular context. For early modern Italy this has meant integrating the study of bone-setters, pedlars, wise women, priests, exorcists, and saints into more traditional explorations of physicians, surgeons, and apothecaries. It has also meant problematizing the body. Accounts of healing miracles have been used to explore the different concepts of the body and disease, held by physicians, churchmen, and laypeople. The whole field of illness was increasingly contested—by being categorized in different ways in different levels of society—especially as one proceeds through the eighteenth century.

The female body in particular might be considered a battlefield. Witchcraft accusations from seventeenth-century Friuli suggest that the particularities of the female body—especially the magical power of the womb to give life and destroy it—were the source of the social perceptions regarding women in general and witches in particular. The Church's opposition to the laity's use of the powers of the sacred for their own ends was behind its campaign against magic—and this included the mostly corporeal magic of female witches. In the same way, understanding notions of procreation and conception can lead us back to the wider cultural contexts. Such is the case with Ottavia Niccoli's study of conception and the menstrual taboo in the fifteenth and sixteenth centuries. Niccoli suggests that the link between menstruating women, conception, and monstrous births is not a timeless given—as a merely anthropological approach might suggest. Rather, the link was made at a precise historical moment, in a treatise of 1559. It was only possible as long as the nascent science of embryology took a back seat to theology. Once this ceased to be the case, during the eighteenth century, the belief disappeared from the learned strata of society, only to resurface at the end of the nineteenth century as a folkloric 'relic'. It thus ends up in the anthropological sphere from which it first arose. Niccoli provides a useful example of the often troubled but ultimately complementary relationship between history and anthropology.

In 1972 E. P. Thompson warned that anthropology offered no easy short cuts for the historian.[6] Both anthropology and history have come a long way since then, but the advice is still valid. The risks are just as evident: the applicability of models and concepts derived from one place and time to another quite different one; the assumption that there exists a body of material somewhere conveniently packaged and labelled 'anthropology' which we can dip into at will, rather than a range of conflicting, disputed, and evolving areas and sub-disciplines; and the problem of time—balancing accounts of 'structure' and 'event', and elucidating changes in structure over longer spans of time.

The best anthropological history—including numerous examples of Italian microhistory—has recognized the complementarity of social and cultural analysis. It has focused on the harmonies and tensions which existed at different levels, large and small. The reasons that tempted many historians to turn to anthropology still remain valid: the desire to develop a better understanding of the behaviour, thought, and action of those persons usually ignored in traditional historiography or treated as the passive subjects of history. It allows us to turn to our period in a new way, asking new questions of the past.

[6] E. P. Thompson, 'Anthropology and the Discipline of Historical Context', *Midland History* 1(3) (1972), 45.

PART IV

THE CHALLENGE AND CRISIS OF THE OLD REGIME

11

The public sphere and the organization of knowledge

Brendan Dooley

Introduction: the marketplace of ideas

'The kittens have opened their eyes.'[1] So proclaimed Lionardo Fioravanti in 1576, commenting on the distribution of knowledge about nature to wider and wider audiences. No longer, in his view, could the specialists count on popular ignorance for guaranteeing their prestige. And his statement about the effects of the printing press was applied by Costantino Saccardino, practically word for word, some forty years later, to knowledge about religion. Around the same time that Saccardino was burned for heresy in Bologna, Traiano Boccalini in Rome remarked about the large number of curious minds to which politics was now being exposed. When Ferrante Pallavicino finally added the field of sexual experience to this growing list, no one could deny that a significant change was under way. What was to be this brave new world, in which the secret nostrums and enchantments of the philosophers would be put to everyday use? What would happen if the true nature of religion were revealed, and

[1] Fioravanti quotes the proverb in *Dello specchio di scientia universale* (Venice, 1583), 42; quoted in P. Camporesi, 'Cultura popolare e cultura di élite fra medioevo ed età moderna', in C. Vivanti (ed.), *Storia d'Italia Annali*, iv: *Intellettuali e potere* (Turin, 1981), 87–8.

the techniques used by rulers for gaining and losing states made objects for conversation by the many? What were the risks, if new knowledge of the body were to put the deepest sources of pleasure, so to speak, at the fingertips of all? Political and religious authorities thought they knew. Discipline would slacken. Obedience would disappear. And the tradition-honoured distinctions between categories of people would be erased. In short, a world of lewdness, licence, and libertinism would replace the more ordered one in which they lived.

Almost no one, before the eighteenth century, argued that information of all sorts ought to circulate with total freedom. But between the sixteenth and the eighteenth centuries a developing market for information and knowledge overwhelmed all efforts to hold it back. Few were the ideas, originating in high culture and tending toward the modification or destruction of traditional thought patterns, that did not find their way into academic discussions or even, on occasion, university lesson plans; and few were the popular commonplaces of rebellion that did not find an eventual outlet in the printed word— openly or clandestinely. The wider marketplace of ideas appeared to have enormous consequences for the organization of power. Discussion and debate of issues whose control had previously defined the very categories of authority now took place in a public sphere, potentially open to anyone who wished to take part. From the sixteenth to the eighteenth century, the emergence of this public sphere was itself an object of debate. And one of the great contributions of the Italian Enlightenment philosophers was to recognize a fait accompli—the new organization of knowledge—and to form programmes for social renewal based on what they perceived as a newly instituted power.

Recent research has drawn attention to the precocity of Italy's contribution to this leading European trend. New sources and new methods have helped distinguish the new emerging world from the old disappearing one, during the period covered by this book. This chapter can only trace the bare outlines of a theme that regarded literary history as much as political history, the history of science as well as the history of knowledge, the history of aesthetics as well as the history of conversation.

None of this, of course, is to imply that the mechanisms for the repression of knowledge were not everywhere present or, where present, were ineffective. And discussions about the necessity for censorship and other controls among ecclesiastical authorities were exactly matched by discussions among civil ones. They need no further elaboration here. However, in the minds of the authorities involved, the difficulties of successfully repressing dangerous ideas seemed to be somehow offset by the advantages of encouraging possibly useful cultural expressions in the academies, in the universities, and, especially, in the press. To be sure, the cultivation of favourable expressions in the arts and humanities was nothing new. In the new environment that began to emerge in the early modern period, efforts to direct expressions to the interests of Church and state encountered powerful competition in what was becoming a veritable marketplace of ideas.

Print culture

Already in the sixteenth century, presses were at work in over a 100 centres, from Venice to Palermo, and from Cagliari in Sardinia to Eboli in the kingdom of Naples. Books are difficult to count, and for the two following centuries no complete catalogue yet exists. The information we have indicates a remarkable increase across the period. The early eighteenth-century Venetian printer Girolamo Albrizzi could be excused for the exaggeration when he remarked that 'more books are born today every year than previously in an entire century'.[2] He well knew that judging their quality was no easy task. Half a century later, the Modena-based scholar and journalist Francesco Antonio Zaccaria quipped, 'If the good Lord does not send down some paper-eating pestilence to get so many bad and useless writings out of the way, we will pretty soon have to abandon our homes to give way to these honoured guests, whose indiscretion becomes more odious as their number increases.'[3]

A major change between the sixteenth and eighteenth centuries was the emergence of new instruments intended to convey larger quantities of information to larger numbers of readers. Smaller formats could make printing less expensive, and text from a quarto edition could be squeezed into a duodecimo with considerable

---

[2] *Galleria di Minerva* 1 (n.p., 1696).
[3] Storia letteraria d'Italia 1 (1750), p. vi.

savings in paper—still a precious commodity in the age before wood pulp. No one knew this better than Antonio Bulifon, printer in Naples, whose experiments earned him the epithet, 'inventor of the duodecimo'. A small pamphlet could even be condensed into a single handbill. And by the seventeenth century, even scientists such as Giovanni Domenico Cassini and Marcello Malpighi either had such handbills printed up containing works of theirs, or else considered doing so. Indeed, so widespread did the literature in flysheet, pamphlet, duodecimo, ventiquattresimo, and so on, become that Giovanni Cinelli Calvoli devised a special tool called the *biblioteca volante* ('flying library') in order to keep track of it.

To the many new genres of publication introduced in the first years of printing, the seventeenth century added printed newspapers. Political information that once circulated in manuscript newsletters, commercial correspondence, and diplomatic reports could now be put at the disposal of many. First introduced in Italy by the Genoese writer Pietro Castelli in 1639, on the model of Theophraste Renaudot's *Gazette de France*, and spurred on by the events of the Thirty Years War, newspapers were an instant success. They soon spread to Florence, and eventually they appeared in Venice, Rimini, Mantua, Milan, Ancona, Foligno, Turin, Bologna, Macerata, Messina, Naples, Perugia, Fermo, Sinigaglia, and Fano (to name the centres so far identified). By the end of the century, they were a thriving industry. In the cities of the Papal States, monopolies on certain kinds of news went for twenty to thirty *scudi* apiece, when the entire value of a print shop rarely exceeded 150 *scudi*. In Florence, the state monopoly was bid up from 400 ducats a year to 425. In Naples, where a numerous population made for brisk business, the monopoly cost no less than 800 ducats.

Of course, print was no greater guarantee of the accuracy of information at the time than it is in our own. The government pensions awarded to some journalists, for instance in the duchy of Savoy, to ensure the production of favourable news did little to increase credibility. Lorenzo Magalotti, naturalist and secretary of the Accademia del Cimento in Florence, found news writing to be a source of despair so painful that he included it along with the other causes of philosophical scepticism. But in order for information to become a subject of discussion, it was not necessary to believe the sensationalist stories invented by subscription-hungry journalists or the news about far-fetched achievements planted by publicity-seeking governments. The bad faith of the people who made up such stories became itself a subject of discussion in the public sphere. The Milanese adventurer Gregorio Leti noted, 'Everyone knows that very frequently princes turn losses into victories in order to terrify the people; and, indeed, to bring them into ever greater affection. There-fore, the people, so frequently hoodwinked, always turn victories into losses, forming squadrons at their pleasure and princes to their tastes.'[4]

The variety magazine, another seventeenth-century invention, increased still more the scope for the regular publication of quantities of information. The new genre emerged directly from earlier media for exchanging cultural news, like book catalogues and handbills, as well as manuscript letters, still valid conduits between scholars and amateurs alike. From these occasional media to the regular weekly or monthly issue, with a promise of indefinite continuation, of volumes concerning every aspect of cultural activity interesting to amateurs and specialists alike, was not a very great step, and the first to take it was Denis de Sallo in his Paris *Journal des sçavans*, published from 1665. Soon afterwards came the Roman *Giornale dei letterati*, directed by the mathematician Michelangelo Ricci and collaborators. Ricci's publication was so successful that a pirate version was started up by a printer in Bologna, and it was soon imitated in Ferrara, Parma, and elsewhere. Nor, in spite of the term 'letterati' or 'learned' included in many of the titles, were the new periodicals entirely aimed at a single audience. Giuseppe Malatesta Garuffi explicitly addressed his variety magazine, *Il genio dei letterati appagato* ('The Satisfaction of the Inclinations of the Learned'), to 'whoever, being rather uncultivated, [desires] to throw off [his] own rusticity [*ruvidezza*]'. Many were the readers who fitted that description.

Whether the more voluminous production and importation of printed books during the course of the eighteenth century was any more effective, for communicating to larger numbers of readers, than the 2,200 or so periodicals published in over fifty locations all over Italy during the same period is difficult to say. A few of the more

---

[4] Gregorio Leti, *Dialoghi politici, ovvero, la politica che usano in questo tempo i principi e repubbliche italiane per conservare i loro stati e signorie* (2 vols., Geneva, 1666), i. 255.

specialized examples of the latter, such as the *Saggi* of the Etruscan Academy of Cortona, the *Memorie sopra la fisica e la scienza naturale* of Lucca, and the *Commentarii* of the Bolognese *Istituto*, most probably did not contribute significantly to the sphere of public knowledge we are analysing here, except to the extent that information seeped out of their formula-bespattered pages and into the general stream of culture. We can safely assume that a much more crucial role was played by the many entirely new genres that attempted to break down barriers between reader and writer by introducing a more informal mode of expression. In the *Novelle letterarie* (1740–92) of Florence, compiled at first by Giovanni Lami, shorter articles, more frequent (weekly) publication, and a captivating style made a powerful new appeal. Gasparo Gozzi in Venice, creator of the *Gazzetta veneta* (1660–2) and the *Osservatore veneto* (1761–2), contributed an even more appealing format, drawing upon the experience of the *Spectator* of Richard Steele and Joseph Addison. For his *Frusta letteraria* (1763–5), first published in Venice, Giuseppe Baretti invented an unforgettable journalistic persona: Aristarco Scannabue.

Among eighteenth-century publications, if only for the sheer quantity of information they diffused, the eighteenth-century newspapers would deserve special mention. But the newly expanded formats and double columns, with headlines and characteristic titles to draw readers' interest, were not the only innovations. A century after their first arrival in Italy, newspapers were better written and more critical—although not necessarily more trustworthy. Most importantly, they were run by successful entrepreneurs who sought to offset the rising cost of local monopoly rights by wider distribution. For this reason, the modern historian Franco Venturi was able to use these sources for reconstructing what—to put it in his own words— 'the Florentine reader' of the 1760s (or the Milanese reader or the Venetian reader) 'really kn[ew]' about events going on around them.[5]

We would like to extend Venturi's formula to the entire early modern period, and turn it into a question: what indeed did people know, when did they know it, and how did they know it? Obviously much depended on who and where they were. And in the hundreds, indeed

---

[5] Venturi's analysis is in his *Settecento riformatore*, espec. vol. iii: *The First Crisis*, trans. R. Burr Litchfield (Princeton, NJ, 1989), where I quote from the original Italian p. xvi, and vol. iv: *The End of the Old Regime in Europe*, 1776–1789, trans. R. Burr Litchfield (2 vols., Princeton, 1991).

thousands, of villages and hamlets that dotted the countryside of the various states of Italy, it was still possible to get along without any great awareness of what was going on in the larger cities of the same state, much less elsewhere. But Italy was still a land of large and medium-sized cities. In Venice, Florence, Milan, Naples, Genoa, and the rest of the two dozen or so semi-independent lesser administrative centres, people who did not read for pleasure read for necessity. While their relations with government were mediated more and more by printed proclamations, broadsheets, and even newspapers, their work and home lives were informed by the various trade manuals and books of secrets offering everything from cooking recipes to miracle cures.

To be sure, early modern literacy did not guarantee access to modern culture, but it was a start. In spite of the low profits customarily reported by Italian printers' guilds to their governments at tax time, there was no shortage of readers—or of writers. Gregorio Leti, whom we have already met, was probably not the most dispassionate observer, and we have no way of knowing exactly whom he was attempting to flatter when he noted the extraordinary reading habits of the common people in and around the city of Bologna. Yet his comments, minus some exaggeration, could be extended to almost everywhere else. 'Not only does one very frequently see tailors, cobblers, and other artisans leave their manual work, by which they earn their daily bread, to read some book of history or poetry,' he observed, 'but even the peasants in the provinces around the city mainly talk about poetry and history, and frequently with some intelligence.'[6] Certain satirical prints by Giuseppe Mitelli of common people at their tasks seem to confirm Leti's observations.

Instructional programmes put in place to prevent vagrancy or to win more souls to the truths of faith could plant seeds that might grow in many directions. Male literacy rates of 40 per cent or better were common in the larger cities. In Naples, this required a considerable structure, beginning with literacy training imparted gratis by the religious orders and their lay associates. And in Venice, at the most basic level, there were private instructors—both at home and in the numerous private schools. Next came the six Venetian government-funded humanist schools, one to each section of the city, and parallel

---

[6] Gregorio Leti, *L'Italia regnante* (4 vols., 'Valenza' [= Venice], 1675–6), ii. 81.

to these, the Church's schools for young clerics. In Rome, state-salaried masters in each of the city districts or *rioni* taught poor students gratis and were allowed to charge a fee to whoever could pay. In addition, sixty or so independent schools were registered with the papal government and inspected from time to time.

The university milieu

Beyond the level of basic skills, a lucky few might attend one of the fifteen or so universities scattered around the peninsula. Although this education was still mostly restricted to youths belonging to the elites of Italy and the rest of Europe, enrolments were less than exclusive. Scholarships were provided by some cities to enable poorer students to attend. And for those without a sufficient grammar school background, remedial instruction was usually available in the university town, sometimes as part of the university's official programme.

True, university education before the eighteenth century was more suited to delivering well-tried formulas than to imparting the most recent conceptions in the fields of the arts and humanities. That a good portion of the faculties should be dedicated to preparing candidates for jobs in the bureaucracies and public health services was an important mission for the state officials who ran the universities. The professional associations responsible for accrediting new physicians and lawyers ensured that examinations should be based on proficiency in traditional practices as expounded in a selection of standard texts—Galen and Hippocrates in medicine, Justinian and Gratian in law. Most students came hoping to gain just enough knowledge of these texts to be able to pass the exams. Not surprisingly, for the most part, lessons were still based on the familiar model of text and commentary.

However, universities were by no means dead to the world of ideas developing around them. Let us take, for instance, the fields of natural knowledge. If the mass of instruction in these fields was probably distinguished only by a general mediocrity, some students had the opportunity to hear Andreas Vesalius, Galileo Galilei, Giovanni Alfonso Borelli, Marcello Malpighi, and any of the other top figures who taught at universities in Italy at some point, or even for their entire careers. Some of these figures are known to have sprinkled their university lessons, or even filled them, with ideas based on their own research, at times deviating significantly from the material students might need to know for professional accreditation. And most of these figures are known to have given private or informal instruction to small groups of disciples hand-picked from among the best students.

Nor were regularly enrolled students the only persons likely to gain access to what went on in the university classroom. Apart from the publications whereby university professors customarily diffused the best of their classroom teaching, the public lectures at the beginning of each term might attract members of the city bureaucracy and anyone else in the vicinity. Then as now, professors dared to make more adventurous affirmations by voice alone, on the impulse of the moment, than they would ever make in print. This, presumably, is how some of the notions of Paduan Aristotelianism and its esoteric offshoots, including the mortality of the soul and the spontaneous generation of all living things including humans, passed from elite culture into the popular culture of someone like the Friulian miller Menocchio, where they may have mixed with unorthodox pre-existing conceptions of how the world works.

Eighteenth-century reformers attempted to bring an ever-larger portion of university lessons up to date with respect to contemporary needs. Rather than as repositories of past knowledge, they conceived of the universities as institutions for the production of ideas and concepts useful for modern life. In tune with plans to overhaul the criteria for professional accreditation to reflect this change, they called for the suppression or replacement of study programmes derived from older ways of thought and the introduction of new programmes. By way of new university chairs, they promised instruction in mathematical analysis, natural history, experimental science, hydraulic architecture, military architecture, surgery, veterinary medicine, agriculture, obstetrics, political economy, non-Roman law, notarial arts, and more. To support the new programmes they inspired the establishment of new laboratories furnished with the latest instruments, more abundant collections of natural specimens, better-designed models, and other teaching tools, along with new spaces for practical demonstrations.

The reform of the university of Padua aimed explicitly to deliver more useful knowledge into the public sphere. Reformers proposed a university journal that might inspire professors to outdo one another in the publication of their research results, while providing a place for students and the general public to sample the professors' ideas. The best of the professors would be invited to take part in a new academy of 'science, letters and arts' under the jurisdiction of the Venetian magistrates responsible for the university, where they would be rewarded for their extra work by additional stipends. Spaces for the academy's investigations were to be supplied by the various new structures that had been built or institutions created to supplement the new university curricula. Now these structures would be put at the service of a more broadly based programme of public education.

An environment was thus created for the late eighteenth-century resurgence of Italian universities. And in halls and buildings refitted to accommodate larger enrolments, greater numbers of students were able to profit from the instruction of Antonio Genovesi in Naples, Lazzaro Spallanzani and Alessandro Volta in Pavia, Luigi Galvani in Bologna. At Bologna, the number of yearly graduates increased by a third. At Pavia, enrolments that oscillated between 100 and 150 students at the beginning of the century had doubled by the 1770s, and by 1788–9 had reached over 1,000. Obviously the city of Pavia could not supply a sufficient number of entrants; and among those from outside the state of Lombardy were considerable contingents from the adjacent Savoy states and also from northern Europe.

The urban academies

University culture has often been viewed in opposition to the urban academies dedicated to the arts and sciences. And in the early part of our period, this was certainly the case. Indeed, the dynamic new contexts developing within the academies bore little resemblance to even the most creative of university environments. By a clever system of whimsical pseudonyms and a pseudo-republican form of governance, the academy of the Oziosi (Leisured Ones) in Naples, for instance, cast a subtle veil of courtesy over the deep rifts within a status-conscious society. During their meetings, 'Il Fisso' (the Solid

One), i.e. the poet Giambattista Composta, and 'Il Solitario' (the Solitary One), i.e. Luigi Caraffa, the Prince of Stigliano, might for a moment be judged only on the basis of the poetry they submitted for approval to fellow academicians or the academic orations they gave concerning the nature of beauty, the glories of Naples, the advantages of youth. By insisting on both halves of the Horatian formula—usefulness and pleasure—and not just the first, the academies managed to join amateurs and experts in a common endeavour. In the opinion of their contemporary theorist Scipione Bargagli, they provided spaces where 'a conversational being', by exercising his reason and his intellect with others of his species, 'might easily come to know the truth and understand the good'.[7]

Of course, not all civil conversations were of the same calibre; and few, if we are to judge by the results, could match those held among members of the Accademia della Crusca in Florence. In the first year of their meetings, under the guidance of Leonardo Salviati, they discussed the relative merits of the Latin, Greek, and Tuscan languages, and whether all the sciences could be rendered into the latter. Their project for a scholarly edition of Dante's *Divine Comedy* established their credentials in linguistic matters. When they turned to the compilation of a new vocabulary for use by all Italians, the apportionment of the various vocabulary entries among members was alternated, in their meetings, with questions such as whether to add more words from foreign languages, whether well-known Latin words ought to be included, and whether plebeian as well as elite usage should be represented. These disquisitions bore fruit in the first edition of the vocabulary in 1612, followed by a second, a third, a fourth, by that time well into the eighteenth century.

For sheer transgressiveness, the Accademia degli Incogniti was unsurpassed. Begun by the Venetian nobleman Giovanni Francesco Loredan and collaborators in 1630, it included some of the most important libertine writers of the time—from Loredan himself to Ferrante Pallavicino and Antonio Rocco, and a good many of the novelists as well. The same circles welcomed works by the celebrated Venetian feminist Arcangela Tarabotti and the lascivious poet

---

[7] Scipione Bargagli, *Delle imprese* (Venice, 1594), 516, cited in A. Quondam, 'Le accademie', in Alberto Asor Rosa (ed.), *La letteratura italiana*, i: *Il letterato e le istituzioni* (Turin, 1982).

Giambattista Marino. A chief activity of the academy was to be the publication of works of its members and their associates, under agreements with the printers Giacomo Sarzina and Giovanni Valvasense—including, under false place name, prohibited books and dangerous books still unexamined by the censors. And before a series of trials brought the clandestine branch of this activity to a standstill, it had placed on the market some of the period's most notorious classics on sexual mores, republicanism, and philosophical freedom.

Among the 870 or so academies founded in over 227 centres throughout Italy in the seventeenth century, few were devoted specifically to science. Those few were supposed by members to be better adapted for the free exchange of natural knowledge than the outmoded universities. Already with the Accademia dei Lincei, founded in Rome in 1603, the trend toward specialization began, as also the attempt to limit membership, if possible, to those with something truly original to contribute. No other academy demanded total withdrawal from worldly concerns and collaboration with colleagues in a monastery-like compound. But all the academies in this category, even the Accademia del Cimento founded in Florence in 1657, were committed to some sort of public role, and especially to the publication of results, often in printed form.

At the end of the seventeenth century, the first academy to function as a guide to general cultural endeavour in Italy was the Accademia degli Arcadi, founded in 1690. The reform of poetic taste might seem a field far too esoteric to serve as the basis for any sort of cultural movement at all. But the organizers of Arcadia, Gian Vincenzo Gravina and Giammaria Crescimbeni in Rome, were more than just poets; nor did they compose their verses merely to please the eye and ear. They shared with their Renaissance forebears the conviction that poetry was a branch of rhetoric, and rhetoric a gateway to moral philosophy. In the free spaces they helped create around Italy for the exchange of ideas, reading the great poetry of the past was to serve as an effective public education programme. Writing poetry would focus the minds of dilettantes in every community on the most important values. Within three years of the academy's inauguration in Rome, successful colonies were announced in Arezzo and Macerata. Before long colonies had spread to most of the main cities of Italy and as far as Venetian Dalmatia, with total membership exceeding 1,300.

In the early years of the eighteenth century, Ludovico Antonio Muratori sought to bring independent cultural organization to the next level of social utility. Part programme and part provocation, his 'literary republic', had it gone beyond the planning stage, would have resembled the Accademia degli Arcadi only in its geographical extension. Public education, in Muratori's view, was useless until intellectual culture itself had been improved. He proposed to assemble all the best minds on the peninsula and direct their efforts to the reform and renewal of the disciplines of the arts and sciences. Then and only then, he believed, could new answers be expected for some of the economic and social problems in the Italian states. A series of anonymous diatribes drew attention to these objectives, creating expectations about each successive list of members. Interrupted by the War of the Spanish Succession, Muratori's effort nonetheless set the agenda for the academic movement of the eighteenth century.

In spite of the earlier antagonisms, by the eighteenth century the culture of the urban academies had begun more and more to coincide with university culture. In 1711, Luigi Ferdinando Marsili organized the Istituto di Bologna, Italy's first functioning scientific academy, with the specific intention of making the highest intellectual endeavours known to the local citizenry. Inevitably, members of the faculty at the Institute included faculty members at the University of Bologna. And while the academicians published the more detailed results of their expertise in the volumes of the Institute's *Commentarii*, they gave public lectures in the evening, when university classes were not in session. Subjects ranged from animal respiration to chronometry; from the composition of water to atmospheric electricity; from fossilized wood to the medical uses of camphor; as well as descriptions of natural history expeditions by top members.

In subsequent decades, members of some of the more productive older academies, such as the Aletofili of Verona, the Ricovrati of Padua, and the Fisiocritici of Siena, attempted to adjust the activities of their respective institutions to the new criterion of social utility. The pressing problems of food production and distribution during the middle decades of the eighteenth century spurred a new wave of foundations more specifically dedicated to economic issues. In Florence, Ubaldo di Montelatici founded the Accademia dei Georgofili in order to discover ways of applying scientific expertise to agricultural productivity. His efforts were emulated by a score of similar foundations around Italy; and eventually the Venetian government undertook to place those in its territories under its own protection and furnish them with funding.

From the start, the new academies offered something more than solutions for improving agriculture. They contributed a considerable impetus to discussions about joining intellectual interests to practical ones, theory to practice, and science to technology. There was already considerable precedent for this. Antonio Genovesi was not the first to suggest that 'everything in the sciences that is not useful for mankind is a waste of time'. He only expressed it most forcefully. 'If philosophy has helped us in anything,' he went on, 'it is precisely this: in having disabused us of so many useless applications of our forefathers.' In his view, natural history was the particular field which, pursued at the expense of other more abstract studies, was most likely to 'make Italy less unhappy'.[8] Antonio Zanon joined to this field the study of physics, claiming Voltaire as his authority in this regard.

In fact, the academies were as much fomenters as symptoms of a major change in what might be called the public sphere of science in the latter half of the century. And the publications that purported to cover their activities, such as the *Giornale d'Italia*, run by Francesco Griselini in Venice, or the *Magazzino toscano*, run by Saverio Manetti and collaborators in Florence, helped turn the campaign for more useful applications of science and technology into a commonplace. Manetti's journal claimed to extend its purview to 'the sciences, the arts, economics, erudition, poetry', but especially 'medicine, physics, natural history and agriculture', the latter being not only 'among the most useful' but also 'the most requested from the authors of this work'.[9] Articles concerning ways to bring more marginal land under cultivation appeared alongside reports on the prices of telescopes on the London market. Articles concerning winemaking could be found next to studies on the application of chemical theories to enamelling processes. Public health was a recurring theme in discussions about

[8] Letter to Francesco Griselini, 1764, in G. Giarrizzo, G. Torcellan, and F. Venturi (eds.), *Illuministi italiani*, vii: *Riformatori delle antiche repubbliche, dei ducati, dello stato pontificio e isole* (Turin, 1965), 104.

[9] *Magazzino toscano* 3, pt. 2 (16 July 1772). Cf. *Giornale d'Italia spettante alla scienza naturale e principalmente all'agricoltura e al commercio* 1 (1764), 65, 68, 124, 167, 416; 2 (1765), 57, 78.

the nutritional value of different types of bread and in discussions about methods for smallpox vaccination perfected by Thomas Dimsdale. And public health was joined to social criticism. From the journal's standpoint, it was not enough to criticize mortmain and excessively large property holding as blocks to social progress. Political arithmetic had to be brought to bear on an exact reading of the evidence from parish registers to show what progress had been made.

Although praised by some of the protagonists of the Italian Enlightenment, such as Antonio Genovesi and Cesare Beccaria, for their attention to economic matters, the agricultural academies were criticized by others such as Alberto Fortis for their lack of attention to social and political issues. In the 1760s a new set of institutions emerged, devoted more specifically to such issues. The Accademia dei Pugni (Academy of the Fists), founded by Pietro Verri and collaborators in Milan, joined members in the common task of bringing about more general and incisive reforms in the Italian old regimes. The group's collective efforts not only strongly affected important publications by individual members, such as Cesare Beccaria's *On Crimes and Punishments*; they bore fruit also in a periodical called *Il Caffè* (Milan, 1764–6), whose easy conversational style helped popularize opposition to received opinions and propagate a programme of social and political change. Meanwhile in Bologna, Giovanni Ristori and Sebastiano Canterzani formed a kind of academy known as the Società Enciclopedica, dedicated to the importation, study, and discussion of the French *Encyclopédie* and other foreign publications. Among the many activities of the academy was the printing of works by members; and a major result of the efforts of Ristori and Canterzani was a journal reflecting all these interests, the *Memorie enciclopediche* (Milan, 1781–7).

There is no way of assessing the precise contribution of the agricultural academies, the Accademia dei Pugni, the Società Enciclopedica, and all their imitators and their spin-off publications, to the complex intellectual developments that eventually led to the formation of a science of humanity in late eighteenth-century Italy. At least as important must have been the contribution of the specialized scientific associations newly founded during the course of the eighteenth century, including the Institute of Bologna, the Academy of Sciences in Naples, and the Royal Academy of Science in Piedmont, as well as the combined science and arts academies in Verona and Padua, many of which survived the Napoleonic period and in some form or other exist to this day. All these institutions constituted an important part of the thriving environment around Luigi Galvani, Lazzaro Spallanzani, Alessandro Volta, and the other protagonists of the great eighteenth-century resurgence of Italian science.

The salon

The role of the academies in the history of eighteenth-century knowledge cannot be analysed without taking account also of the classic type of informal sociability known as the salon. Although Baldassare Castiglione furnished the model, in his account of the sixteenth-century salon of Elisabetta Gonzaga, duchess of Urbino, two centuries later there was still no sharp distinction between this type and other more formal private cultural organizations. At times, salons became academies bearing the names of their founders. That was the case of the Accademia di Medinacoeli in Naples, which originated as a discussion group at the home of the duke of Medinacoeli, including the heirs of the tradition of the Accademia degli Investiganti and representatives of the Neapolitan pre-Enlightenment. Alternatively, private schools of eminent educators might function like salons. This was certainly the case at the palazzo in Castelfranco belonging to the Ricatti family, where the quality of discussions, particularly on philosophical matters, impressed a visitor like Leibniz. And although the discussion group of the Dominican friar Tommaso Pio Maffei at S. Giovanni e Paolo in Venice, which inspired Venetian disciples of Isaac Newton including Antonio Conti and Giovanni Poleni, might more properly be called a school, certainly the name 'salon' belongs to the group which sat at the feet of the Franciscan friar Carlo Lodoli at S. Francesco della Vigna, including eminent Venetian patricians like Andrea Memmo as well as visual artists, to discuss the application of modern principles to architecture and city planning. After all, Lodoli himself had benefited from discussions carried on in the palazzo of Venetian nobleman Girolamo Ascanio Giustinian, whose brilliant salon in the 1730s hosted the reformer Pietro Giannone, in flight from Naples. Lodoli's group, and its successor, acquired more of the trappings of worldly sociability than a convent could provide, when it moved into the palazzo of the English consul Joseph Smith, eminent patron of the arts and formidable collector of books including those by the French *philosophes*. Whether Laura Bassi's famous home academy in Bologna ought to be considered a salon is difficult to say. In either case, the practical aspects of experimental philosophy were discussed and demonstrated there, often in the presence of Bassi's students from the university, by the use of a considerable repertoire of electrical instruments and paraphernalia belonging to her husband, the physicist Giuseppe Veratti. Lazzaro Spallanzani is known to have been inspired by her in his eventual choice of a career.

The art of conversation flourished in the capitals of the Italian Enlightenment. The Milanese salon of the duchess Maria Vittoria Serbelloni-Ottoboni was frequented by Pietro Verri and Giuseppe Parini. And although the presence of Parini in the salon belonging to the marquise Paola Castiglione Litta at her palazzo in Porta Orientale is only enough to suggest an interest in modern literature, and not the Enlightenment per se, surely the receptions held at the Palazzo Melzi by Carlo Firmian, the minister of the Austrian government, must have aided their host in his task of implementing many of the reforms suggested by the Milanese Enlightenment philosophers Pietro and Alessandro Verri, Cesare Beccaria, and others. Neapolitan salons in the mid-eighteenth century include the informal gatherings held by Raimondo di Sangro, prince of San Severino, alchemist, naturalist, and collector. Perhaps Raimondo's masonic connections are no more certain indications of his Enlightenment sympathies than his publication of an anti-ecclesiastical tract later placed on the Index of Forbidden Books. Much better documented are the sympathies of Bartolomeo Intieri, the Tuscan economist whose Neapolitan villa became a gathering place for local Neapolitan intellectuals. We know less about the salon belonging to the De Gennaro family in Posilippo, where the Neapolitan cultural luminaries included a future Jacobin, Francesco Maria Pagano.

Renowned more for brilliant company than for contributions to the Enlightenment was the salon of Maria Pizzelli in Rome in the last decades of the century; and the same went for the fashionable circles of the Niccolini and Corsini families in Florence. But even Madame de Staël is reported to have admired the conversations that went on in the home of Luisa d'Albany in Palazzo San Clemente in Florence from the 1770s. The attachment formed by Luisa to the Piedmontese poet Vittorio Alfieri during such meetings determined her eventual transfer to Paris. On her return to Florence in 1792, the salon met every Saturday, reinvigorated by a common animus against the French Revolution, with the hostess occasionally masquerading as Marie Antoinette, and always parading the scandalous *ménage à trois* between herself, Alfieri, and Xavier Fabre. With Alphonse Lamartine among the distinguished guests, the group's interests at this point had already begun to foreshadow the aesthetic of Romanticism.

Café society

For extending the sphere of civil conversation, social intercourse, and informal exchange out of the elegant private homes and into the streets and squares, cafés played a key role. And although coffee as a beverage existed already in the late seventeenth century, a definite café culture did not develop until the eighteenth century. Then, the relaxed environment depicted by Carlo Goldoni in his play *The Coffee Shop* (1750) was repeated in innumerable places all along the peninsula—in over 100 shops in Venice alone. Goldoni's view of the squalid clientele—from careless husbands to hucksters and public whores—did not uniformly apply, if we are to judge from the distinguished histories left by a few of the better-known shops. Gasparo Gozzi furnished a rich testimony of Florian's in Venice, as 'the true school of hospitality', a place where discussions might range from contemporary visual and performing arts to literature and public morals, and where he could count on selling a good portion of the press run of his sophisticated *Gazzetta veneta*.[10] In the same league as Florian's was Caffè Pedrocchi in Padua, frequented by some of the more interesting professors at the university as well as their local adversaries, and, in Rome, Caffè Greco, where the presence of Keats, Shelley, and Goethe has been hypothesized but never proven.

To Pietro Verri fell the task of explaining what could possibly be the lasting social impact of a stimulating beverage sold in the genial environment and relative freedom of a public locale. 'However grave

---

[10] *Il Caffè*, ed. S. Romagnoli (Milan, 1960), 1.

a man may be, even the most leaden on this earth, he will inevitably reawaken, and at least for a half hour, become a reasonable person.' When the remarkable properties of the beverage were combined with places to sit or stand at ease, and the best company to be found in Rome, Padua, Venice, Pisa, Luca, Florence, or, as in this case, Milan, there was no telling what might happen. In Verri's view, published in the pages of the characteristic periodical *Il Caffè*, high-spirited persons and cultivated intellects turned their meditations and their discussions to love of the public good and the search for truth, which, paraphrasing Pythagoras, 'are the only things whereby ... humans resemble gods'.[11]

Conclusion: the court of public opinion

When did the modern public sphere of persons making public use of their reason emerge in contrast to traditional authorities in Church and state? In a widely quoted formulation, Jürgen Habermas saw the first signs of change in seventeenth-century England, followed by the various parts of continental Europe well into the following century. Yet the story we have told in these pages suggests some refinements at least to the Italian portion of this scheme. Gregorio Leti noted that the allotment of praise and blame was effective in holding governments accountable for their actions already in the 1660s. Tyrants, he explained, used to commit crimes knowing that their evil actions would never be made public, and that their very presence would inspire awe and adoration. All this had now changed. Now rulers, fearing adverse publicity, kept their more irresponsible impulses in check. 'They see their peoples all set with their tongues wagging ready to spread throughout the public squares the poison of discord that can turn monarchies into republics,' he said. 'Therefore, if people's silence turned princes into tyrants, peoples' constant jabbering has turned tyrants into princes.'[12] The historian Vittorio Siri, writing some twenty years after John Milton penned the *Areopagitica*, referred to public opinion as a virtual court of law. 'The generality of

---

[11] Quoted by Alberto Lorenzi in E. Falqui (ed.), *Caffè letterari* (Rome, 1962), 273.

[12] *Dialoghi politici*, i. 250.

men', he claimed, 'consists of an inexorable tribunal instituted by nature to judge with the fullest liberty and to pronounce upon the actions not only of rulers but also of private and humble persons, to allot to them the blame or praise that they deserve.'[13]

From these affirmations to the modern formulation of the public sphere was only a small step. And the Neapolitan legal theorist Gaetano Filangieri took that step in the 1780s, when he proclaimed that public opinion had become an immovable fixture of life all across Europe. This 'tribunal', as he called it, 'stronger than magistrates and laws promulgated by ministers and kings', stood 'inexorable and indomitable', demonstrating that 'sovereignty is constantly and really with the people'.[14] To him, and to many others by the end of the eighteenth century, the only public sphere worthy of the name was the public sphere of democracy.

[13] Vittorio Siri, *Mercurii*, vii (Casale, 1667), 382.
[14] F. Venturi (ed.), *Illuministi italiani*, v: *Riformatori napoletani* (Milan, 1962), 748.

12

Enlightenment and reform[1]

Anna Maria Rao

Introduction: the relationship between Enlightenment and reform

For Italy, too, the eighteenth century was the age of Enlightenment and reform. But, as in the rest of Europe, this did not mean that the institutions of government in Italy suddenly became the object of an irresistible desire for reform, nor were Enlightenment and reform linked directly as cause and effect. In fact, much of recent historical debate on eighteenth-century Italy has been devoted to exploring how the Enlightenment and reform were linked, and also the extent to which it would be more correct to think in terms of distinct 'national' enlightenments, each with features that made them specific and hence different from France.

Since the 1960s study of the Enlightenment in Italy has been profoundly influenced by the work of Franco Venturi. Venturi's studies set out a clear general interpretation as well as a critical periodization of the main developments. In particular, Venturi has shown convincingly that it was not until after the War of Austrian Succession (1740–48) that much broader and more effective reform policies began to be shaped. These initiatives coincided with the birth of a new intellectual movement that was deeply influenced by the ideas coming from France and the rest of Europe. This movement's inspiration

[1] Translated from the Italian by John A. Davis.

came from a new concern to pursue knowledge free of all forms of censorship or self-censorship, with the aim not of accumulating abstract learning, but of acquiring knowledge of public and practical utility in order to change the existing world.

Some have argued that Venturi's interpretation returned to the tradition of idealistic history inspired in Italy by Benedetto Croce, in which ideas would seem to be the principal motor of historical change. But this is to miss the point that Venturi's interpretation and periodization are convincing, precisely because it was in these years that a remarkable convergence of different economic, social, political, and cultural developments took place. In fact, from the 1750s onwards, it was these changes that were the real driving force behind reform initiatives taken by the Italian rulers. In contrast to the past, however, these initiatives were no longer addressed simply at solving specific financial or fiscal issues, but reveal more ambitious projects for changing society and the state as a whole. It was through the writings and ideas of numerous independent intellectuals and thinkers that this great reform project was constructed and defined.

The motives for the reforms, their objectives, and the means employed to realize them varied according to time and place. Most reforms originated as empirical solutions to specific problems and were implemented according to need and opportunity. Nonetheless, they shared many common features, in particular, the central and increasing role of state intervention, which now reached out to extend and strengthen its authority to fields like education and public welfare that had been previously controlled by the Church, the family, or the community in ways that began to redefine the boundaries between public and private spheres. In the early decades of the eighteenth century the pressing financial burdens arising from warfare and military expenses had been the principal motives for a variety of attempts to reorganize state administration. Such initiatives were directed at increasing the rulers' control over fiscal revenues and devising more effective and rational ways of distributing and raising taxes. But after the mid-century, and especially after the 1760s, a new spirit inspired the reform initiatives and spread the need in civil society to reorganize the whole structure of the state, to establish bodies of political representation, and to practice civil equality and liberty. The aspirations for change were never clear-cut, and from the start they also echoed forms of opposition to absolutism that had very different roots in the defence of older corporate or regional autonomies.

The thinkers and writers of the Enlightenment, as well as the masonic lodges that were rapidly expanding throughout Italy, gave great prominence to the role allocated to the 'philosopher-king' in the reform process. The principle was that rulers needed first to be virtuous in order to perform satisfactorily their highest mission, which was to promote 'public happiness'. This ideal, which historians of the eighteenth century have termed 'enlightened despotism' or 'total absolutism', influenced both the policies adopted by many rulers as well as the ways in which many eighteenth-century rulers consciously chose to represent themselves.

The increasingly public nature of the debates on reform, together with the circulation of men and ideas from one state to another, made possible the construction of political and administrative reform projects in which different governments shared common goals. The reform movement took different forms in each state, but it was still remarkably unified in its aims and goals. This was in large part because of the debates that were now being conducted from one end of Italy to the other through newspapers and journals, literary and scientific societies, and private correspondence. Freemasonry and masonic associations also played a critical role in the dissemination of the new ideas and the creation of new forms of public opinion.

The reform movement was deeply influenced by economic events, in particular the terrible famines of the 1760s and 1780s, and by major international events such as the Seven Years War (1756–63), the American War of Independence (1776–81), and the French revolutionary wars after 1789. Thus, specific economic, social, political, and cultural developments explain why, at the very moment when it seemed to have attained its greatest influence in the 1780s, when its followers began for the first time to reach beyond the capital cities to the main provincial centres, the reform movement entered into crisis. This linkage to internal and external events makes it clear that the crisis of the reform movement in Italy predated the Revolution of 1789 in France, which would bring with it very different models for changing the world.

The Wars of Succession

The Italian states were deeply affected by the European wars that were fought to settle the succession of the crowns of Spain (1701–14), Poland (1733–38), and Austria (1740–48). As a consequence of these wars, Spain's two-century domination of Milan, Naples, Sardinia, and Sicily gave way to a situation in which power was shared between Bourbon Spain and Habsburg Austria. In addition to the Duchy of Milan, Austria now controlled the Duchy of Parma and Piacenza (which had formerly been possessions of the Farnese family), as well as Tuscany where the Habsburg Dukes of Lorraine replaced the ancient Medici dynasty when it ran out of male heirs. In 1734 the kingdom of Naples was reunified with Sicily and acquired its own king, Charles of Bourbon, the son of Philip V of Spain and Elisabeth Farnese. But in 1748, under the terms of the Treaty of Aix-la-Chapelle, the Duchy of Parma passed to another son of the king of Spain, Philip of Bourbon. The annexation of Sardinia to the Piedmontese state ruled by the Dukes of Savoy brought into being a new monarchy, with the title of the kingdom of Sardinia. The temporal possessions of the Papacy, the ancient Republics of Genoa, Venice, and Lucca, and the Duchy of Modena and Reggio ruled by the Este family all survived in the former state, but the ancient Duchy of Mantua that had formerly been ruled by the Gonzaga family now disappeared to be partitioned between the House of Savoy and Austria.

In 1737, Scipio Maffei—a noble and erudite scholar from Verona, as well as a friend and correspondent of Ludovico Antonio Muratori, with whom he championed the common struggle for the freedom of historical research—wrote in a tract entitled *A Proposal for the Permanent Preservation of the Republic of Venice in the Present State of Italy and Europe*: 'When Italy is discussed, its peoples are treated as though they were flocks of sheep or some other lowly animals. In the great international peace congresses, Italian ambassadors are either no longer admitted or else are left to cut a sad and wretched figure'. Maffei's treatise was not published until much later in 1797, when it appeared under the title *Political Advice*.[2] This was shortly after

---

[2] *Consiglio politico. Finora inedito. Presentato al governo veneto nell'anno 1736. Dal marchese Scipione Maffei. Diviso in tre parti* (Venice, 1797).

French republican armies led by Napoleon Bonaparte invaded Italy in 1796 and founded the short-lived Italian Republics (1796–99). In these years Maffei's text was widely cited in the post-invasion debates, which focused on the contrasts between liberation and conquest, between the Mother Nation (France) and its sister Republics, and also on the prospects for Italy's political unification which, during the three-year period of the Italian Republics, set the supporters of the Revolution in Italy (who called themselves 'patriots') in opposition to the government of the Directory in France.

When it was first written 60 years earlier, however, Maffei's tract had been more specifically concerned with finding ways to halt the decline of the Venetian Republic. But beyond that immediate aim, it also offered important insights into the political situation in Italy during the Wars of Succession, which had already stimulated thought about the proper relationship between rulers and their subjects, the best means of fighting successful wars, of maintaining peace within individual states, and on the reasons for the decline of great empires. It was not military might that guaranteed the survival of monarchies, Maffei insisted, but good laws and the happiness of their subjects. Those views had been expressed earlier in Naples in 1709 by another learned nobleman of Genoese origin, Paolo Mattia Doria, who had written that only 'those peoples who are united, virtuous and strong' are able to 'defend their Prince and their State'. In his *Treatise on Taxation* (1743), the economist Carlantonio Broggia also argued that the existing tax systems needed to be reformed not simply to improve the finances of the state, but above all to acquire and maintain popular support: 'More than the armies of his enemies, the Prince should fear and take careful heed of the discontent of the poor, especially when that discontent is caused by unjust taxes'.[3]

In this early period, however, attempts to reorganize the administration of taxes were driven primarily by the need to meet the costs of warfare rather than any desire to gain the support or promote the well-being of the ruled. Newly installed dynasties, as well as local ruling elites, often attempted to reorganize public administration with a view to extending their respective authority and power. This

---

[3] Carlantonio Broggia, *Trattato de' tributi* (1743), cited in Anna Maria Rao, 'Organizzazione militare e modelli politici a Napoli fra Illuminismo e rivoluzione', in *Modelli nella storia del pensiero politico*, vol. II: *La rivoluzione francese e i modelli politici*, Vittor Ivo Comparato (ed.) (Florence 1989), 43–6.

was the case in the kingdom of Sardinia where the so-called 'constitutions' of 1723 and 1729 created a uniform code of law, gave the ruler control over the entire school system, and at the same time established the first public secondary schools. Following the model of absolutist monarchy set by Louis XIV in France, the reforms of this period aimed at increasing the centralized powers of the state, reducing privilege, and establishing administrative uniformity.

One of the central aims was to regain control over public finances, which was done by establishing central and provincial administrative institutions and offices (such as the office of the provincial Intendant in Piedmont) that were either new or else endowed with new powers. Their purpose was to redistribute taxes and to limit the rights of others to raise taxes at a local level. But the starting point for any broader reorganization of the tax system was the compilation of registers of land ownership known as *catasti* (cadastral surveys). These registers were an essential instrument for achieving more rational distribution of the tax burden and also for reducing the fiscal immunities enjoyed by feudal landowners and the Church. Compilation of the cadastral surveys was a massive and time-consuming undertaking, and in practice they were often far from complete. In Piedmont work on compiling the land register had been started in the late seventeenth century and was completed in 1731. In Naples it was not launched until 1740, but was completed in the 1750s. In Milan the register was started in 1718, but was then suspended in 1733; it was then completed in 1758 thanks to the creation in 1749 of a special commission or 'junta' headed by the Tuscan Pompeo Neri. In Lombardy, the introduction of the land register was accompanied in 1755 by the reorganization and standardization of local government, while in 1751 all previous tax-farms were unified in a single General Tax Farm that greatly simplified the raising of indirect taxes.

The new property registers dealt a heavy blow to the tax privileges enjoyed by the Church, while a spate of new laws eliminated jurisdictional privileges formerly enjoyed by the clergy and ecclesiastical institutions (including abolishing the right of sanctuary and the jurisdiction of the Inquisition courts). The rulers' control over the nomination of bishops and the exercise of censorship was also extended. All these changes were reflected in the Concordats drawn up between the Papacy and the kingdom of Sardinia (1727 and 1740), the kingdom of Naples (1741), and Austrian Lombardy (1757).

The rulers also made great efforts to reorganize their armies and navies, especially (but not only) in the states that were most closely involved in international affairs like the kingdoms of Sardinia and Naples. The reorganization of public administration also encouraged professional training for public employees and officials in civil administration and in the armed forces, and the new military colleges that many rulers set up to train officers for their armies quickly became the principal means for acquiring scientific and technical knowledge. The reorganization of fiscal and military institutions had important implications for the role of the nobility, too, and edicts redefining the status of the nobility with a view to transforming them into a class of public servants and military officers in the service of the state were issued in Piedmont in 1720–22, in Rome in 1746, in Tuscany in 1750, and in Naples in 1756.

The 1760s: famine and the 'patriotic turn'

The relative political stability and peace that followed the Treaty of Aix-la-Chapelle (1748) concluding the War of the Austrian Succession also had far-reaching economic and cultural consequences. Once the danger of a single foreign power taking on the hegemonic role that Spain had held in Italy in the two previous centuries was averted, the two major independent Italian rulers—the king of the Two Sicilies and the king of Sardinia—seemed finally free to assume leadership in the Italian states of the centuries-old struggle to reduce the political influence of the Church. Freedom from warfare and relative political stability also created the opportunity to address a wide range of other domestic problems. This new balance of power did not mean that Italy was no longer an object of the expansionist or dynastic intrigues of the other European powers. Until the start of the revolutionary wars at the end of the century, the great European powers no longer pursued hegemony in Italy by military means, but rather they created spheres of influence through public opinion, through propaganda, through the networks of Masonic associations, and through trade and commercial pressures.

In addition to the favourable international situation, other and more general developments were also creating pressure for broader reform projects. Expanding population, rising prices for agricultural products, the more general economic recovery, and growing external demand for agricultural products and raw materials increased the importance of those social groups who had the strongest interest in changing the existing distribution of land-ownership and the organization of agriculture. At the same time merchants and manufacturers were also beginning to call for measures that would unify domestic markets, improve access to external markets, provide incentives for production, restrict feudal and ecclesiastical property, bring better roads and infrastructures, and shorten cumbersome bureaucratic procedures.

Voltaire wrote that in France after the 1750s 'the nation began talking about corn', that is to say about economic, political, and social issues, and this was true in Italy as well. For the first time economic issues began to be discussed in the universities, and in 1754 a chair of 'Mechanical Arts and Commerce' was created in the University of Naples where the first courses in political economy in the whole of Europe were now taught. Antonio Genovesi was the first incumbent of the chair; and in his *Discourse on the True Object of Letters and the Sciences* (1753), he insisted that philosophy should be 'concerned only with things', in other words, with acquiring the practical knowledge needed to change the economy and society.

Between 1700 and 1750 the population of the Italian peninsula had risen from 11.5 million to 15.5 million inhabitants. The rate of increase was highest in southern Italy and on the islands of Sicily and Sardinia, but overall was a modest 35 per cent in comparison with an average of 64 per cent for the rest of Europe in the same period. The ways in which the population was distributed revealed many of the distinctive features of Italian society, however, and most obviously the very high density of the urban population. Five capital cities, for example, had populations that exceeded 100,000: Milan, Venice, Rome, Palermo, and Naples, which with 350,000 inhabitants remained the third largest city in Europe. As elsewhere in Europe, the vast majority of the population was nonetheless rural and agriculture remained the principal economic resource of Italian society. Forms of agriculture varied enormously from one end of the peninsula to the other, and included both the large and smaller feudal estates that were found throughout the kingdom of Naples and Sicily, in southern Lazio, in the Duchy of Modena and in Savoy, as well as the small and middling peasant farms that were the most distinctive feature of the states of central and northern Italy. In addition to feudal estates, Church properties were extensive and included not only land, but also a vast range of buildings, dues, and taxes held under various titles. As well as being subject to the burdens of seigneurial, Church, and state taxes and levies, the countryside was also obliged to meet the subsistence needs of the cities through provisioning regulations that were believed to be essential for the maintenance of public order and 'tranquillity' in the towns.

The terrible famine of 1763/64 that struck the cities of Naples, Rome, and Florence with particular severity shook the climate of confidence that had grown up with the return of peace to Italy. The disastrous effects of the famine demonstrated that peace alone had not been sufficient to guarantee economic revival and confirmed the urgent need for reform. The Lisbon earthquake of 1755 had already dramatically raised questions throughout Europe about human ability to oppose the forces of destruction that were inevitably present in nature, and the Italian famines of 1763 and the epidemics that followed them revealed in no less dramatic terms the fraught relationship between man and nature and the fragility of human life.

For the thinkers of the Enlightenment, however, famine and disease were no longer signs of inscrutable divine will. Instead, they were seen as the consequences of bad institutions, which could be corrected by informed government intervention. As a result, the famines came to play a critical role in re-launching the debates on economic reform and on the jurisdiction and powers that the sovereign should exercise. As they progressed, these debates and inquiries began to expose the defects of the existing organization of agriculture and to focus attention on the conditions of the provinces. If the provinces were the granaries of the capital cities, their condition also revealed the tremendous harm caused by the ways in which the grain trade was organized.

The 1763/64 famine therefore strengthened and gave new urgency to the calls for greater freedom of domestic trade and for doing away with the provisioning regulations that had paralysed the government's capacity for responding to the crisis caused by the failure of the harvest of the early 1760s. However, these regulations continued to find strenuous defenders among the urban consumers who were the principal beneficiaries of price controls imposed by paternal rulers. But the famine and the epidemics that followed also focused new attention on the issues of poverty, on the marginal groups in society, on living conditions and public hygiene in the major cities, and on topics like the need to build cemeteries outside densely inhabited urban areas.

Such considerations led Pompeo Neri and a group of Tuscan agronomists to propose the radical reorganization of urban provisioning through the removal of controls on the price of bread and the introduction of new farming methods and leases to improve agricultural productivity. Similarly, the provisioning crisis lay behind Grand Duke Peter Leopold's decision to convert the ecclesiastical and public lands managed by the state in Tuscany into quit-rent leases that were to be granted in perpetuity to peasant farmers, and to abolish all internal customs duties as well as the guilds. In his *Lessons on Commerce* delivered at the University of Naples, Antonio Genovesi also proposed that all Church land should be converted into peasant lease-holds.

Even in those parts of Italy that escaped the worst of the famine, the condition of agriculture was still very much at the centre of attention. In Milan Cesare Beccaria lectured on the 'Science of Administration' ('Scienze camerali'), while in Genoa Gerolamo Gnecco published his *Reflections on the Conditions of Agriculture in the Province of Genoa* in 1770. Everywhere proposals were put forward designed to rescue the peasants from oppression and ignorance, and as a result of these debates the government decided to abolish controls on bread prices in Milan in 1770–71.

Discussion of the obstacles to economic development took on a greater sense of urgency as awareness grew of the gap that separated the Italian states from the most advanced European countries. But the widely shared belief that the Italian states were backward in comparison with the leading European powers in both economic and military terms served to place even greater importance on the need to discover the means that would enable Italy to achieve economic development and hence catch up with its rivals. Without discarding their cosmopolitan outlook, among writers and thinkers these concerns gave rise to a new sense of being part of a specifically Italian cultural community with its own linguistic and literary patrimony.

This was very clearly stated in an article by Gian Rinaldo Carli that was published in the journal *Il Caffé* in Milan in 1765. Carli appealed for men of letters to join in a common effort to achieve scientific and artistic progress 'for the universal good of our nation' and he also called for a broader sense of patriotism to replace more localized identities:

No matter whether cities be large or small . . . are situated in one place rather than another . . . are separated in different domains or are subject to different rulers, when it comes to the progress of the sciences and the arts they are all part of a single system; let the love of patriotism, which is to say, of the universal good of our nation, be the Sun that illuminates and attracts them. Let us love the good wherever we may find it, and let us seek to promote and inspire it wherever we find it to be lifeless and languishing . . . By so doing we shall all once more become Italians, without ceasing to be human beings.[4]

During the period of the struggles for national independence in the nineteenth century, Gian Rinaldi Carli's appeal was frequently cited as an example of the dawning of a new Italian national identity. But it is probably better understood as an expression of a more widespread 'patriotic turn' that was taking place throughout the Italian states towards the end of the 1760s. More than a sense of attachment to a specific place of birth or the defence of its traditions, this sentiment derived from Rousseau's description of the *patria* as a community founded on the virtuous pursuit of the public good and public happiness through the implementation of good laws. During the Corsican revolt against Genoa in 1755 led by Pasquale Paoli, this patriotism openly took the form of the demand for constitutional government that anticipated forms of representative democracy. However, the cession of Corsica to France in 1768 meant that the realization of these aspirations would have to be deferred to other times.

Milan and Naples were the principal centres for the diffusion of Enlightenment culture, in the first case thanks to the activities of Verri, Beccaria, and the group associated with the journal *Il Caffé*, and in the second because of the influence of Antonio Genovesi's teaching at the university. The principal topics of debate were the system of urban grain-provisioning, agriculture, land reclamation projects, and monetary issues. It was this essentially pragmatic and applied

---

[4] *Il Caffé 1764–1766*, Giovanni Francioni and Sergio Romagnoli (eds.)(Turin 1993), 422–7.

character of Enlightenment thought in Italy that made it distinct from its French counterpart, and many of the leading Italian thinkers—Pietro Verri, Cesare Beccaria, Gaetano Filangieri, and Giuseppe Palmieri to name only a few—held important and influential positions in public administration. In Piedmont many of the reformers were public officials or technical experts, as in the case of Giambattista Bogino who served as a Minister of State from 1750 to 1773. In Tuscany Francesco Maria Gianni was also the principal architect of the reforms introduced in the name of the Grand Duke Peter Leopold after 1765.

For the realization of their projects the intellectuals initially looked above all to the state and to the 'enlightened' rulers. Not all the rulers could boast the training in philosophy that the Duke of Parma, Ferdinand of Bourbon, had received from the French philosopher Condillac, but most understood the advantages of employing senior officials who were strongly committed to the idea of the State and its autonomy vis-à-vis the Church. Their mobility from state to state also played an important role in the circulation of ideas and reform projects. Pompeo Neri, for example, served in the administrations of the Dukes of Lorraine and then of Peter Leopold in Tuscany, but was also active in Maria Teresa's administration in Lombardy where he helped complete the land register. The Piedmontese reformer Paolo Paciaudi also contributed to the enlightened policies introduced in the Duchy of Parma as an adviser during the ministry of Du Tillot. Bernardo Tanucci came to Naples from Tuscany, and his long ministry from 1755 to 1776 marked a critical moment in the struggle against both feudal and ecclesiastical privilege. In Milan, the ministers Kaunitz and Firmian were the true authors of Maria Teresa's reform progamme, while the Lombard land register—the most advanced in Italy—was the collaborative work of specialists and technical experts from all over and has been described as 'the fruit of the joint efforts of reformers from all over the peninsula, supported by a foreign dynasty that had sufficient strength to overcome the resistance of the local ruling groups'.[5]

Once the famines of the 1760s had passed, the reformers began to think about agriculture in terms that went beyond the simple issue of fiscal revenues. Agriculture now became a science and proposals for

[5] Carlo Capra, 'Il Settecento', in Domenico Sella and Carlo Capra, *Il Ducato di Milano dal 1535 al 1796* (Turin 1984), 350.

agricultural improvements were increasingly linked to projects for broader social reforms. There was now broad agreement that traditional ways of organizing peasant labour were counter-productive and damaged the productivity of the land. At the same time the gradual diffusion of the economic theories of the French physiocrats and the *laissez-faire* economists, together with the increase in the number of newspapers, academies, and agricultural societies enabled those engaged in these debates to acquire new forms of self-awareness, new forms of organization, and new ways of expressing their ideas. As a result, they began to put forward proposals for the redistribution of landownership by arguing that the expansion of small and middle-sized peasant proprietors was a necessary premise for improving the ways in which the land was cultivated. In line with contemporary population theories that identified the wealth of a nation with the number of its inhabitants and of labourers available for agriculture, they also argued that these measures would also cause the population to increase. Similar concerns about labour productivity gave rise to new proposals for assisting the unemployed and for reducing the numbers of beggars and vagabonds, many of whom were now to be shut up in specially designed hospices and work-houses.

From the 1760s economic issues were at the centre of the attention not only of men of letters and science but also of governments, and this would have important consequences for the administrative organization of the states. Pretty much everywhere special ad hoc commissions staffed by economists and technical experts were set up in the attempt to overcome the opposition to change mounted by the tribunals and magistrates. The Supreme Council for Economic Affairs that was created in Milan in 1765, for example, signalled a decisive shift in the politics of reform. Carli was its president and Pietro Verri was also a member, whereas members of the traditional patriciate and magistracy were excluded. Similar tasks were assigned in 1771 to the newly formed Magistrato Camerale. In Genoa, a Deputation of Commerce was created at the end of the 1770s to advise the government on technical and economic matters, while in Naples a Supreme Council of Finance was established in 1782.

The problems relating to the Church now began to be tackled in a more comprehensive manner and in ways that went beyond purely jurisdictional issues. The spiritual offices of the clergy were redefined, limits were placed on the wealth that religious foundations might accumulate, and the number of regular orders was reduced since they were considered to be damaging to the economy. In the year that the Jesuits were expelled from the Italian states, Carlantonio Pilati, a former professor of civil laws in Turin, published the first volume of his treatise *Concerning the Question of Reform in Italy* (1767 and 1770), in which he listed among the 'devastating wounds' that afflicted Italy: the overweening power of the clergy, superstition, economic backwardness, legislative disorder, and the maladministration of justice. He concluded with an appeal for a radical and comprehensive reform of Church and state. In 1768 a Tuscan writer named Cosimo Amidei published anonymously a tract entitled *The Church and the Republic, Each Within its Limits*, in which he appealed to the rulers to protect 'the philosophical spirit' and the sovereignty of the state from all forms of ecclesiastical intervention.

The expulsion of the Jesuits in 1767 and their suppression as a religious order by Pope Clement XIV in 1773 placed vast tracts of land at the disposition of rulers and made possible a general reform of schools and public education. New laws on mortmain limited the size of donations that might be bequeathed to religious foundations. In Milan decrees of 1768 and 1779 halted recruitment to mendicant orders and suppressed many smaller convents. In Naples Charles of Bourbon had already used the revenues of suppressed monasteries to finance the city's monumental new Poor House (Albergo dei Poveri, 1751) and in 1783 his successor Ferdinand IV seized the lands and possessions of the Calabrian monasteries to finance the work of reconstruction following the devastating earthquake that struck vast areas of Calabria and Sicily in 1783.

Measures to limit the jurisdiction of the Church were being vigorously pursued everywhere. These policies dated back to the early seventeenth century when they had found a distinguished early champion in Paolo Sarpi. But it was only towards the end of the eighteenth century that the rulers set out to address the general problems posed by ecclesiastical interference in economic as well as jurisdictional terms. Responsibility for censorship of the press, for example, was transferred from the courts of the Inquisition to secular censors appointed by the state. This was important because in the eighteenth century ecclesiastical censorship remained a dramatic reality in Italian cultural life. In 1734 Pope Clement XII had banned John

Locke's *Essay Concerning Human Understanding*. In 1751, the year in which its first Italian translation was published in Naples, Montesquieu's *Esprit des Lois* was also placed on the Index. After the pope's condemnation of his *Civil History of the Kingdom of Naples* (1723), the Neapolitan writer Pietro Giannone had been forced into exile, and after wandering between Vienna, Modena, and Geneva, he died in prison in Turin in 1748. In 1739 Tommaso Crudeli was arrested in Florence and charged by the Inquisition with anticlericalism and supporting free masonry, which Clement XII had banned in 1738. Beccaria's essay on *Crimes and Punishments* and Gaetano Filangieri's *Science of Legislation* were also placed on the Index of Prohibited Books. But secular censorship could be no less severe, and in Naples in 1753 Paolo Mattia Doria's posthumous work *The Idea of the Perfect Republic* was burned by the public hangman because it criticized absolutist policies. In 1755 Carlantonio Broggia was also condemned to exile for having publicly criticized the government's financial policy. Yet these measures did not prevent the condemned books from circulating, and indeed they contributed indirectly to the formation of a public opinion that was sympathetic to the very ideas that the censors sought to proscribe.

The triumph and the crisis of reform

Whether we take the Piedmont of Victor Amadeus III of Savoy, the Lombardy of the Habsburg rulers Maria Teresa and Joseph II, the Tuscany of Grand Duke Peter Leopold, the Naples of Ferdinand IV of Bourbon, the temporal dominions of the Pope, or the oligarchic Republics of Genoa and Venice that acted as fortresses to defend their ancient patrician orders, the central slogan of politics, literature, and science in Italy in the 1770s and 1780s was 'public happiness'. That phrase started to appear even in the prologues of legislative documents, which indicates the importance that governments now attached to 'public opinion' and its approval. In the collection of laws known as the Este Code that was promulgated in 1771 by Duke Francis III of Modena, for example, it was stated that the new limits imposed on feudal jurisdictions had been inspired by the 'principles of equity and reason' and for the good and happiness of the duke's subjects. Similar principles were invoked in the law of 1774 by which King Ferdinand IV of Naples limited the arbitrary power of the Neapolitan judges by requiring them to give full written and published explanations of their judgments.

Whether they were motivated by intellectual conviction or by necessity, by propaganda aims, or by genuine humanitarian concern, the Italian rulers now began to engage in reforms that were designed to improve the conditions of their subjects. In some cases this led to the introduction of new law codes inspired by the principles that Cesare Beccaria had championed. In the Duchy of Savoy feudalism was abolished in an edict of King Charles Emanuel III dated 1771, which was then put into effect by Victor Amadeus III in 1778. Throughout the territories ruled by the House of Savoy local government was placed under much closer control by the government in Turin. Between 1784 and 1785 the Milanese state was also thoroughly reorganized and centralized, while the domination of the nobility in local provincial government was also ended. In 1786 the traditional stronghold of noble power, the Senate, was also abolished. So too were the guilds, while the state took on responsibility for the provision of public welfare, and work began in redrafting the criminal law code. In Tuscany, Grand Duke Peter Leopold's penal code of 1786 abolished the use of torture and the death penalty. In Sicily, the Neapolitan Viceroy Domenico Carracciolo led a vigorous campaign against feudal privilege and power, gave new powers to local government, and abolished the tribunal of the Inquisition. The principles of *laissez-faire* and the ideas of the physiocrats were invoked even in the Papal States, where the customs system and the urban provisioning regulations were reformed in the same years.

The reform initiatives gathered pace, but they were no longer driven simply from above or by purely fiscal or military needs. There were important pressures coming from below as well, and they ensured that the tradition of piecemeal initiatives designed to solve specific financial needs would give way to more comprehensive forms of intervention. Behind these pressures lay the new social forces which were urging for reforms that would make political and administrative institutions responsive to the needs of a rapidly changing society. Indeed, the state's intervention in this period was possible because it was widely supported by the groups who favoured reform and believed that this could only be achieved by strengthening and extending the state's capacity to intervene. The changes taking place in society and in public opinion, together with demographic expansion and the emergence of a nucleus of new private property owners, all contributed to strengthen support for the reform programme. Whereas in the 1730s and 1740s reform had run up against the immovable resistance of the privileged orders, especially the clergy and the nobility, by the 1770s and 1780s large sections of the clergy and the nobility had now been won over to the cause of reform.

Many leading figures in the reform movement were men of the Church, many of whom were sincerely convinced that the clergy should return to their original mission of 'caring for souls' and what Muratori had called 'disciplined devotion'. There were deep divisions within the clergy, which were increased by the spread of Jansenist ideas, and the synod convened at Pistoia in 1786 by bishop Scipio de Ricci to discuss these issues led to open confrontation between the orthodox and the innovators.

Many noblemen took an interest in agricultural improvement, either because they were open to the ideas of their age or because they needed to increase their rent-rolls. But the works of Montesquieu also encouraged the idea that the nobility had a new political role to play, one that would no longer be linked to birth and honour but rather to their economic influence and their experience. The urban patriciates also divided into rival factions, some seeking stubbornly to defend their privileges while others were more willing to acknowledge that certain skills and knowledge were desirable for those who held civic office.

It was, above all, within the ranks of those 'middling groups' to whom Antonio Genovesi had addressed his teaching, however, that the need was felt most strongly for a radical renewal that would bring into being a new regime of private property, free trade, and rational bureaucracies that were less cumbersome and more responsive to the needs of the people. Once the old urban provisioning regulations had been dismantled in the name of free trade, once Church properties and feudal jurisdictions began to be reduced, new pressure from private landowners and from those who hoped to join them brought into question the future of the vast tracts of royal demesne and the extensive common lands owned by rural communities. The first measures to divide the common lands among local communities were taken in the late 1780s.

Among the young, and especially among the cadet sons of noble families who found themselves excluded from inheritance of land and family assets, hostility towards the privileges of birth was especially strong. They now called most loudly for careers commensurate with their economic, scientific, and technical knowledge, and refused to enter the traditional careers in the magistracy, the Church, and the army. It was not by chance that the 21-year-old Gaetano Filangieri addressed his fellow young men in his *Reflections* on the law of 1774 that required Neapolitan judges to give written explanations of their judgements: 'Unhappy youth that is destined to pass its best years in frustration; but do not let yourselves be halted by the confused clamour of those who would bid you keep silent when it comes to supporting the cause of your Sovereign and your Fatherland'.[6]

The educational reforms introduced in the 1770s and 1780s were addressed particularly to the needs of the young. This was also an indication that the rulers no longer looked on education as a threat to public morality and public order. Instead, they saw education as a means to ground their own political programme in a greater understanding of the condition and opinions of their subjects, and also on their consent. In fact, they were now prepared to invoke the support of a public opinion to whose formation they had directly contributed. Science and culture had become essential features of the image that the state sought to project of itself. Meanwhile, reform of secondary and primary schools, the founding of scientific associations, of libraries and museums, provided new jobs for the *literati*, while reform of the universities increased the supply of trained administrators and technical experts.

With the creation of academies directly sponsored by the state, such as the Milanese Patriotic Society, the Neapolitan Academy of Science and Letters in 1778, or the Genoese Society for Arts and Manufactures in 1786, men of letters and philosophers finally won recognition for their skills. Nor was this merely honorific. The academies created important new opportunities for disseminating and promoting research and scholarship. In this way, the theoretical projects of the intellectuals and reform policies of the rulers seemed

---

[6] Gaetano Filangieri, *Riflessioni politiche su l'ultima legge del Sovrano, che riguarda la riforma dell'amministrazione della giustizia* (Naples 1774), 94–5.

to come even closer. The rapid expansion of literary and scientific periodicals, the increasingly intense exchanges between the centre and the periphery, between the capital cities and the principal provincial centres, meant too that they attracted ever-greater publicity.

In Milan men like Verri and Beccaria had never been simply 'thinkers' but also administrators in the employ of the state, while in Naples too some of the leading figures in the reform movement in the 1780s accepted government office. Gaetano Filangieri and Giuseppe Palmieri were members of the Council of Finance that had been created in 1782, and as Visitor-General Giuseppe Maria Galanti was able to collect the mine of data and information that was subsequently published in his *Description of the Kingdom of the Sicilies*, a work that in large part anticipated the collection of local statistics that was introduced only later in the Napoleonic era. But entry into public administration was also the ultimate acknowledgement of the merit and talents of the *literati*, whose knowledge and practical skills were in stark contrast to the aimlessness associated with the nobility, the clergy, and the lawyers. They had won at least partial recognition as being creative and life-giving.

However, many of the contradictions that were embedded in the partnership between philosophy and politics can be seen in the case of Naples. In practice the reformers' projects were invariably emptied of their broader and more radical aims. Once they came into contact with the realities of traditional bureaucratic lethargy, the lack of financial means, and the resistance of the most reactionary sections of the nobility, the clergy, and the magistracy, they were forced back into the established practices of piecemeal intervention. The Neapolitan Supreme Council of Finance illustrated how not only vested interests but also prevailing juridical and bureaucratic mentalities continued to block reform initiatives. The economist Domenico di Gennaro described such obstacles to reform very vividly in a letter to Melchiorre Delfico on 1 February 1792:

The late abbé Galiani was absolutely right to compare our Council of Finance to Christmas Eve, when everyone eats too much and finishes up with violent indigestion. Things are just like that on the Council: great projects, great plans, much talk of the public good, of trade, agriculture, manufactures and so forth, all hither and thither, sometimes starting again from the beginning but without ever coming to any conclusions, except the most undesirable ones . . . Four lawyers of the utmost tenacity in their despotism disposed at will of all matters that were proposed. The director is a man of the best intentions who delivers whole academies of learned discourses, but lacks what is needed to do the job; and when challenged on the grounds of fiscal need, immediately lays down his arms and surrenders.[7]

Not only in Naples, however, did the initial enthusiasm aroused by the government reform initiatives give way to disillusionment and frustration. Although his reasons were different, Pietro Verri was no less disillusioned when in 1786 he was stripped of his government offices. He too was keenly aware of the ambiguities and precariousness of the partnership between the rulers and 'the philosophers who find themselves ignored, contradicted, and persecuted in their own lifetime'. The enlightened despotism that he had always looked on only as 'a transient [system] but one that is necessary to bring corrupted nations back to correct principles' now seemed to be overbearing and oppressive.[8]

Verri had looked forward to a system of political representation based on property and education, but in the meantime the American Revolution had brought forth more radical political and social models. This meant that the overthrow of the feudal regime could no longer be thought of simply in terms of converting the nobility into landowners, and questions about how to achieve a more equal distribution of economic resources began to be raised. The social issues exposed by the famine of 1763/64 were also becoming more pressing. In his *Political Essays* (1783) Francesco Maria Pagano, for example, argued that: 'We find the people are divided between the powerful corporations of the nobles, the Churchmen and the magistrates, yet it is the poor oppressed plebes who are destined to carry on their backs the massive burden of these three orders'.[9] The Sicilian Giovanni Agostino de Cosmi wrote in similarly severe and despairing terms about the weakness of the 'middling orders':

No body of citizens can ever be called prosperous, rich, or cultured if they are divided into only two classes, one disproportionately rich and the other forced to live in poverty and beg for a living; one fully educated and the other

---

[7] Letter of Domenico di Gennaro to Melchiorre Delfico (1 February 1792), cited in Franco Venturi (ed.), *Riformatori napoletani* (Milan/Naples 1962), 1111.

[8] Cited in Carlo Capra, 'Alle origini del moderatismo e del giacobinismo in Lombardia: Pietro Verri e Pietro Custodi', *Studi storici* 4 (1989), 875, 878.

[9] Francesco Maria Pagano, *Saggi politici* (1783), cited in Venturi (ed.), *Riformatori napoletani*, 898.

totally ignorant; one industrious while the other is base and without work; one full of all the virtues and the other without any sense of morality.[10]

Peter Leopold had considered introducing a constitution in Tuscany in the late 1780s, but by then even the more 'enlightened' forms of absolutism were showing signs of internal contradictions that could not be resolved. The partnership that had in theory linked the reform initiatives of the rulers to the broader expectations of change among the intellectuals and within Italian society was already an illusion. The political initiatives of the rulers, which many reformers had considered to be the best means for achieving reform, had proven to be ineffective, while absolutism showed itself to be fundamentally opposed to the growing demands for greater political liberty. What had begun among the intellectuals as a struggle against the abuses of the old system was now being transformed into a struggle against the whole existing political system; the reform initiatives of the rulers had stimulated and strengthened the demand for real reform, but by now the reform movement had moved beyond this and was setting its own objectives.

Gaetano Filangieri's *Science of Legislation* (1780–85) can be seen as the authentic manifesto of both the triumph and the crisis of the partnership between Enlightenment and reform. Although it was held in high esteem by the Neapolitan minister John Acton for the force of its critique of the feudal system, Filangieri's work set out a reform programme that no absolutist ruler could possibly have wanted to adopt. Much earlier in 1741 Ludovico Antonio Muratori had denounced the obsolete and ineffective administration of justice in his essay *On the Defects of Jurisprudence*. In 1764 in his essay *On Crimes and Punishments* Cesare Beccaria had launched a piercing denunciation of the existing criminal law, of the Church, the lack of clear distinctions between crime and sin, and a society of orders based on the privileges of birth. But it was only with the publication of Filangieri's great work that a comprehensive reformulation of the nature and underlying principles of the state and of society finally emerged. In his study Filangieri effectively dismantled the Ancien Regime in its entirety, using concepts and language that were no longer compatible with the juridical and

---

[10] Cited in Giuseppe Giarrizzo, *Cultura e economia nella Sicilia del '700* (Caltanissetta-Roma 1992), 155.

administrative arguments that sought to preserve or modify the existing order.

From that point onwards the reform movement became linked to demands for constitutional reform that were inevitably incompatible with the blind defence of absolutist power by Italy's Savoyard, Bourbon, and Habsburg rulers. An important example of this came from Sardinia. When in the 1790s Sardinian demands for the restoration of the island's ancient representative institutions within the monarchy met with unyielding opposition from the absolutist Savoyard rulers, the island became a theatre for open revolt against Piedmont.

Conclusion: Enlightenment and revolution

Historians of Italy's nineteenth-century Risorgimento have often looked on writers like Scipio Maffei and Gian Rinaldo Carli as forerunners of a new sense of Italian national identity. While there can be no doubt that the economic and cultural changes that took place in the eighteenth century did give rise to a new sense of belonging to a common 'patria' among the elites, by the close of the century Italy was still a country of deep internal contrasts and differences. Indeed, in many cases these internal contradictions had become greater as a result of the changes that had taken place, and despite the fact that men of letters could continue to think of themselves as members of a 'Republic of Letters' that was as much European as Italian.

Most conspicuously, the differences between North and South had grown greater. In the North the impact of the reforms was greater in terms of administrative organization, of the expansion of new cultural and scientific institutions, and the adoption of new forms of agriculture. In the South, the contrast between the theoretical propositions of what was nonetheless a broad and vigorous intellectual movement and the practical interventions of a monarchy that remained weak and subject to endless internal and external constraints was more evident.

Throughout Italy the eighteenth century also saw the contrasts between city and countryside increase, as well as those that separated the educated classes from the vast mass of the illiterate poor, even though notable efforts had been made, especially in Piedmont and

Lombardy, to provide elementary schooling for the rural populations. The reformers had placed great emphasis on the need for the wider dissemination of knowledge. 'The enlightenment of a nation is not the result of the actions of some few men of learning, but rather derives from the expansion and multiplication of learning through the contributions of great numbers of enlightened.persons', Pietro Verri had written in 1766.[11]

The rapid expansion of the publishing trade after the 1760s was an important sign of the growth of a new reading public consisting of men and women who were curious to follow the latest innovations and read books. The expansion of teaching in the universities had also increased the size of the reading public, but this had no impact at all on the poor, especially not in rural areas and in the South. Recent studies have also shown how the emergence of a new and strongly lay culture served to widen the gap between the educated classes and the masses, who were considered by the former to be irrevocably incarcerated in ignorance and superstition. The reformers were also convinced that what the peasant population needed above all was practical knowledge useful for the development of agriculture, and they excluded them from any form of higher education on the grounds that it would lead to a shortage of labour for agriculture.

By the end of the century the contrasts between the increasingly radical demands of the reformers and the resistance of the rulers and the privileged corporate bodies of society could no longer be contained. Eighteenth-century reformism had proved to be riddled with contradictions and ambiguities. The measures adopted to free the trade in grain and to remove controls on the price of necessities had proved very damaging to the poorest consumers and were the cause of protests and riots that served to curtail rather than encourage new reforms. The declining power exercised by the privileged orders and corporate bodies also gave rise to new fears that in the absence of those intermediary forces whose political importance Montesquieu had emphasized, absolutist power would degenerate into mere despotism.

The attempts by the rulers to do away with the forms of self-government that had survived in many regions also struck at

---

[11] Cited in Franco Venturi, *Settecento riformatore*, vol. 1: *Da Muratori a Beccaria* (Turin 1969), 432.

traditions that found fierce defenders, and even inspired local academies and cultural associations to begin writing and researching the histories of their own localities. Yet the reforms that had taken root thanks to the pressures of economic expansion and new cultural outlooks made the remaining obstacles to change all the more difficult to tolerate. If this made the opposition of the privileged orders and the defenders of older forms of self-government more determined, it also gave rise to more radical reform projects.

Riots and revolts had occurred frequently during the course of the century, but with no clear pattern or frequency, although they became more frequent and more extensive in the final decades of the century. There had been revolts in the cities of the Republic of Genoa, bread riots in Milan and Naples, violent protests in Tuscany against the government's *laissez-faire* economic policies and against its pro-Jansenist religious policies, unrest in the Garfagnana (the Este corridor along the edge of Tuscany linking Modena to the Tyrrhenian) in protest against high taxes and administrative centralization, and anti-feudal movements in many provinces of the kingdom of Naples. When the Revolution took place in France in 1789, therefore, it did no more than confirm the belief shared by most Italian rulers and their ministers that the reform movement had been the portent of revolution. With the outbreak of war in 1793 and the involvement of many of the Italian states in the First Coalition against the French Republic, all forms of innovation became synonymous with subversion. For the Church, which had for long been preparing its forces against the reformers and had adopted the same means of communicating with and mobilizing public opinion that had been developed by the reformers, the revolution in France was the perfect opportunity for launching a massive propaganda campaign against the Enlightenment and reform. It was on these terms that Italy entered the era of the revolutions, when the deep contrasts and conflicts that had been accumulating during the course of the century of reform would finally burst into the open.

Conclusion

John A. Marino

Lorenzo da Ponte's Italian libretto of a French drama on a Spanish subject for an Austrian composer—Mozart's *The Marriage of Figaro* (1786)—captures the cosmopolitan conversation and conscience of cities and courts at the end of the Old Regime. The plot turns on the moral corruption of a possible double adultery. Count Almaviva designs to exercise his alleged droit de seigneur (the right to enjoy the first night with his servant Figaro's bride Susanna), and his wife, the Countess, in a retaliatory flirtation toys with the androgynous Cherubino. Sexual immorality becomes a metaphor for the crisis of the nobility and the Old Regime in general. The question of noble pretension to property, privilege, and power thus emerges as the underlying problem of the old order.

Decadence and decline have long demonized the period of foreign domination between Renaissance humanism and Enlightenment reform in Italy. Salient examples abound. The 1737 death of Gian Gastone de' Medici, the last of his dynasty, and the passing of Tuscany to Lorraine and Austria epitomized the fall. Grand duke of Tuscany at 52 years of age upon his brother's death in 1723, Gian Gastone was prematurely senile, often drunk in public, surrounded by sycophants, and for months at a time, never out of bed. In that same year, 1737, the international singing sensation and later impresario, the Neapolitan *castrato* Farinelli, came to Spain. For the next ten years until the death of Philip V (the first Spanish Bourbon and father of the first Neapolitan Bourbon), Farinelli lullabied the depressed king to sleep with the same four songs every night!

Such impressionistic vignettes, however, discount the dynamism at the heart of early modern Italian society and culture. Rather than an anachronistic history of blame for the supposed delayed political unification of the peninsula's myriad independent states and centuries of foreign occupation, of scorn for a so-called diverted religious reformation and centuries of clerical authoritarianism, or of regret for the presumed failed transition to industrialization and centuries of peripheralization in the developing world economy, the continuities of land and labour, law and religion, language and family across the early modern period now loom larger than the fissures. Neither its rigid social hierarchy nor its Habsburg and Bourbon overlords, neither Catholicism nor the papacy, neither economic impediments nor guild intransigence caused or sustained Italy's relative decline. Conquered in the sixteenth century by the greater manpower and resources of the new monarchies in Spain and France, three territorial states (Milan, Naples, and Sicily) became a part of the Spanish empire and a source of revenue to support Habsburg Spain's ventures. These three pacified provinces and the peninsula's other petty polities had their internecine warfare quelled and became a bulwark against the Ottoman advance. As the first global world economy centred in north-west Europe took shape and the Thirty Years War squandered Spain's imperial patrimony, Italy lost its former economic leadership and had its economy restructured. To simplify the trajectory of western civilization as a predetermined, unilinear progression of power and culture from Venice to Antwerp, Madrid, Amsterdam, Paris, and London is to distort the multiple nodes and divergent paths to modernity that made Italy an integral part of the cosmopolitan world of early modern Europe.

Throughout these forgotten centuries, Italy's early modern urban infrastructure and intra-urban networks fostered and furthered traditions and techniques in political practice and thought from reason of state to political economy, as much as in the arts and sciences from Marinism to the Arcadians or from the Accademia del Cimento to the Bologna Academy of Sciences. From a post-nationalist, post-colonial, post-Tridentine, and post-industrial perspective, we should not let the unification fervour and liberal optimism of early modern Italy's Risorgimento heirs blind us to the bright lights of architecture in Rome and the opera in Venice, or to the bellicose polemics on the socio-political front waged between the 'old' and 'new' nobility in Genoa and the 'ancients' and 'moderns' in Naples. At the same time, we should not ignore early modern Italy's high negatives and low lights—material constraints on life (poverty, famine, and disease), political and ideological limitations on liberty, and the persistence of patriarchal and patrician power.

Such a polycentric world does not mean that all regions and towns developed uniformly, that some parts did not dominate and subordinate others, and that the inequalities did not exacerbate divisions both internally and externally. What it does mean, however, is that Italy's long history of familial and corporate identity and of communal and regional localism prevailed. Despite the absence of a unifying centre or polity, the collective contributions of the Old Regime states continued to be greater than the sum of their parts.

If we look back from the early modern period to the medieval characterization of Italy as the 'garden of the Mediterranean'—the centre of productivity and abundance in the civilized world—we can see that much had changed in Italy and outside. Soon after Padua and Pisa in 1545 (followed in the next decade by the medical schools of Florence and Ferrara, and in 1568 at Bologna) created the first botanic gardens—collections of rare herbs and plants for study, experiment, and medicines—imitation outside Italy saw seven other botanic gardens founded for medical instruction across Europe by the end of the century, at Vienna, Göttingen, Leipzig, Leyden, Basel, Fronecker, and Montpellier. But the flattery of imitation soon gave way to the condescension of tourists, as all Italy itself was already on the way to becoming a hothouse and museum.

An Atlantic-centred world in the seventeenth and eighteenth centuries saw Italy as a stop on the Grand Tour, a school for gentlemen and scholars to test themselves against the past. The romanticism of foreigners such as Goethe or Stendhal rediscovered what Italians themselves had known and practised all along: namely, Italian passion's connection with thought and action. That restless passion, with its unexpected flash of light and colour, was the distinctive feature of Italy's reigning aesthetic throughout most of the early modern period. What seemed to be so at odds with the Tridentine Church and the staid conservatism of the Old Regime state (or its Restoration afterlife) in fact expressed the underlying logic of immanent faith and power. Petrarch's first proclamation of modernity in the fourteenth century resonated through the contrasts and contradictions, censorship, and circumspection of the early modern era. The peninsula's multiplicity of social and political forms, its innovative aesthetic imagination, its literature and learning, its philosophical speculation and scientific inquiry, its popular fantasies and practice of everyday life, and its circulation of news, ideas, goods, and people established the foundation for its democratic and industrial revolutions, and beyond. It was a foundation, however, fraught with fissures and fault lines—increased inequalities between the haves and have-nots, producers and consumers, religious and lay culture, educated elites and a superstitious populace, the city and the countryside, the North and the South. The Risorgimento did not reinvent Italy from an ancient or Renaissance past, but would build upon this precarious infrastructure that it loved to hate and had so long endured.

Further reading

Introduction: on the Grand Tour

For general overviews of the period, see Eric Cochrane, *Italy, 1530–1630*, ed. Julius Kirshner (London, 1985); D. Sella, *Italy in the Seventeenth Century* (London, 1997); D. Carpanetto and G. Ricuperati, *Italy in the Age of Reason, 1685–1789* (London, 1987); Gregory Hanlon, *Early Modern Italy, 1550–1800* (London, 2000); Christopher F. Black, *Early Modern Italy: A Social History* (London, 2001); Stuart J. Woolf, 'Italy, 1600–1796', and Robert Oresko, 'Culture in the Age of Baroque and Rococo', in George Holmes (ed.), *The Oxford History of Italy* (1997), 113–76; Stuart J. Woolf, *A History of Italy 1700–1860: The Social Constraints of Political Change* (London, 1979); Fernand Braudel, *Out of Italy, 1450–1650*, trans. Siân Reynolds (Paris, 1991); and Eric Cochrane (ed.), *The Late Italian Renaissance* (New York, 1970). The standard textbook on the visual arts is Rudolf Wittkower, *Art and Architecture in Italy, 1600–1750*, 6th edn., rev. Joseph Connors and Jennifer Montagu (New Haven, Conn., 1999). An extensive bibliography has been compiled by Gregory Hanlon, 'Early Modern Italy: A Comprehensive Bibliography of Works in English and French' (available from www.EarlyModernItaly.com).

For general overviews in Italian, see Nicola Tranfaglia and Massimo Firpo (eds.), *La Storia: I grandi problemi dal Medioevo all'età contemporanea*, vols. iii–v, of *L'età moderna* (Turin, 1986–7); Giovanni Cherubini et al. (eds.), *Storia della società italiana*, vols. x–xii (Milan, 1987–9); Luigi De Rosa (ed.), *La storiografia italiana degli ultimi vent'anni*, vol. ii: *Età moderna* (Rome, 1989); Gaetano Greco and Mario Rosa (eds.), *Storia degli antichi stati italiani* (Rome, 1996).

For pioneering studies, see Eric Cochrane, *Florence in the Forgotten Centuries 1527–1800* (Chicago, 1973) and Franco Venturi, *The First Crisis*, trans. R. Burr Litchfield (Princeton, NJ, 1989) and *The End of the Old Regime in Europe, 1776–1789*, trans. R. Burr Litchfield (2 vols., Princeton, 1991), which are part of Venturi's magisterial *Settecento riformatore* (5 vols., Turin, 1969–90).

On the Grand Tour, see Margaret M. McGowan, *The Vision of Rome in Late Renaissance France* (New Haven, Conn., 2000); Edward Chaney, *The Evolution of the Grand Tour: Anglo-Italian Cultural Relations since the Renaissance* (London, 1998); Christopher Hibbert, *The Grand Tour* (London, 1987); Jeremy Black, *The British Abroad: The Grand Tour in the Eighteenth Century* (New York, 1992); and *Grand Tour: The Lure of Italy in the Eighteenth Century*, exhibition catalogue, ed. Andrew Wilton and Ilaria Bignamini (London, 1996).

For an introduction to a broad range of original sources in translation, see Brendan Dooley (ed. and trans.), *Italy in the Baroque: Selected Readings* (New York, 1995) and Jeanne Chenault Porter (ed.), *Baroque Naples: A Documentary History, 1600–1800* (New York, 1999).

Chapter 1

For some fundamental primary sources, see Robert Bellarmine, *The Supreme Pontiff* [*De Summo Pontifice*], in *Opera Omnia*, ed. Justin Fèvre (12 vols., Paris, 1870–74); Jean Bodin, *The Six Books of a Commonweal*, trans. Richard Knolles and ed. Kenneth D. McRae (Cambridge, 1962); Giovanni Botero, *The Reason of State* (1589), trans. P. J. Waley and D. P. Waley (London, 1956); Tommaso Campanella, *A Discourse Touching on the Spanish Monarchy*, trans. Edmund Chilmend (London, 1654); Francisco Suárez, *A Treatise on the Laws and God the Lawgiver* [*Tractatus de Legibus ac Deo Legislatore*] (2 vols., Naples, 1872); and Paolo Sarpi, *Istoria dell'Interdetto e altri scritti*, ed. M. D. Brusnelli and G. Gambarin (2 vols., Bari, 1940).

On early modern Italian politics and political thought in general, see Giorgio Chittolini, 'The "Private", The "Public", the State', in Julius Kirschner (ed.), *The Origins of the State in Italy*, (Chicago, 1996), 34–61; Roland Mousnier, 'The Exponents and Critics of Absolutism', in J. P. Cooper, (ed.), *The New Cambridge Modern History*, vol. iv: *The Decline of Spain and the Thirty Years War* (Cambridge, 1970), 104–31; Daniela Frigo (ed.), *Politics and Diplomacy in Early Modern Italy*, (Cambridge, 2000); Quentin Skinner, *The Foundations of Modern Political Thought* (Cambridge, 1978).

On Spanish Italy and Spanish policy in Italy, see A. Calabria and J. Marino (ed. and trans.) *Good Government in Spanish Naples* (New York, 1990); Aurelio Musi, *L'Italia dei viceré* (Rome, 2000); Aurelio Musi (ed.), *Nel sistema imperiale. L'Italia spagnola* (Naples, 1994); Helena Puigdomènech, ' "La lunga practica e continua lezione delle cose del mondo" nella politica spagnola di fine Cinquecento e inizio Seicento', in Jean-Jacques Marchand (ed.) *Niccolò Machiavelli* (Rome, 1996); Manuel Rivero, *Felipe II y el gobierno de Italia* (Madrid, 1998); Jack Beeching, *The Galleys at Lepanto* (London, 1982); L. Serrano, *España en Lepanto* (Madrid, 1984); and Anthony Pagden, *Spanish Imperialism and the Political Imagination* (New Haven, Conn., 1990).

On Rome and Venice, see: Thomas J. Dandelet, *Spanish Rome, 1500–1700* (New Haven, Conn., 2001); P. Nores, 'Storia della guerra degli spagnoli contra papa Paolo IV', *Archivio storico italiano*, 1st ser., 12(1) (1847); Paolo Prodi, *The Papal Prince*, trans. Susan Haskins (Cambridge, 1987); William Bouwsma, 'The Venetian Interdict and the Problem of Order', in *A Usable Past: Essays in European Cultural History* (Berkeley, Calif., 1990), 97–111; Robert Finlay, *Politics in Renaissance Venice* (London, 1980); and Richard Mackenney, 'A Plot Discover'd? Myth, Legend, and the "Spanish" Conspiracy against Venice in 1618', in John Martin and Dennis Romano (eds.), *Venice Reconsidered*, (Baltimore, 2000), 185–216.

Chapter 2

For an introduction to the historiography of early modern Catholicism, see John O'Malley, *Trent and All That: Renaming Catholicism in the Early Modern Era* (Cambridge, Mass., 2000); both N. S. Davidson, *The Counter Reformation* (Oxford, 1987) and Ronnie Po-Chia Hsia, *The World of Catholic Renewal, 1540–1770* (Cambridge, 1998) offer useful global overviews of the broader context of change and renewal in early modern Catholicism. Bibliographies with a focus on Italy may be found in David Gentilcore, 'Methods and Approaches in the Social History of the Counter-Reformation in Italy', *Social History* 17(1) (1992), 73–96; William V. Hudon, 'Religion and Society in Early Modern Italy: Old Questions, New Insights', *American Historical Review* 101 (1996), 783–804; John Martin 'Recent Italian Scholarship on the Renaissance: Aspects of Christianity in Late Medieval and Early Modern Italy', *Renaissance Quarterly* 48 (1995), 593–610; and Anne Jacobson Schutte, 'Periodization of Sixteenth-Century Italian Religious History: The Post-Cantimori Paradigm Shift', *Journal of Modern History* 61 (1989), 269–84.

On prophetic currents, see Ottavia Niccoli, *Prophecy and People in Renaissance Italy*, trans. Lydia G. Cochrane (Princeton, NJ, 1990) and Gabriele Zarri, 'Living Saints: A Typology of Female Sanctity in the Early Sixteenth Century', in Daniel Bornstein and Roberto Rusconi (eds.), *Women and Religion in Medieval and Renaissance Italy*, trans. Margery J. Schneider (Chicago, 1996), 219–304; cf. Marion L. Kuntz, *The Anointment of Dioniso: Prophecy and Politics in Renaissance Italy* (University Park, Pa., 2001).

The history of Catholic spirituality in the sixteenth century received its classic formulation in H. Outram Evennett, *The Spirit of the Counter Reformation* (Cambridge, 1968). Among the more significant biographical studies are Hubert Jedin, *Papal Legate to the Council of Trent: Cardinal Seripando*, trans. Frederic C. Eckhoff (St Louis, 1947); Adriano Prosperi, *Tra evangelismo e riforma. G. M. Giberti (1495–1543)* (Rome, 1969); Elisabeth G. Gleason, *Gasparo Contarini: Venice, Rome and Reform* (Berkeley, Calif., 1993); and Thomas F. Mayer, *Reginald Pole: Prince and Prophet* (Cambridge, 2000). But 'heretical' currents also challenged the basic presuppositions of the Catholic Church. Here the work of Delio Cantimori, *Eretici italiani del Cinquecento* (Florence, 1939; new edn. Turin, 1992) remains fundamental, but see now Silvana Seidel Menchi, *Erasmo in Italia, 1520–1580* (Turin, 1987) and Massimo Firpo, *Inquisizione romana e controriforma. Studi sul cardinal Giovanni Morone* (Bologna, 1992) and, by the same author, *Tra alumbrados e 'spirituali'. Studi su Juan de Valdés e il valdesianesimo nella crisi religiosa del '500 italiano* (Florence, 1990). For an attempt to interpret reform currents in their social context, see John Martin, *Venice's Hidden Enemies: Italian Heretics in a Renaissance City* (Berkeley, Calif., 1993). For a micro-historical approach to heresy, see Carlo Ginzburg, *The Cheese and the Worms: The Cosmos of a Sixteenth-Century Miller*, trans. John and Anne Tedeschi (Baltimore, 1980). We lack sufficient analysis of the ways in which religious ideas were diffused, though two studies, in addition to the work of Ginzburg just cited, provide points of departure: Paul Grendler, *The Roman Inquisition and the Venetian Press* (Princeton, NJ, 1977) and Claudia di Filippo Bareggi, *Il mestiere di scrivere. Lavoro intellettuale e mercato libraio a Venezia nel Cinquecento* (Rome, 1988).

On the institutional history of this period, the best studies have been those devoted to confraternities. An overview is provided by Christopher F. Black, *Italian Confraternities in the Sixteenth Century* (Cambridge, 1989), but see especially the works of Brian Pullan, *Rich and Poor in Renaissance Venice: The Social Institutions of a Catholic State* (Cambridge, Mass., 1975) and Ronald F. E. Weismann, *Ritual Brotherhood in Renaissance Florence* (New York, 1982), both model studies of religious institutions in their historical context. On the Jesuits, see John O'Malley, *The First Jesuits* (Cambridge, Mass., 1993); students must look to more specialized literature for the study of particular reform movements, but see Richard L. DeMolen (ed.), *Religious Orders of the Catholic Reformation* (New York, 1996). For an important work on monastic reform, see Barry Collett, *Italian Benedictine Scholars and the Reformation: The Congregation of Santa Giustina of Padua* (Oxford, 1985). On the history of cardinals in this period, see Barbara McClung Hallman, *Italian Cardinals, Reform, and the Church as Property, 1492–1563* (Berkeley, Calif., 1985); on bishops, Giuseppe Alberigo, *I vescovi italiani al Concilio di Trento (1545–1547)* (Florence, 1959); on the Inquisition, John Tedeschi, *The Prosecution of Heresy: Collected Studies on the Inquisition in Early Modern Italy* (Binghamton, NY, 1991); on the Index, Jesus Maria de Bujanda (ed.), *Index de Rome, 1557, 1559, 1564. Les premiers Index romains et l'index du Concile de Trente* (Geneva, 1990); and on the papal monarchy, Paolo Prodi, *The Papal Prince—One Body and Two Souls: The Papal Monarchy in Early Modern Europe*, trans. Susan Hankins (Cambridge, 1987). For Trent, the definitive work remains Hubert Jedin, *History of the Council of Trent* (London, 1957–61), a translation of the first two volumes of his magisterial *Geschichte der Konzils von Trient* (4 vols. in 5, Freiburg, 1949–75).

But the most exciting developments have been efforts, often inspired by social anthropology, to explicate the religious practices of the early modern period from a more socio-cultural perspective. On Savonarola, see Donald Weinstein, *Savonarola and Florence: Prophecy and Patriotism in the Renaissance* (Princeton, NJ, 1970). For some stimulating work on saints, see Edward Muir, 'The Virgin on the Street Corner', in Steven Ozment (ed.), *Religion and Culture in the Renaissance and Reformation* (Kirksville, Mo., 1989), 25–40; and several of the essays in Peter Burke, *The Historical Anthropology of Early Modern Italy: Essays on Perception and Communication* (Cambridge, 1987); and especially Rudolph Bell and Donald Weinstein, *Saints and Society: The Two Worlds of Western Christendom, 1000–1700* (Chicago, 1982). For an insightful case study of the interplay of Catholicism with rural customs, see Carlo Ginzburg, *The Night Battles: Witchcraft and Agrarian Cults in the Sixteenth and Seventeenth Centuries*, trans. John and Anne Tedeschi (Baltimore, 1983). John Bossy was a pioneer in a sociological approach to late medieval and early modern Catholicism, though his book *Christianity in the West, 1400–1700* (Oxford, 1985) should be read in conjunction with his many essays, frequently cited. A landmark work that synthesizes the new religious history with the history of institutions is Adriano Prosperi, *Il tribunali della coscienza. Inquisitori, confessori, missionari* (Turin, 1996), while Ottavia Niccoli's *La vita religiosa nell'Italia moderna* (Rome, 1998) provides a useful overview of early modern Italian Catholicism. For an excellent local study, see Wietse de Boer, *The Conquest of the Soul: Confession, Discipline, and Public Order in Counter-Reformation Milan* (Leiden, 2001).

Finally, selected primary texts are available in English: *Reform Thought in Sixteenth-Century Italy*, ed. and trans. Elisabeth G. Gleason (Ann Arbor, Mich., 1981); John C. Olin (ed.), *The Catholic Reformation: Savonarola to Ignatius Loyola* (New York, 1992); William V. Hudon (ed.), *Theatine Spirituality: Selected Writings* (New York, 1996); and *The Canons and Decrees of the Council of Trent*, trans. H. J. Schroeder (Rockford, Ill., 1978).

Chapter 3

For a general overview of the pre-industrial economy and its development, see Carlo M. Cipolla, *Before the Industrial Revolution: European Society and Economy 1000–1700*, 3rd edn. (New York, 1994); Jan de Vries, *The Economy of Europe in an Age of Crisis: 1600–1750* (Cambridge, 1976); and Paolo Malanima, *Economia preindustriale. Mille anni: dal IX al XVIII secolo* (Milan, 1995). For Italy, see Paolo Malanima, 'L'economia', in G. Greco and M. Rosa (eds.), *Storia degli antichi stati italiani*, (Rome, 1996), 249–95; Domenico Sella, *Italy in the Seventeenth Century* (London, 1997); and D. Carpanetto and G. Ricuperati, *Italy in the Age of Reason, 1685–1789* (London, 1987). For sources, see Giuseppe Felloni, 'Italy', in Charles Wilson and Geoffrey Parker (eds.), *An Introduction to the Sources of European Economic History, 1500–1800*, (Ithaca, NY, 1977), 1–36.

On demography, see Lorenzo Del Panta, 'I processi demografici', in Greco and Rosa, *Storia degli antichi stati italiani*, 215–47; and Gérard Delille, 'Agricultural Systems and Demographic Structures in the Kingdom of Naples', in Antonio Calabria and John A. Marino (eds. and trans.) *Good Government in Spanish Naples*, (New York, 1990), 79–126. For the countryside, see Emilio

Sereni, *History of the Italian Agricultural Landscape*, trans. R. Burr Litchfield (Princeton, NJ, 1997); Silvio Zotta, 'Agrarian Crisis and Feudal Politics in the Kingdom of Naples: The Doria at Melfi (1585–1615)', in Calabria and Marino, *Good Government*, 127–203; and Domenico Sella, *Crisis and Continuity: The Economy of Spanish Lombardy in the Seventeenth Century* (Cambridge, Mass., 1979). On urban industry, see Richard Mackenney, *Tradesmen and Traders: The World of the Guilds in Venice and Europe, 1250–1650* (London, 1987); Herman Van der Wee, *The Rise and Decline of Urban Industries in Italy and the Low Countries: Late Middle Ages–Early Modern Times* (Leuven, 1988); Simona Cerutti, 'Group Strategies and Trade Strategies in Turin', in Stuart Woolf, (ed.), *Domestic Strategies: Work and Family in France and Italy, 1600–1800* (Cambridge, 1990), 102–47; and Luca Mola, *The Silk Industry of Renaissance Venice* (Baltimore, 2000). On the seventeenth-century crisis and Italian economic decline, see the fundamental articles by Carlo M. Cipolla, 'The Economic Decline of Italy', in Brian Pullan (ed.), *Crisis and Change in the Venetian Economy in the Sixteenth and Seventeenth Centuries*, (London, 1968), 127–45, and Ruggiero Romano, 'Italy in the Crisis of the Seventeenth Century', in Peter Earle (ed.), *Essays in European Economic History: 1500–1800* (Oxford, 1974), 185–98.

On Venice, see Pullan, *Crisis and Change*; Frederic C. Lane, *Venice: A Maritime Republic* (Baltimore, 1973); Ugo Tucci, 'The Psychology of the Venetian Merchant in the Sixteenth Century', in J. R. Hale (ed.), *Renaissance Venice*, (London, 1973), 346–78; Richard Rapp, *Industry and Economic Decline in Seventeenth-Century Venice* (Cambridge, Mass., 1976); idem, 'The Unmaking of the Mediterranean Trade Hegemony: International Trade Rivalry and the Commercial Revolution', *Journal of Economic History* 35(3) (1975): 499–525; Robert C. Davis, *Shipbuilders of the Venetian Arsenal: Workers and Workplace in the Preindustrial City* (Baltimore, 1991). On Florence, see Judith C. Brown, *In the Shadow of Florence: Provincial Society in Renaissance Pescia* (New York, 1982); idem, 'A Woman's Place Was in the Home: Women's Work in Renaissance Tuscany', in Margaret W. Ferguson et al. (eds.), *Rewriting the Renaissance: The Discourses of Sexual Difference in Early Modern Europe* (Chicago, 1986), 206–24; Judith C. Brown and Jordan Goodman, 'Women and Industry in Florence', *Journal of Economic History* 40(1) (1980), 73–80; and Frank McArdle, *Altopascio: A Study in Tuscan Rural Society, 1587–1784* (New York, 1978). On Naples and the South, see Maurice Aymard, 'From Feudalism to Capitalism in Italy: The Case that Doesn't Fit', *Review* 6 (1982), 131–208; Patrick Chorley, *Oil, Silk, and Enlightenment: Economic Problems in XVIIIth Century Naples* (Naples, 1965); John A. Marino, *Pastoral Economics in the Kingdom of Naples* (Baltimore, 1988); and Antonio Calabria, *The Cost of Empire: The Finances of the Kingdom of Naples in the time of Spanish Rule* (New York, 1991).

Chapter 4

For a general overview, see David I. Kertzer and Richard P. Saller (eds.), *The Family in Italy from Antiquity to the Present* (New Haven, Conn., 1991); Marzio Barbagli, *Sotto lo stesso tetto. Mutamenti della famiglia italiana dal XV al XX secolo* (Bologna, 1984); Cesarina Casanova, *La famiglia italiana in età moderna. Ricerche e modelli* (Rome, 1997).

On the legal construction of gender, see Thomas Kuehn, *Law, Family and Women: Toward a Legal Anthropology of Renaissance Italy* (Chicago, 1991), and idem, 'Person and Gender in the Laws', in Judith C. Brown and Robert C. Davis (eds.), *Gender and Society in Renaissance Italy* (London, 1998); Renata Ago, 'Ruoli familiari e statuto giuridico', *Quaderni storici* 30(1) (1995), 111–33. On the legal history of the family, see Paolo Ungari, *Storia del diritto di famiglia in Italia* (Bologna, 1974).

On family and gender in Renaissance Florence, besides Christiane Klapisch-Zuber's classic *Women, Family and Ritual in Renaissance Italy* (Chicago, 1985), see also Isabelle Chabot, 'Widowhood and Poverty in Late Medieval Florence', *Continuity and Change* 3(2) (1988), 291–311; 'La loi du lignage. Notes sur le système successoral florentin (XIVe–XVe, XVIIe siècles)', *Clio. Histoire, femmes et sociétés* (1998), 51–72; 'Lineage Strategies and the Control of Widows in Renaissance Florence', in Sandra Cavallo and Lyndan Warner (eds.), *Widowhood in Medieval and Early Modern Europe* (London, 1999), 127–44; 'Seconde nozze e identità materna nella Firenze del tardo Medioevo', in Silvana Seidel Menchi, Anne Jacobson Schutte, and Thomas Kuehn (eds.), *Tempi e spazi della vita femminile nella prima età moderna* (Bologna, 1999), 493–523. See also Elaine Rosenthal, 'The Position of Women in Renaissance Florence: Neither Autonomy nor Subjection', in Peter Henley and Caroline Elam (eds.), *Florence and Italy: Renaissance Studies in Honour of Nicolai Rubinstein* (London, 1988), 369–81.

On family and gender in Renaissance Venice, see Stanley Chojnacki, *Women and Men in Renaissance Venice* (Baltimore, 2000) and Elisabeth Crouzet-Pavan, '*Sopra le acque salse*'. *Espace, pouvoir et société à Venise à la fin du Moyen Âge* (Rome, 1992).

On the triumph of the patriliny, see D. E. Zanetti, *La demografia del patriziato milanese nei secoli XVII, XVIII, XIX* (Pavia, 1972); and F. W. Kent, *Household and Lineage in Renaissance Florence: The Family Life of the Capponi, Ginori, and Rucellai* (Princeton, NJ, 1977).

On the forcing of patrician girls into convents in late Renaissance Venice, see Jutta Gisela Sperling, *Convents and the Body Politic in Late Renaissance Venice* (Chicago, 1999); for a more general survey, see Francesca Medioli: 'To Take or Not to Take the Veil: Selected Italian Case Histories, the Renaissance and after', in Letizia Panizza (ed.), *Women in Italian Renaissance Culture and*

Society (Oxford, 2000), 122–37; Francesca Medioli, 'Lo spazio del chiostro. Clausura, costrizione e protezione nel XVII secolo', in Seidel Menchi, Schutte, and Kuehn, *Tempi e spazi di vita femminile*, 353–76. On gender and religion in early modern Catholicism, see Gabriella Zarri's excellent essay 'Gender, Religious Institutions and Social Discipline: The Reform of the Regulars', in Brown and Davis, *Gender and Society in Renaissance Italy*, 193–212. On the forcing of sons into monastic life, see F. Tamburini, *Santi e peccatori. Confessioni e suppliche dai Registri della Penitenzieria dell'Archivio Segreto Vaticano (1451–1586)* (Milan, 1995); and G. Dall'Olio, 'La disciplina dei religiosi all'epoca del Concilio di Trento. Sondaggi bolognesi', in *Annali dell'Istituto Storico Italo-Germanico di Trento* 21 (1995), 93–140.

On the family's political role, see: Joanne M. Ferraro, *Family and Public Life in Brescia, 1580–1650: The Foundations of Power in the Venetian State* (Cambridge, 1993); Cesarina Casanova, 'Potere delle grandi famiglie e forme di governo', in Lucio Gambi (ed.), *Storia di Ravenna*, vol. iv: *Dalla dominazione veneziana alla conquista francese* (Venice, 1994); Renata Ago, *Carriere e clientele nella Roma barocca* (Rome, 1990), 39–129; Renata Ago, 'Giochi di squadra: uomini e donne nelle famiglie nobili del XVII secolo', in Maria A. Visceglia (ed.), *Signori, patrizi, cavalieri nell'età moderna* (Rome, 1992), 256–64.

For an overview of women's property rights (limited to northern and central Italy), see Isabelle Chabot, 'Risorse e diritti patrimoniali', in Angela Groppi (ed.), *Storia delle donne italiane*, vol. ii: *Il lavoro delle donne* (Rome, 1996), 47–70. See also the essays in Isabelle Chabot and Giulia Calvi (eds.), *Le ricchezze delle donne. Diritti patrimoniali e poteri familiari in Italia (XIII–XIX sec.)* (Turin, 1998); Renata Ago, 'Oltre la dote: i beni femminili', in Groppi, *Il lavoro delle donne*, 164–82; Sandra Cavallo, 'What Did Women Transmit? Ownership and Control of Household Goods and Personal Items in Early Modern Italy', in Moira Donald and Linda Harcernbe (eds.), *Gender and Material Culture in Historical Perspective* (London, 2000), 38–53.

On southern Italy, see Gérard Delille's fundamental book, *Famiglia e proprietà nel regno di Napoli* (Turin, 1988), and Maria Antonietta Visceglia, *Il bisogno d'eternità. I comportamenti aristocratici a Napoli in età moderna* (Naples, 1988).

On cadets, see Renata Ago, 'Ecclesiastical Careers and the Destiny of Cadets' in *Continuity and Change* 7 (1992), 271–82; R. Bizzochi, *In famiglia. Storie di interessi e affetti nell'Italia moderna* (Rome, 2001).

On marriage, see Michela De Giorgio and Christiane Klapisch-Zuber (eds.), *Storia del matrimonio* (Rome, 1996) and Silvana Seidel Menchi and Diego Quaglioni (eds.), *Coniugi nemici. La separazione in Italia dal XII al XVIII secolo* (Bologna, 2000); Volker Hunecke, 'Matrimonio e demografia del patriziato veneziano (secc. XVII–XVIII)', *Studi veneziani* 15 (1991), 269–319; Daniela Lombardi, 'Fidanzamenti e matrimoni dal Concilio di Trento alle riforme settecentesche', in De Giorgio and Klapisch-Zuber, *Storia del matri-monio*, 215–50. On separation, see O. Di Simplicio, *Peccato, penitenza, per-dono. La formazione della coscienza nell'Italia moderna*, (Milan, 1994). On clandestine marriage, see G. Cozzi, 'Padri, figli e matrimoni clandestini (metà sec. XVI–metà sec. XVIII)', *La cultura* 14 (1976); V. Hunecke, 'Matrimonio e demografia del patriziato veneziano (secc. XVII–XVIII)', *Studi veneziani* 15 (1991), 269–319.

On motherhood and women's guardianship of children, see Giulia Calvi, *Il contratto morale. Madri e figli nella Toscana moderna* (Rome, 1994) and Giovanna Fiume (ed.), *Madri. Storia di un ruolo sociale* (Venice, 1995).

On nineteenth-century developments, see Paolo Macry, *Ottocento. Famiglia, élites e patrimoni a Napoli* (Turin, 1988); Maura Palazzi, 'Nuovi diritti e strategie di conservazione dopo l'Unità. Le famiglie contadine del bolognese', in Chabot and Calvi, *Le ricchezze delle donne*, 121–48; Maura Palazzi, *Donne sole. Storia dell'altra faccia dell'Italia tra antico regime e società contemporanea* (Milan, 1997); Manuela Martini, 'Doti e successioni a Bologna nell'Ottocento. I comportamenti patrimoniali del ceto nobiliare', *Quaderni storici* 92 (1996), 269–304; Ida Fazio, 'Valori economici e valori simbolici: il declino della dote nell'Ottocento', *Quaderni storici* 79 (1992), 291–316.

Chapter 5

For a general orientation, see: D. Sella, *Italy in the Seventeenth Century* (London, 1997), D. Carpanetto and G. Ricuperati, *Italy in the Age of Reason, 1685–1789* (London, 1987), and P. Burke, 'The Language of Orders in Early Modern Europe', in M. L. Bush (ed.), *Social Orders and Social Classes in Europe since 1500* (London, 1992), 1–12. On court society in Italy, see S. Bertelli, F. Cardini, and E. G. Zorzi (eds.), *The Courts of the Italian Renaissance* (New York, 1986).

Trends of urban population are traced in J. De Vries, *European Urbaniza-tion, 1500–1800* (Cambridge, Mass., 1984) and in K. J. Beloch, *Bevölkerungs-geschichte Italiens* (Berlin, 1937). Some recent studies of particular cities are M. Pollak, *Turin, 1564–1680: Urban Design, Military Culture, and the Creation of the Absolutist Capital* (Chicago, 1991), L. Nussdorfer, *Civic Politics in the Rome of Urban VIII* (Princeton, NJ, 1992), and H. Gross, *Rome in the Age of Enlightenment: The Post-Tridentine Syndrome and the Ancien Regime* (Cambridge, 1990).

For the Italian nobility in general, the best study is C. Donati, *L'idea di nobiltà in Italia, Secoli XIV–XVIII* (Bari, 1988); on feudal nobles in the south, see T. Astarita, *The Continuity of Feudal Power: The Caracciolo di Brienza in Spanish Naples* (Cambridge, 1990); for infeudation in the north, see D. Sella, *Crisis and Continuity: The Economy of Spanish Lombardy in the Seventeenth Century* (Cambridge, Mass., 1979). On patricians, see R. Burr Litchfield,

Emergence of a Bureaucracy: The Florentine Patricians, 1530–1790 (Princeton, NJ, 1986), idem, 'Un mercante Fiorentino alla corte dei Medici. Le "Memorie" di Roberto di Roberto Pepi (1572–1634)', *Archivio storico italiano* 47 (1999), 727–81, and J. C. Davis, *The Decline of the Venetian Nobility as a Ruling Class* (Baltimore, 1962).

The older works on guild organization, A. Fanfani, *Storia del lavoro in Italia dal secolo XV agli inizii del XVIII* (Milan, 1959) and L. Dal Pane, *Il tramonto delle corporazioni in Italia. Secoli XVIII e XIX* (Milan, 1959) are now augmented by A. Guenzi, P. Massa, and F. P. Caselli (eds.), *Guilds, Markets and Work Regulations in Italy: 16th–19th Centuries* (Aldershot, 1998) and R. Mackenney, *Tradesmen and Traders: The World of the Guilds in Venice and Europe, ca. 1250–1650* (Totowa, NJ, 1987). On artisans, see R. C. Davis, *Shipbuilders of the Venetian Arsenal* (Baltimore, 1991) and R. T. Rapp, *Industry and Economic Decline in 17th Century Venice* (Cambridge, Mass., 1976). On women, see D. Romano, 'Gender and the Urban Geography of Renaissance Venice', *Journal of Social History* 23 (1989), 339–53, and J. C. Brown and J. Goodman, 'Women and Industry in Florence', *Journal of Economic History* 40 (1980), 73–80. On migration to cities, see G. Levi, 'Mobilità della popolazione e immigrazione a Torino nella prima metà del settecento', *Quaderni storici* 6(17) (1971), 510–44; on the poor, see G. Politi, M. Rosa, and F. della Peruta (eds.), *Timore e carità. I poveri nell'Italia moderna* (Cremona, 1982).

On aspects of the Church, see Beloch, *Bevölkerungsgeschichte Italiens*, and Gross, *Rome in the Age of Enlightenment*; on Jewish communities, Attilio Milano, *Storia degli ebrei in Italia* (Turin, 1992). On confraternities, see B. Pullan, *Rich and Poor in Renaissance Venice* (Cambridge, Mass., 1971) and C. Black, *Italian Confraternities in the 16th Century* (Cambridge, 1989).

On ceremonial, see S. Bertelli, *The King's Body: The Sacred Rituals of Power in Medieval and Early Modern Europe*, trans. R. Burr Litchfield (University Park, Pa., 2001). M. Casini, *I gesti del principe. La festa politica a Firenze e Venezia in età rinascimentale* (Venice, 1996), E. Muir, *Civic Ritual in Renaissance Venice* (Princeton, NJ, 1981), and R. C. Davis, *The War of the Fists: Popular Culture and Public Violence in Late Renaissance Venice* (New York, 1994). On outbreaks of plague, see L. Dal Panto, *Le epidemie nella storia demografica italiana: Secoli XIV–XIX* (Turin, 1980), and on popular reactions, C. M. Cipolla, *Cristofano and the Plague: A Study in the History of Public Health in the Age of Galileo* (Berkeley, Calif., 1973) and G. Calvi, *Histories of a Plague Year: The Social and the Imaginary in Baroque Florence*, trans. Dario Biocca and Bryant T. Ragan (Berkeley, Calif., 1984). On the revolt of Naples in 1647, see R. Villari, *The Revolt of Naples*, trans. James Newell with John A. Marino (Cambridge, 1993).

On aspects of the emergence of a modern public sphere, see C. Capra, V. Castronovo, and G. Ricuperati, *La stampa Italiana dal Cinquecento all'Ottocento* (Bari, 1986), E. W. Cochrane, *Tradition and Enlightenment in the Tuscan Academies, 1690–1800* (Chicago, 1961), and F. Venturi, *The End of the Old Regime in Europe, 1768–1789*, trans. R. Burr Litchfield (Princeton, NJ, 1989).

Chapter 6

For the general political history of Italy in the seventeenth and eighteenth centuries, see the relevant chapters in Daniela Frigo (ed.), *Politics and Diplomacy in Early Modern Italy: The Structure of Diplomatic Practice 1450–1800* (Cambridge, 2000); Gregory Hanlon, *Early Modern Italy, 1550–1800* (London, 2000); Yves-Marie Bercé et al., *L'Italie au XVIIe siècle* (Paris, 1989); Stuart J. Woolf, *A History of Italy 1700–1860: The Social Constraints of Political Change* (London, 1979). See also Helmut G. Koenigsberger, 'The Italian Parliaments from their Origins to the End of the Eighteenth Century', *Journal of Italian History* 1(1) (1978), 18–49; Claudio Donati, *L'idea della nobiltà in Italia, secoli XIV–XVIII* (Bari, 1988); Gregory Hanlon, *The Twilight of a Military Tradition: Italian Aristocrats and European Conflicts 1560–1800* (London, 1998).

For the seventeenth century, see Geoffrey Parker, *The Army of Flanders and the Spanish Road, 1567–1659* (Cambridge, 1972), chs. 2 and 3; David Parrott, 'The Mantuan Succession, 1627–1631: A Sovereignty Dispute in Early Modern Europe', *English Historical Review* 112 (1997), 20–65; David Parrott and Robert Oresko, '*Reichsitalien* and the Thirty Years War', in Klaus Bussmann and Heinz Schilling (eds.), *1648: War and Peace in Europe* (3 vols., Munich, 1998), i: *Politics, religion, law and society*, 141–60; Christopher Storrs, 'The Army of Lombardy and the Resilience of Spanish Power in Italy in the Reign of Carlos II', in *War and History* 4(4) (1997), 371–97, and 5(1) (1998), 1–22; Karl O. Von Aretin, 'L'ordinamento feudale in Italia nel XVI–XVII secolo e le sue ripercussioni sulla politica europea', *Annali dell'Istituto Storico Italo-Germanico in Trento* 4 (1978).

For the eighteenth century, see Guido Quazza, 'Italy's Role in the European Problems of the First Half of the Eighteenth Century', in Matthew S. Anderson and Ragnhild M. Hatton (eds.), *Studies in Diplomatic History: Essays in Memory of D. B. Horn* (Harlow, 1970), 138–54; Spenser Wilkinson, *The Defence of Piedmont 1742–1748* (Oxford, 1927); Jeremy Black, 'The Development of Anglo-Sardinian Relations in the First Half of the Eighteenth Century', *Studi piemontesi* 12(1) (1983), 48–60. On the eighteenth-century reforms, see Giuseppe Ricuperati and Dino Carpanetto, *Italy in the Age of Reason, 1685–1789* (London, 1987); Matthew S. Anderson, 'The Italian Reformers', in Hamish Scott (ed.), *Enlightened Absolutism* (Basingstoke, 1990), 55–74; Franco Venturi, *Italy and the Enlightenment: Studies in a Cosmopolitan Century*, trans. Susan Corsi (London, 1972).

Works on individual states.

For Naples and Sicily, see Benedetto Croce, *A History of the Kingdom of Naples*, trans. Frances Fenaye (Chicago, 1970); Rosario Villari, *The Revolt of Naples*, trans. James Newell (Cambridge, 1993); Antonio Calabria, *The Cost of Empire: The Finances of the Kingdom of Naples in the Time of Spanish Rule* (Cambridge, 1991); John Marino and Antonio Calabria (eds.), *Good Government in Spanish Naples* (New York, 1990); Peter Burke, 'The Virgin of the Carmine and the Revolt of Masaniello', in his *The Historical Anthropology of Early Modern Italy* (Cambridge, 1987), 191–206; Anthony Pagden, '*Fede Pubblica* and *Fede Privata*: Trust and Honour in Spanish Naples', in his *Spanish Imperialism and the Political Imagination* (New Haven, Conn., 1990), 65–89; Moses I. Finley and Denis Mack Smith, *A History of Sicily* (3 vols., London, 1968), vols. ii and iii; Tommaso Astarita, *The Continuity of Feudal Power: The Caracciolo di Brienza in Spanish Naples* (Cambridge, 1991); Helmut G. Koenigsberger, 'The Revolt of Palermo in 1647', in his *Estates and Revolutions* (Ithaca, NY, 1971), 253–77; Girolamo Imbruglia (ed.), *Naples in the Eighteenth Century: The Birth and Death of a Nation State* (Cambridge, 2001).

For the Papal States, see Laurie Nussdorfer, *Civic Politics in the Rome of Urban VIII* (Princeton, NJ, 1992); Paolo Prodi, *The Papal Prince—One Body and Two Souls: The Papal Monarchy in Early Modern Europe* (Cambridge, 1987); Wolfgang Reinhard, 'Papal Power and Family Strategy in the Sixteenth and Seventeenth Centuries', in Ronald G. Asch and Adolf M. Birkle (eds.), *Princes, Patronage and the Nobility: The Court at the Beginning of the Modern Age, ca.1450–1650* (Oxford, 1991).

For Tuscany, see Eric Cochrane, *Florence in the Forgotten Centuries 1527–1800* (Chicago, 1973); Furio Diaz, *Il granducato di Toscana. I Medici* (Turin 1987); Furio Diaz, Luigi Mascilli Migliorini, and Carlo Mangio, *Il granducato di Toscana. I Lorena dalla Reggenza agli anni rivoluzionari* (Turin, 1997); R. Burr Litchfield, *Emergence of a Bureaucracy: The Florentine Patricians 1530–1790* (Princeton, NJ, 1986); Jean-Claude Waquet, *Corruption: Ethics and Power in Florence 1600–1770* (Philadelphia, 1992), and his *Le Grand-Duché de Toscane sous les derniers Médicis* (Paris, 1990).

For Genoa, see Edoardo Grendi, *La repubblica aristocratica dei genovesi* (Bologna 1987); Osvaldo Raggio, *Faide e parentele. Lo stato genovese visto dalla Fontanabuona* (Turin, 1990).

For Venice, see James C. Davis, *The Decline of the Venetian Nobility as a Ruling Class* (Baltimore, 1962); Kenneth M. Setton, *Venice, Austria and the Turks in the Seventeenth Century* (Philadelphia, 1991); Alberto Tenenti, *Piracy and the Decline of Venice 1580–1615* (London, 1968).

For Milan and Lombardy, see Daniel Klang, *Tax Reform in Eighteenth-Century Lombardy* (New York, 1977); 'Reform and Enlightenment in

Eighteenth-Century Lombardy', *Canadian Journal of History* 19(1) (1984), 39–70; his 'Economics and Political Economy in Eighteenth-Century Lombardy', *Italian Quarterly* 114 (1988), 37–53; and his 'Cesare Beccaria and the Clash between Jurisprudence and Political Economy in Eighteenth-Century Lombardy', *Canadian Journal of History* 23(3) (Dec. 1988), 305–36; Alexander Grab, 'Enlightened Despotism and State-Building: The Case of Austrian Lombardy', *Austrian History Yearbook* 19 and 20 (2) (1983–4), 43–72; his 'The Politics of Subsistence: The Liberalization of Grain Commerce in Austrian Lombardy under Enlightened Despotism', *Journal of Modern History* 57 (June 1985), 185–210; and his 'Enlightened Absolutism and Commonlands Enclosure: The Case of Austrian Lombardy', *Agricultural History* 63(1) (1989), 49–72; Cesare Mozzarelli, *Sovrano, società e amministrazione locale nella Lombardia teresiana* (Bologna, 1982); Carlo Capra, *La Lombardia austriaca nell'età delle riforme* (Turin, 1987).

For Piedmont-Savoy, see Guido Quazza, 'Guerra civile in Piemonte (1637–1642). Nuove ricerche', *Bollettino storico-bibliografico subalpino* 57 and 58 (1959–60); Robert Oresko, 'The House of Savoy in Search of a Royal Crown in the Seventeenth Century', in Oresko et al. (eds.), *Royal and Republican Sovereignty in Early Modern Europe* (Cambridge, 1997), 272–350; Christopher Storrs, *War, Diplomacy and the Rise of Savoy, 1690–1720* (Cambridge, 1999); Geoffrey Symcox, *Victor Amadeus II: Absolutism in the Savoyard State 1675–1730* (London, 1983); Sabina Loriga, *Soldati. L'istituzione militare nel Piemonte del Settecento* (Venice, 1992); Andrea Merlotti, *L'enigma delle nobiltà. Stato e ceti dirigenti nel Piemonte del Settecento* (Florence, 2000).

Chapter 7

New paradigms of interpretation.

Assessment of interpretive frameworks: John W. O'Malley, *Trent and All That: Renaming Catholicism in the Early Modern Era* (Cambridge, Mass., 2000). Confessionalization: Gerhard Oestreich, *Neostoicism and the Early Modern State*, ed. Brigitta Oestreich and H. G. Koenigsberger, trans. David McLintoch (Cambridge, 1982); Wolfgang Reinhard, 'Pressures towards Confessionalization? Prolegomena to a Theory of the Confessional Age', in C. Scott Dixon (ed.), *The German Reformation: The Essential Readings* (Oxford, 1999), 169–92. Excellent recent general accounts: Domenico Sella, *Italy in the Seventeenth Century* (London, 1997), chs. 5 and 6; Robert Bireley, SJ, *The Refashioning of Catholicism, 1450–1700: A Reassessment of the Counter-Reformation* (Basingstoke, 1999).

Inquisition and prohibited books.

Waldensians: Euan Cameron, *The Reformation of the Heretics: The Waldenses of the Alps, 1480–1580* (Oxford, 1984); Gabriel Audisio, *The Waldensians: Dissent, Persecution and Survival, c. 1170–c. 1570* (Cambridge, 1999). Jews: Brian Pullan, *The Jews of Europe and the Inquisition of Venice, 1550–1670* (Oxford, 1983); Pier Cesare Ioly Zorattini, 'Jews, Crypto-Jews, and the Inquisition', in Robert C. Davis and Benjamin Ravid (eds.), *The Jews of Early Modern Venice* (Baltimore, 2001), 97–116. Roman Inquisition: John Tedeschi, *The Prosecution of Heresy: Collected Studies on the Inquisition in Early Modern Italy* (Binghamton, NY, 1991). Witchcraft: Ruth Martin, *Witchcraft and the Inquisition in Venice, 1550–1650* (Oxford, 1989); Anne Jacobson Schutte, ' "Saints" and "Witches" in Early Modern Italy: Stepsisters or Strangers?', in Anne Jacobson Schutte, Thomas Kuehn, and Silvana Seidel Menchi (eds.), *Time, Space, and Women's Lives in Early Modern Europe* (Kirksville, Mo., 2001), 153–64. Pretence of holiness and related issues: Anne Jacobson Schutte, *Aspiring Saints: Pretense of Holiness, Inquisition, and Gender in the Republic of Venice, 1618–1750* (Baltimore, 2001).

Contours of holiness.

Changing models of saintliness: Donald Weinstein and Rudolph Bell, *Saints and Society: The Two Worlds of Western Christendom, 1000–1700* (Chicago, 1982); Peter Burke, 'How to be a Counter-Reformation Saint', in his *The Historical Anthropology of Early Modern Italy: Essays on Perception and Communication* (Cambridge, 1987), 48–62; Simon Ditchfield, *Liturgy, Sanctity and History in Tridentine Italy: Pietro Maria Campi and the Preservation of the Particular* (Cambridge, 1995). Menocchio: Carlo Ginzburg, *The Cheese and the Worms: The Cosmos of a Sixteenth-Century Miller*, trans. John and Anne Tedeschi (Baltimore, 1980); Andrea Del Col, *Domenico Scandella Known as Menocchio: His Trials before the Inquisition (1583–1599)*, trans. John and Anne C. Tedeschi (Binghamton, NY, 1996). 'Failed' and 'successful' holy women: Anne Jacobson Schutte, 'Little Women, Great Heroines: Simulated and Genuine Female Holiness in Early Modern Italy', in Lucetta Scaraffia and Gabriella Zarri (eds.), *Women and Faith: Catholic Religious Life in Italy from Late Antiquity to the Present* (Cambridge, Mass., 1999), 144–58.

Pastors and sheep.

Popes as ordinaries in the States of the Church: Paolo Prodi, *The Papal Prince—One Body and Two Souls: The Papal Monarchy in Early Modern Europe*, trans. Susan Haskins (Cambridge, 1987). Diocesan reform in Milan:

Wietse de Boer, *The Conquest of the Soul: Confession, Discipline and Public Order in Counter-Reformation Milan* (Leiden, 2001). Priests and preaching: Frederick J. McGinness, *Right Thinking and Sacred Oratory in Counter-Reformation Rome* (Princeton, NJ, 1995); Benjamin W. Westervelt, 'The Prodigal Son at Santa Justina: The Homily in the Borromean Reform of Pastoral Preaching', *Sixteenth Century Journal* 32 (2001), 109–26. Bishops, lay people, and piety in a southern region: David Gentilcore, *From Bishop to Witch: The System of the Sacred in Early Modern Terra d'Otranto* (Manchester, 1992). Confraternities: Nicholas Terpstra, *Lay Confraternities and Civic Religion in Renaissance Bologna* (Cambridge, 1995); John Patrick Donnelly and Michael H. Maher (eds.), *Confraternities and Catholic Reform in Italy, France, and Spain* (Kirksville, Mo., 1999); Nicholas Terpstra (ed.), *The Politics of Ritual Kinship: Confraternities and the Social Order in Early Modern Italy* (Cambridge, 2000). Convents: Jutta Gisela Sperling, *Convents and the Body Politic in Late Renaissance Venice* (Chicago, 1999). Involuntary monachization: Anne Jacobson Schutte, 'Legal Remedies for Forced Monachization in Early Modern Italy', in Michelle Fontaine, Paul Murphy, and Ronald Delph (eds.), *Venice, Rome, and Reform in Early Modern Italy: Essays in Honor of Elisabeth G. Gleason* (forthcoming).

Enlightenment and reform.

Indispensable: Franco Venturi's classic *Settecento riformatore, i: Da Muratori a Beccaria* (Turin, 1960); ii: *La chiesa e la repubblica dentro i loro limiti, 1758–1774* (Turin, 1976). Some relevant primary sources in English (1583–1704) may be found in *Italy and the Baroque: Selected Readings*, ed. and trans. Brendan Dooley (New York, 1995).

Chapter 8

For a general introduction to the relationship between the early modern arts, society, and politics in Southern Europe, see José Antonio Maravall, *Culture of the Baroque: Analysis of a Historical Structure*, trans. Terry Cochran (Minneapolis, 1986 [1975]). See also Fernand Braudel, *Out of Italy, 1450–1650*, trans. Siân Reynolds (Paris, 1991); Shearer West (ed.), *Italian Culture in Northern Europe in the Eighteenth Century* (Cambridge, 1999). Lina Bolzoni, *La stanza della memoria. Modelli letterari e iconografici nell'età della stampa* (Turin, 1995); and Jon R. Snyder, *Dissimulation and the Culture of Secrecy in Early Modern Europe* (Berkeley, Calif., 2002). On the universality of early modern Italian art, see Robert Williams, 'The International Style', in Martin Kemp (ed.), *The Oxford History of Western Art* (Oxford, 2000), 180–83.

Painting and sculpture.

On anamorphosis, see Lyle Massey, 'Anamorphosis through Descartes or Perspective Gone Awry', *Renaissance Quarterly* 50(4) (1997), 1148–89. On art academies, see Anton W. A. Boschloo, Elwin J. Hendrikse, Laetitia C. Smit, and Gert Jan van der Sman (eds.), *Academies of Art between Renaissance and Romanticism* (The Hague, 1989). On art markets, see Michael North and David Ormrod (eds.), *Art Markets in Europe, 1400–1800* (Aldershot, 1998). On the burgeoning field of Artemisia studies, see R. Ward Bissell, *Artemisia Gentileschi and the Authority Of Art : Critical Reading and Catalogue Raisonné* (University Park, Pa., 1998) and Mary D. Garrard, *Artemisia Gentileschi: The Image of the Female Hero in Italian Baroque Art* (Princeton, NJ, 1989). Oddly, some of the most significant recent research is found in Alexandre Lapierre, *Artemisia: A Novel*, trans. Liz Heron (New York, 2000 [1998]). Sofonisba Anguissola (*c.*1532–1625) was the most prominent early modern female painter before Artemisia; see *Sonfonisba Anguissola e le sue sorelle*, exhibition catalogue (Milan, 1994) and Fredrika H. Jacobs, 'Woman's Capacity to Create: the Unusual Case of Sofonisba Anguissola', *Renaissance Quarterly* 47(1) (1994), 74–101. On Pietro da Cortona, see Carole Paul, 'Pietro da Cortona and the Invention of the Macchina', *Storia dell'arte* 89 (1997), 74–99, and Anna Lo Bianco (ed.), *Pietro da Cortona 1597–1669*, exhibition catalogue (Milan, 1997). On Caravaggio, see Catherine Puglisi, *Caravaggio* (London, 2000 [1998]). On Vasari, see Patricia L. Rubin, *Giorgio Vasari: Art and History* (New Haven, Conn., 1995). On Rosa, see Jonathan Scott, *Salvator Rosa: His Life and Times* (New Haven, Conn., 1995). Many new and important works appeared for the Bernini commemoration of 1998; see Anna Coliva and Sebastian Schütze (eds.), *Bernini scultore. La nascita del barocco in casa Borghese*, exhibition catalogue (Rome, 1998); and Aidan Weston-Lewis (ed.), *Effigies and Ecstasies: Roman Baroque Sculpture and Design in the Age of Bernini*, exhibition catalogue (Edinburgh, 1998).

Architecture.

The best overall introduction in English to early modern architecture in Italy is Henry A. Millon (ed.), *The Triumph of the Baroque: Architecture in Europe, 1600–1750*, exhibition catalogue, 2nd rev. edn. (New York, 1999). On early modern architectural writing, see Alina A. Payne, *The Architectural Treatise in the Italian Renaissance: Architectural Invention, Ornament, and Literary Culture* (Cambridge, 1999); and Vaughan Hart and Peter Hicks (eds.), *Paper Palaces: The Rise of the Renaissance Architectural Treatise* (New Haven, Conn., 1998). Palladio's great treatise has been reprinted as *The Four Books of Architecture*, trans. Robert Tavernor and Richard Schofield (Cambridge, Mass.,

1997). On the villa, see James S. Ackerman, *The Villa: Form and Ideology of Country Houses* (Princeton, NJ, 1990). On Borromini, see Joseph Connors, *Borromini and the Roman Oratory: Style and Society* (New York, 1980). On Juvarra, see *Filippo Juvarra 1678–1736. De Mesina al Palacio Real de Madrid* (Madrid, 1994).

On the Grand Tour, see Andrew Wilton and Ilaria Bignamini (eds.) *Grand Tour: The Lure of Italy in the Eighteenth Century*, exhibition catalogue (London, 1996).

Music.

Lorenzo Bianconi, *Music in the Seventeenth Century* (Cambridge, 1987) remains an invaluable introduction to early modern Italian music. The three-volume sequence—Curtis Price (ed.), *The Early Baroque Era: From the Late 16th Century to the 1660s* (London, 1993); George J. Buelow (ed.), *The Late Baroque Era: From the 1680s to 1740* (Englewood Cliffs, NJ, 1993); and Neal Zaslaw (ed.), *The Classical Era: From the 1740s to the End of the 18th Century* (London, 1989)—contain a number of excellent essays. James M. Saslow, *The Medici Wedding of 1589: Florentine Festival as 'Theatrum Mundi'* (New Haven, Conn., 1996) offers a detailed analysis of the *intermedi* performed in Florence in 1589. Detailed documentation on the festival itself can be found in Maurizio Fagiolo dell'Arco, *La festa barocca* (Rome, 1997). On early modern opera, see Ellen Rosand, *Opera in Seventeenth-Century Venice: The Creation of a Genre* (Berkeley, Calif., 1991); Ian Fenlon and Peter N. Miller, *The Song of the Soul: Understanding 'Poppea'* (London, 1992); and Paolo Fabbri, *Il secolo cantante. Per una storia del libretto d'opera nel Seicento* (Bologna, 1990).

Literature.

On 'civility', see Peter Burke, *The Fortunes of the 'Courtier': The European Reception of Castiglione's 'Cortegiano'* (University Park, Pa., 1995). On academic culture in Italy, see Daniel Javitch, *Proclaiming a Classic: The Canonization of 'Orlando Furioso'* (Princeton, NJ, 1991), and Jon R. Snyder, *Writing the Scene of Speaking: Theories of Dialogue in the Late Italian Renaissance* (Stanford, Calif., 1989). On Marino's poetry and the visual arts, see Elizabeth Cropper, 'The Petrifying Art: Marino's Poetry and Caravaggio', *Metropolitan Museum Journal*, 26 (1991), 193–212. An English translation of the contest between the singer and the nightingale is available in Paschal C. Viglionese, *Italian Writers of the Seventeenth and Eighteenth Centuries* (Jefferson, NC, 1988), 44–9. On Basile's masterpiece, see Nancy L. Canepa, *From Court to Forest: Giambattista Basile's 'Lo cunto de li cunti' and the Birth of the Literary*

Fairy Tale (Detroit, 1999). On Ariosto versus Tasso, see Valeria Finucci (ed.), *Renaissance Transactions: Ariosto and Tasso* (Durham, NC, 1999). On Veronica Franco and women's writing, see Margaret F. Rosenthal, *The Honest Courtesan: Veronica Franco, Citizen and Writer of Sixteenth-Century Venice* (Chicago, 1992). One of the most important works on the early modern Italian theatre is Siro Ferrone, *Attori mercanti corsair. La commedia dell'arte in Europa tra Cinque e Seicento* (Turin, 1993). On the 'Arte', see Paul C. Castagno, *The Early 'Commedia dell'arte' (1550–1621): The Mannerist Context* (New York, 1994).

Chapter 9

Readers interested in knowing more about science in Renaissance Italy should begin with the following works: Charles Schmitt, 'Science in the Italian Universities in the Sixteenth and Early Seventeenth Centuries', in Maurice Crosland (ed.), *The Emergence of Science in Western Europe* (New York, 1976), 35–56; Paul Lawrence Rose, *The Italian Renaissance of Mathematics* (Geneva, 1975); Massimo Bucciantini and Maurizio Torrini (eds.), *La diffusione del Copernicanesimo in Italia, 1543–1600* (Florence, 1997); William Eamon, *Science and the Secrets of Nature* (Princeton, NJ, 1994); Paula Findlen, *Possessing Nature: Museums, Collecting, and Scientific Culture in Early Modern Italy* (Berkeley, Calif., 1994); idem, 'The Formation of a Scientific Community: Natural History in Sixteenth-Century Italy', in Anthony Grafton and Nancy Siraisi (eds.), *Natural Particulars: Nature and the Disciplines in Renaissance Europe* (Cambridge, Mass., 1999), 369–400; Nancy G. Siraisi, *The Clock and the Mirror: Girolamo Cardano and Renaissance Medicine* (Princeton, NJ, 1997); Anthony Grafton, *Cardano's Cosmos: The Worlds and Works of a Renaissance Astrologer* (Cambridge, Mass., 1999); and Andrea Carlino, *Books of the Body: Anatomical Ritual and Renaissance Learning*, trans. John Tedeschi and Anne C. Tedeschi (Chicago, 1999).

The problems of science and heresy can be further explored in such works as: Paul Oskar Kristeller, *Eight Philosophers of the Italian Renaissance* (Stanford, Calif., 1964); Frances Yates, *Giordano Bruno and the Hermetic Tradition* (Chicago, 1964); Luigi Firpo, 'The Flowering and Withering of Speculative Philosophy—Italian Philosophy and the Counter Reformation: The Condemnation of Francesco Patrizi', in Eric Cochrane (ed.), *The Late Italian Renaissance* (New York, 1970), 266–84; Pietro Redondi, *Galileo Heretic*, trans. Raymond Rosenthal (Princeton, NJ, 1987); Richard J. Blackwell, *Galileo, Bellarmine, and the Bible* (Notre Dame, Ind., 1991); John Headley, *Tommaso Campanella and the Transformation of the World* (Princeton, NJ, 1997); and Hilary Gatti, *Giordano Bruno and Renaissance Science* (Ithaca, NY, 1999).

Different aspects of seventeenth century Italian science are explored in:

Corrado Dollo, *Modelli scientifici e filosofici nella Sicilia spagnola* (Naples, 1984); Michael Segre, *In the Wake of Galileo* (New Brunswick, NJ, 1991); Ugo Baldini, *Legem impone subactis. Studi su filosofia e scienza dei gesuiti in Italia 1540–1632* (Rome, 1992); Mario Biagioli, *Galileo, Courtier: The Practice of Science in an Age of Absolutism* (Chicago, 1993); Cesare S. Maffioli, *Out of Galileo: The Science of Waters 1628–1718* (Rotterdam, 1994); Brendan Dooley, 'The Communications Revolution in Italian Science', *History of Science* 33 (1995), 469–96; Domenico Bertoloni Meli (ed.), *Marcello Malpighi: Anatomist and Physician* (Florence, 1997); Walter Bernardi and Luigi Guerrini (ed.), *Francesco Redi. Una protagonista di scienza moderna* (Florence, 1999); John L. Heilbron, *The Sun in the Church: Cathedrals as Solar Observatories* (Cambridge, Mass., 1999); Paula Findlen (ed.), *Baroque Imaginary: The World of Athanasius Kircher* (forthcoming).

On Italian scientific academies, see especially: Max H. Fisch, 'The Academy of the Investigators', in E. Ashworth Underwood (ed.), *Science, Medicine, and History* (2 vols., Oxford, 1953), i: 521–63; W. E. Knowles Middleton, *The Experimenters: A Study of the Accademia del Cimento* (Baltimore, 1971); idem, 'Science in Rome, 1675–1700: The Accademia Fisicomatematica of Giovanni Giustino Ciampini', *British Journal of the History of Science* 8 (1975), 138–54; Paolo Galluzzi, Carlo Poni, and Maurizio Torrini (eds.), *Accademie scientifiche del '600*, special issue of *Quaderni storici* 48 (1981); and Marta Cavazza, *Settecento inquieto. Alle origini dell'Istituto delle Scienze di Bologna* (Bologna, 1990).

Eighteenth-century Italian science has not been as well studied as the earlier periods and there is very little to consult in English, though comments on eighteenth-century Italian activities are scattered throughout histories of science dealing with this period. The best starting point is Vincenzo Ferrone, *The Intellectual Roots of the Italian Enlightenment: Newtonian Science, Religion, and Politics in the Early Eighteenth Century*, trans. Sue Brotherton (Atlantic Highlands, NJ, 1995). See also Eric Cochrane, *Tradition and Enlightenment in the Tuscan Academies 1690–1800* (Chicago, 1961); Peter K. Knoefel, *Felice Fontana: Life and Works* (Trento, 1984); Walter Bernardi, *La metafisica dell'embrione. Scienza della vita e filosofia da Malpighi a Spallanzani (1672–1793)* (Florence, 1986); Brendan Dooley, *Science, Politics, and Society in Eighteenth-Century Italy: The* Giornale de' letterati d'Italia *and its World* (New York, 1991); Marcello Pera, *The Ambiguous Frog: The Galvani–Volta Controversy on Animal Electricity*, trans. Jonathan Mandelbaum (Princeton, NJ, 1992); Paula Findlen, 'Science as Career in Enlightenment Italy: The Strategies of Laura Bassi', *Isis* 83 (1993), 441–69; idem, 'A Forgotten Newtonian: Women and Science in the Italian Provinces', in William Clark, Jan Golinski, and Simon Schaffer (eds.), *The Sciences in Enlightenment Europe* (Chicago, 1999), 313–49; Gabriella Berti Logan, 'The Desire to

Contribute: An Eighteenth-Century Italian Woman of Science', *American Historical Review* 99 (1994), 785–812; and Vincenzo Ferrone, 'The Accademia Reale delle Scienze: Cultural Sociability and Men of Letters in Turin of the Enlightenment under Vittorio Amedeo III', *Journal of Modern History* 70 (1998), 519–60.

Chapter 10

The obvious place to start is Peter Burke's thought-provoking collection of articles, *The Historical Anthropology of Early Modern Italy: Essays on Perception and Communication* (Cambridge, 1987). Other important examples of Italian anthropological history and microhistory can be found in two collections edited by E. Muir and G. Ruggiero, *Sex and Gender in Historical Perspective* (Baltimore, 1990) and *Microhistory and the Lost Peoples of Europe* (Baltimore, 1991). For the Italian ethnographic tradition, see Per Binde, *Bodies of Vital Matter: Notions of Life Force and Transcendence in Traditional Southern Italy* (Gothenburg, 1999).

Carlo Ginzburg's study of Menocchio's reading habits and cosmology is *The Cheese and the Worms: The Cosmos of a Sixteenth-Century Miller*, trans. John and Anne Tedeschi (Baltimore and London, 1980); for a critical discussion, see Andrea Del Col (ed.), *Domenico Scandella known as Menocchio: His Trials before the Inquisition (1583–99)* (Binghamton, NY, 1996), editor's introduction, pp. xi–cxii. On Croce and peasant culture, see Piero Camporesi, *La maschera di Bertoldo. G. C. Croce e la letteratura carnevalesca* (Turin, 1976).

Edward Muir's *Ritual in Early Modern Europe* (Cambridge, 1997) offers a superb survey of ritual practices, theories, and interpretations. On the transformation of witchcraft beliefs, see Carlo Ginzburg, *The Night Battles: Witchcraft and Agrarian Cults in the Sixteenth and Seventeenth Centuries*, trans. John and Anne Tedeschi (London, 1983) and Gustav Henningsen, '"The Ladies from Outside": An Archaic Pattern of the Witches' Sabbat', in B. Ankarloo and G. Henningsen (eds.), *Early Modern Witchcraft: Centres and Peripheries* (Oxford, 1989), 191–215. For a study of how religion and magic could coexist in the wake of the reforms of the Council of Trent, see David Gentilcore, *From Bishop to Witch: The System of the Sacred in Early Modern Terra d'Otranto* (Manchester, 1992). On transformations in the ritual cycle, see Herman Tak, *South Italian Festivals: A Local History of Ritual and Change* (Amsterdam, 2000). The Venetian bridge battles have been the subject of a study by Robert Davis, *The War of the Fists: Popular Culture and Public Violence* (Oxford, 1994). On civic ritual, see Edward Muir, *Civic Ritual in Renaissance Venice* (Princeton, NJ, 1981), and Richard Trexler, *Public Life in Renaissance Florence* (New York, 1980). Courtly ritual is discussed in John Adamson (ed.), *The Princely Courts of Europe: Ritual, Politics and Culture under the Ancien Régime 1500–1750* (London, 1999).

For a nuanced community-based study, see Tommaso Astarita, *Village Justice: Community, Family, and Popular Culture in Early Modern Italy* (Baltimore, 1999). On the individual search for identity among Marranos, see Brian Pullan, *The Jews of Europe and the Inquisition of Venice, 1550–1670* (Oxford, 1983). On Italian 'renegades' to Islam, see Bartolomé and Lucile Bennassar, *Les chrétiens d'Allah* (Paris, 1989). For the relationship between the culture of work, identity, and demarcation disputes, see Carlo Poni, 'Norms and Disputes: The Shoemakers' Guild in Eighteenth-Century Bologna', *Past and Present* 123 (1989), 80–108, and Angela Groppi, 'Ebrei, donne, soldati e neofiti. E'esercizio del mestiere tra esclusione e privilegi (Roma XVII–XVIII secolo)', in A. Guenzi, P. Massa, A. Moioli (eds.), *Corporazioni e gruppi professionali nell'Italia moderna* (Milan, 1999), 533–59. Ethnic identity is explored in H. Soly and A. K. L. Thijs (eds.), *Minorities in Western European Cities (Sixteenth–Twentieth Centuries)* (Rome, 1995); Thomas Cohen, 'The Case of the Mysterious Coil of Rope: Street Life and Jewish Persona in Rome in the Middle of the Sixteenth Century', *Sixteenth Century Journal* 19 (1988), 209–21; and Thomas Dandelet, 'Spanish Conquest and Colonization at the Center of the Old World: The Spanish Nation in Rome, 1555–1625', *Journal of Modern History* 69 (1997), 479–511.

On consumption and clothing, see Patricia Allerston, 'Clothing and Early Modern Venetian Society', *Continuity and Change* 15 (2000), 367–90. On food, Piero Camporesi, *Bread of Dreams: Food and Fantasy in Early Modern Europe*, trans. D. Gentilcore (Cambridge, 1989). The debate over gift-giving and patronage in early modern science is discussed by Giuseppe Olmi, 'Science and the Court: Some Comments on "Patronage" in Italy', in L. Guzzetti (ed.), *Science and Power: The Historical Foundations of Research Policies in Europe* (Luxembourg, 2000), 25–45. On the workings of the honour code, see Thomas Cohen, 'The Lay Liturgy of Affront in Sixteenth-Century Italy', *Journal of Social History* 25 (1992), 857–77; and Lucia Ferrante, 'Honor Regained: Women in the Casa del Soccorso di San Paolo in Sixteenth-Century Bologna', in Muir and Ruggiero, *Sex and Gender*, 46–72.

On saints and bodily suffering (and much else), see Piero Camporesi, *The Incorruptible Flesh: Bodily Mutation and Mortification in Religion and Folklore*, trans T. Croft-Murray (Cambridge 1988). On dissection, see Andrea Carlino, *Books of the Body: Anatomical Ritual and Renaissance Learning*, trans. John and Anne Tedeschi (Chicago, 1999), 69–119. Although it deals with an earlier period, Nancy Caciola's 'Mystics, Demoniacs, and the Physiology of Spirit Possession in Medieval Europe', *Comparative Studies in Society and History* 42 (2000), 268–306, discusses many of the issues relating to possession. On disease, healing, and the body, see David Gentilcore, *Healers and Healing in Early Modern Italy* (Manchester, 1998) and Gianna Pomata, *Contracting a Cure: Patients, Healers, and the Law in Early Modern Bologna*, trans R. Foy

(Baltimore, 1998). Luisa Accati discusses the role of female magic in 'The Spirit of Fornication: Virtue of the Soul and Virtue of the Body in Friuli, 1600–1800' and Ottavia Niccoli the menstrual taboo in '"Menstruum quasi monstruum": Monstrous Births and Menstrual Taboo in the Sixteenth Century', both in in Muir and Ruggiero, *Sex and gender*, 110–140 and 1–25.

Chapter 11

For a general overview of many of the topics in this chapter, in European perspective, see Peter Burke, *The Social History of Knowledge* (Cambridge, 2000). From a mainly political standpoint, see Jürgen Habermas, *The Structural Transformation of the Public Sphere*, trans. Thomas Burger (Cambridge, Mass., 1989). For the Italian case, see Brendan Dooley, 'Political Publishing and its Critics in Seventeenth-Century Italy', in *Memoirs of the American Academy in Rome* (1997), 175–93. Constraints on the diffusion of knowledge are the subject of Mario Infelise, *I libri proibiti. Da Gutenberg all'Encyclopédie* (Rome, 1999). Brendan Dooley, *The Social History of Skepticism: Experience and Doubt in Early Modern Culture* (Baltimore, 1999) shows how the circulation of error, falsehood, and propaganda affected the public sphere. The theme of forbidden knowledge is discussed in several contributions by Carlo Ginzburg, including 'High and Low: The Theme of Forbidden Knowledge in the Sixteenth and Seventeenth Centuries', *Past and Present* 73 (1976), 28–42, and from a different perspective, his *The Cheese and the Worms: The Cosmos of a Seventeenth-Century Miller*, trans. John and Anne Tedeschi (Baltimore, 1980). However, see Paola Zambelli's correctives in *Historical Journal* 28 (1985), 983–99. For the specific case of Venice, see Peter Burke, 'Early Modern Venice as a Center of Information and Communication', in John Martin and Dennis Romano (eds.), *Venice Reconsidered: The History and Civilization of an Italian City-State, 1297–1797* (Baltimore, 2000).

An overview of the Italian printing press in this period is Amedeo Quondam, 'La letteratura in tipografia', in Alberto Asor Rosa (ed.), *La letteratura italiana*, vol. ii: *Produzione e consumo* (Turin, 1983), 555–686. For the seventeenth century, see Brendan Dooley, 'Printing and Entrepreneurialism in Seventeenth-Century Italy', *Journal of European Economic History* 3 (1996), 569–97, and idem, *Science and the Marketplace in Early Modern Italy* (New York, 2001), ch. 3. Newspapers and the periodical press are discussed in articles by Valerio Castronovo, Giuseppe Ricuperati, and Carlo Capra in V. Castronovo and Nicola Tranfaglia (eds.), *La stampa italiana dal Cinquecento all'Ottocento*, 2nd edn., (Bari, 1986). See also Mario Infelise, 'The War, the News and the Curious: Military Gazettes in Italy', in B. Dooley and Sabrina Baron (eds.), *The Politics of Information in Early Modern Europe* (London, 2001), 216–36.

Literacy instruction is the subject of Paul Grendler, *Schooling in Renaissance Italy: Literacy and Learning, 1300–1600* (Baltimore, 1989). In addition, note Peter Burke, 'The Uses of Literacy in Early Modern Italy', in P. Burke and R. Porter (eds.), *The Social History of Language* (Cambridge, 1987). Concerning universities, see Richard Kagan, 'Universities in Italy, 1500–1700', in R. Chartier and J. Revel (eds.), *Les universités dans l'Europe moderne* (2 vols., Paris, 1986), I: 153–86; chs. 4 and 5 of Dooley, *Science and the Marketplace*, and volumes of the annual journal *History of Universities* (1981–).

Academies in general are discussed by Eric Cochrane, 'The Renaissance Academies in their Italian and European Setting', in *The Fairest Flower: The Emergence of Linguistic Consciousness in Renaissance Europe*, proceedings of the conference at UCLA, Dec. 1983 (Florence, 1985). Documents relating to the Accademia dei Lincei have been translated, with introduction and notes, in Brendan Dooley, *Italy in the Baroque: Selected Readings* (New York, 1995). Those from the Accademia del Cimento have been translated, with introduction and notes, by W. E. K. Middleton, *The Experimenters: A Study of the Accademia del Cimento* (Baltimore, 1971). For Arcadia and its critics, see Brendan Dooley, *Science, Politics and Society in Eighteenth-Century Italy: The Giornale de' letterati d'Italia and its World* (New York, 1991). Later academies are analysed by Eric Cochrane, *Tradition and Enlightenment in the Tuscan Academies* (Chicago, 1961).

Chapter 12

The fundamental work on eighteenth-century Italy is Franco Venturi, *Settecento riformatore*, 5 vols. (Turin 1969–90), and especially vol. 1: *Da Muratori a Beccaria* (1969), which covers the period 1734–1764; vol. 2: *La chiesa e la repubblica dentro i loro limiti, 1758–1774* (1976), which maps out the principal phases in the struggle against the Church; vol. 5 (in two parts): *L'Italia dei lumi (1764–1790), Pt. 1: La rivoluzione di Corsica. Le grandi carestie degli anni sessanta. La lombardia delle riforme* (1987) and Pt. 2: *La Repubblica di Venezia (1761–1797)* (1990). English translations are available for vol. 3: *The First Crisis*, trans. R. Burr Litchfield (Princeton, 1989); vol. 4: *The End of the Old Regime in Europe, 1776–1789*, trans. R. Burr Litchfield, 2 vols. (Princeton, 1991); and a collection of essays, Franco Venturi, *Italy and the Enlightenment. Studies in a Cosmopolitan Century*, trans. Susan Corsi (London 1972). Franco Venturi also edited the anthologies of Enlightenment writers *Illuministi italiani*, vol. 46 in the series *La letteratura italiana, Storia e testi* (Milan/Naples), vol. 46, vol. III: *Riformatori lombardi, piemontesi e toscani*, Franco Venturi (ed.) (1958); vol. V: *Riformatori napoletani*, Franco Venturi (ed.) (1962); vol. VII: *Riformatori delle antiche repubbliche, dei ducati, dello Stato pontificio e delle isole*, Giuseppe Giarrizzo, Gianfranco Torcellan, and Franco Venturi (eds.) (1965). In the same collection see also, vol. 46, vol. VI: *Opere di*

Ferdinando Galiani, Furio Diaz and Luciano Guerci (eds.) (1975); vol. 47: *Literati memorialisti e viaggiatori del Settecento,* Ettore Bonora (ed.) (1951).

A more general but nonetheless very wide-ranging survey can also be found in the *Storia d'Italia,* Ruggiero Romano and Corrado Vivanti (eds.), vol. 3: *Dal primo Settecento all'Unità* (Turin, 1973) and in the more recent volume by Dino Carpanetto and Giuseppe Ricuperati, *Italy in the Age of Reason, 1685–1789,* trans. Caroline Higgitt (London/New York, 1987).

Historiographical trends are reviewed in Marcello Verga, 'Le XVIIIᵉ siècle en Italie: le "Settecento" réformateur?', *Revue d'histoire moderne et contemporaine* 45: 1 (janvier-mars 1998): 89–116, which offers an extensive discussion of the relationship between Enlightenment and reform with very useful bibliographical references.

On individual Italian states, see the volumes that have been published to date in the *Storia d'Italia,* Giuseppe Galasso (ed.) (Turin, UTET): Mario Caravale and Alberto Caracciolo, *Lo Stato pontificio da Martino V a Pio IX* (1978); Lino Marini, Giovanni Tocci, Cesare Mozzarelli, and Aldo Stella, *I Ducati padani, Trento e Trieste* (1979); John Day, Bruno Anatra, and Lucetta Scaraffia, *La Sardegna medioevale e moderna* (1984); Domenico Sella and Carlo Capra, *Il Ducato di Milano dal 1535 al 1796* (1984); Gaetano Cozzi, Michael Knapton, and Giovanni Scarabello, *La Repubblica di Venezia nell'età moderna* (1986); Claudio Constantini, *La Repubblica di Genova* (1986); Vincenzo D'Alessandro and Giuseppe Giarizzo, *La Sicilia dal Vespro all'Unità* (1989); Pier Paolo Merlin, Claudio Rosso, Geoffrey Symcox, and Giuseppe Ricuperati, *Il Piemonte sabaudo. Stato e territori in età moderna* (1994); Furio Diaz, Luigi Mascilli Migliorini, and Carlo Mangio, *Il Granducato di Toscana. I Lorena dalla Reggenza agli anni rivoluzionari* (1997).

In the *Storia della società italiana* (Milan), see for the eighteenth century vol. 12: *Il secolo dei lume e delle riforme* (1989).

Recent studies available in English translation include Vincenzo Ferrone, *The Intellectual Tools of the Italian Enlightenment, Newtonian science, religion and politics in the early Eighteenth Century* trans. Sue Brotherton (Atlantic Highlands, N. J. 1995); and for Naples, *Naples in the Eighteenth Century. The Birth and Death of a Nation State,* ed. Girolamo Imbruglia (Cambridge, 2000).

Chronology

1543	Copernicus, *On the Revolutions of the Heavenly Spheres*; Vesalius, *On the Fabric of the Human Body*; publication of *Il Beneficio di Cristo*
1545	Charles V places Milan under rule of his son, Philip, and creates duchy of Parma and Piacenza for Pier Luigi Farnese
1545–63	Council of Trent meets in three sessions: 1545–7, 1551–2, and 1562–3
1546	Michelangelo (1475–1564) begins work on Campidoglio in Rome
1547	Naples rebels against introduction of the Inquisition
	Michelangelo works on the dome of St Peter's Rome
1549	Archbishop Giovanni della Casa publishes first list of prohibited books at Venice
1550	Giorgio Vasari (1511–74) publishes first edition of his *Lives of the Artists*
1551	The Jesuits found the Collegio Romano in Rome
1551–2	Second session of Council of Trent
1554	Benvenuto Cellini completes the *Perseus* for the Loggia dei Lanzi in Florence
1555	Peace of Augsburg between Charles V and the German princes which allows local princes to establish their preferred religion in their own territories
1555–9	Pontificate of Paul IV (Gian Pietro Carafa), strong Counter-Reformation pope
1556	Philip II's first 'bankruptcy' (debt refinancing); Genoese become financiers to Spanish empire
1556–98	Philip II succeeds to Spanish empire, with kingdoms in Italy (Milan, Naples, Sicily, and Sardinia), Spain (Castile and Aragon), the Low Countries, and the New World
1557	Carafa War; Battle of St. Quentin ends Habsburg–Valois Wars with victory of Philip II
1559	Treaty of Cateau-Cambrésis establishes political order after long period of wars from the 1494 invasions; France renounces all claims in Italy except Saluzzo and Pinerolo; Pope Paul IV issues the Index of Forbidden Books

1562–3	Third session of the Council of Trent
1563	Savoy capital moved from Chambéry to Turin
1565–84	Cardinal Charles Borromeo, archbishop of Milan, resident there as model Counter-Reformation bishop
1571	Battle of Lepanto in which Holy League of Western powers defeats Turkish fleet, but Turks eventually take Cyprus from Venice (1573)
1575–6	Plague in Venice reduces population by 30 per cent
1576	Oratory of St Philip Neri (Oratorians) founded
1577	Livorno (Leghorn) founded by Florentine grand duke Francis I.
1580–1630	Charles Emanuel I rules Savoy
1582	Pope Gregory XIII introduces Gregorian calendar
1593	Livorno (Leghorn) declared a free port by Florentine Grand Duke Ferdinand I
1598	Jacopo Peri (1561–1633), *Dafne*, combines orchestral and choral music with the theatre in the first opera
1599	Tommaso Campanella (1568–1639) arrested for conspiracy
1600	Giordano Bruno (1548–1600) executed by the Inquisition for heresy in Campo dei Fiori, Rome; Henry IV of France marries Marie de' Medici
1601	Treaty of Lyons between France and duchy of Savoy; Savoy obtains Saluzzo in exchange for some transalpine territories
1603	Accademia dei Lincei, Italy's premier scientific academy, founded in Rome
1606	Juridical dispute between papacy and Venice, resulting in papal interedict
1607	Claudio Monteverdi (1567–43), *Orfeus*, performed at Mantua
1610	Galileo publishes his *Sidereal Messenger* (*Sidereus Nuncius*), announcing discovery of the first four moons of Jupiter with the telescope
1611	Accademia della Crusca publishes first edition of its dictionary, *Vocabolario italiano*
1613–17	First War of Monferrat
1618–48	Thirty Years War, with direct fighting in Italian territories during the War of Valtellina (1620–26) and the Second War of Monferrat (1627–31).

1620–26	War of Valtellina, named after the strategic pass linking Habsburg Austria and the Spanish Habsburg possessions in Italy
1621–65	Philip IV succeeds to Spanish crown
1623	Gian Battista Marino published l'*Adone* (*Adonis*), chief work of the leader of Italian baroque literature and of the dominant literary movement named after him, *marinismo*
1623–44	War of Castro between papacy and the Farnese
1627–31	Second War of Monferrat, with siege of fortress of Casale (1628–30)
1630	Plague in the North, with Lombardy and Milan later depicted by Manzoni in *I promessi sposi* (1825; 1840–2)
1632	Galileo, *Dialogue Concerning the Two Chief World Systems*
1633	Galileo constrained to abjure and placed under house arrest by the Inquisition
1645–69	War of Candia, resulting in annexation of Crete by Ottomans from Venice
1647–8	Anti-Spanish revolts in Palermo (Giuseppe Alessi) and in Naples (Tommaso Aniello or Masaniello)
1655	Christina of Sweden converts and abdicates throne to reside in Rome as a cultural patron
1656	Plague in Genoa, Naples, and the South
1656–65	Bernini's colonnade at St Peter's constructed
1657	Accademia del Cimento founded in Florence
1659	Treaty of the Pyrenees between Louis XIV and Philip IV marks beginning of French hegemony in Europe
1672–8	Anti-Spanish revolt of Messina (with assistance of French fleet)
1685	Genoa captured by France
1690	Accademia dell'Arcadia, leader of anti-baroque and anti-marinismo aesthetic movement, founded in Rome
1701–14	War of the Spanish Succession resulted in all Spanish Habsburg possessions in Italy passing to Austrian Habsburgs, with the addition of Mantua
1713–14	Treaties of Utrecht and Rastatt confirm result of War of Spanish Succession with Savoy obtaining Sicily, later exchanged with Austria for Sardinia (1720), as well as Monferrat and Allessandria; the heirs of Elisabeth Farnese (second wife of Philip V) recognized as successors to Parma and Tuscany

1717	Free port established at Trieste
1723	Pietro Giannone, *Istoria civile del regno di Napoli*, maintains the autonomy of the lay state
1725	First edition of Giambattista Vico, *Principles of the New Science*
1733–8	War of the Polish Succession, with entry of Charles of Bourbon in Naples and invasion of Lombardy by Charles Emanuel III
1734	Charles of Bourbon becomes king of the Two Sicilies and initiates enlightened reform under his minister, Bernardo Tanucci
1737	Gian Gastone, the last Medici, dies without heirs
1738	Peace of Vienna confirms Austria to retain Lombardy with addition of Parma and Piacenza; Sardinia to add Novara and Tortona; Francis Stephan of Lorraine to be grand duke of Tuscany; and Naples, Sicily, and the Tuscan garrisons made an independent Bourbon dynasty
1740–48	War of the Austrian Succession, which saw on the Italian front a French invasion of Piedmont with eventual Austrian-Piedmontese victory
1748	Treaty of Aix-la-Chapelle confirmed Maria Teresa as Habsburg empress of Italian territories; Sardinia enlarges its territories to include Vigevano, Voghera and Alto Novarese; Parma and Piacenza given to Philip of Bourbon, brother of Charles, king of Naples
1749	Ludovico Antonio Muratori writes *Della pubblica felicità*, a programme for Enlightenment reform.
1749–59	Under Pompeo Neri in Milan, Maria Teresa's Austria conducts a vast census of property (*catasto*)
1753	Accademia dei Georgofili, dedicated to agricultural knowledge, founded in Florence
1754	In Naples, Antonio Genovesi assumes first university chair in 'Mechanical Arts and Commerce' (political economy)
1756–63	Seven Years War
1759	Charles of Bourbon becomes Charles III of Spain (1759–88) and leaves kingdom of Two Sicilies to his son, Ferdinand IV
1759–73	Jesuits begin to be expelled across Europe, with papal decree of suspension in 1773
1763–4	Famine (especially in Naples, Rome, and Florence)
1764	Alessandro and Pietro Verri launch publication of *Il Caffè* Cesare Beccaria publishes *On Crimes and Punishments*

1767	James Watt's first steam engine in England
1773	Jesuit order suppressed by Pope Clement XIV
1776–81	American War of Independence
1780–85	Gaetano Filangieri publishes *Science of Legislation*
1781	Emperor Joseph II issues the 'Edict of Toleration' abolishing serfdom; grand duke of Tuscany, Pietro Leopold, proposes a constitution with election of provincial and of general representative assemblies
1789	Revolution in France
1792	Jacobin movement spreads to Italy under Giovanni Antonio Ranza in Piedmont and Antonio Jerocades and Ignazio Ciaia in Naples; Alessandro Volta invents the first battery
1794–5	Repression and dispersal of Jacobin movements in Italy
1796	Napoleon invades Italy, defeats the Austrians, and enters Milan to establish the Cisalpine Republic

Map section

Map 1 Italy in 1559 (source: G. Holmes (ed.), *The Oxford History of Italy* (Oxford, 1997))

Map 2 Italy in 1748 (source: G. Holmes (ed.), *The Oxford History of Italy* (Oxford, 1997))

Index

Started : 4 Dec 2009